I0820220

AVID
READER
PRESS

HOW TO BE A RICH OLD LADY

YOUR GUIDE TO EASY INVESTING,
BUILDING WEALTH, AND CREATING
THE WILD, BEAUTIFUL LIFE YOU WANT

AMANDA HOLDEN

AVID READER PRESS

New York • Amsterdam/Antwerp • London
Toronto • Sydney/Melbourne • New Delhi

AVID READER PRESS
An Imprint of Simon & Schuster, LLC
1230 Avenue of the Americas
New York, NY 10020

First Avid Reader Press hardcover edition January 2026

Interior design by Joy O'Meara

Manufactured in the United States of America

5 7 9 10 8 6

Library of Congress Control Number: 2025945122

ISBN 978-1-6680-6692-8
ISBN 978-1-6680-6694-2 (ebook)

For Mom and Dad
Who made everything possible

CONTENTS

Introduction ix

PART I: Financial Foundation

1. How to Use This Book 3
2. What First 6
3. Emergency Fund 9
4. Debt Versus Invest 14
5. Budget 22
6. Spending 29
7. Income 36

PART II: Retirement Account Basics

8. Retirement Accounts 51
9. Roth Versus Traditional 57
10. Rules 68

PART III: How to Invest

11. Stocks & Bonds 81
12. Funds 87
13. Risk 89
14. Asset Allocation 96
15. Index 101
16. Index Funds 105
17. Diversification & the Three-Fund Portfolio 110
18. Target-Date Funds 118
19. Expectations 126
20. Market Crashes 134
21. Underperformance (Stock Picking) 143
22. Fees 148
23. Compound Returns 153

PART IV: Building and Maintaining Your Strategy

24. Banks 163
25. Research 167
26. Trade 175
27. Automation 181
28. Upkeep 184
29. Robo-Advisors 191

PART V: Fine-Tuning Things

30. Ethical Investing 203
31. Market Categories 209
32. Real Estate (REITs) 218
33. Cryptocurrency 222

PART VI: Pearls of Wisdom

34. Retirement Calculations 231
35. Social Security 237
36. What Next 241
37. Health Savings Accounts 247
38. Homeownership 251
39. Children 258
40. Hiring Help 264
41. Apocalypse 270
42. Community 275

The End (Delight) 281
Rich Old Lady Resources 285
Acknowledgments 287
Notes 289

INTRODUCTION

Reno, Nevada, 2012. Lisa, who worked with me at a wealth management firm, had invited me to tag along to her friend's birthday party weekend. I didn't know the birthday girl or her friends, but I was *not* the type to turn down a road trip to Reno. Come Friday afternoon, we tore out of San Francisco in Lisa's '96 Kia Spectra. Two hundred and twenty miles, a couple'a Monster Energy tallboys, and an armful of gas station snacks later, we were saddled up at the bar of the Nugget Casino Resort, ready to spend the next forty-eight hours dancing with the devil.

I announced to Lisa that I had to order the Ass Kicker Margarita being advertised behind the bar: a frozen concoction in a vessel so large it required a neck strap. The bartender overheard my proclamation and locked eyes with me, cigarette dangling off her lip: "I'll take you to the back alley if you *really* wanna get your ass kicked." A chill of delight ran through me. This wasn't just a welcome—it was an omen, an unholy baptism. Reno was in charge now. I was in the passenger seat, ready to let the weekend take me where it would. And I certainly had no intention of boring anyone with details of what Lisa and I did for work.

But the very next morning, emerging from a drunken haze at our budget hotel's continental breakfast, I found myself fielding questions about investing. Lisa's friends had learned we worked in finance, and they were curious about it. Someone had a question about her 401(k) plan. Another wasn't sure about choosing her investments. Between mouthfuls of clammy buffet eggs and burnt coffee, Lisa and I trotted out explanations of different investing concepts and strategies. Our ability to go deep on this, even after an evening of swimming laps in pool-sized tequila-based beverages, surprised even us. We had never done anything like that before. At least, not for our friends.

Although I was happy to be helpful for an hour, I didn't think more of it for the remainder of the weekend. To me, our impromptu investing panel was just one in a delightful log of fun interactions with strangers turned new friends (including Debbie, the bartender). It wasn't until the long car ride home, as we were rehashing the weekend's gossip, that Lisa whipped around to me and said, "How wild was that, Mandy? Teaching all those women how to invest?"

Now that she mentioned it, it *was* wild. Not because we did something miraculous. Not because we were particularly smart or accomplished—no!—but because those women were smart and accomplished. One was on her way to becoming a doctor. Another was a professional violinist, for crying out loud. Yet despite their different backgrounds, talents, achievements, and career paths, they all had one thing in common: None of them knew anything about investing. Because *of course* they didn't! How could they, if no one ever taught them? From within the self-absorbed fog of early twentysomething life, it hadn't occurred to me that not everyone was learning about investing on the job like Lisa and me.

We were very young women paid to peer into the bank accounts and behaviors of wealthy retirees, and I mostly took our vantage point for granted. And even though my thinking about money was still very much forming, a few things had already come into focus. First, I'd come to understand there's a direct connection between the size of an investment portfolio and the quality of a person's retired life. And second, the people who owned those big, life-sustaining investment accounts? They were all men. So no, I didn't know everything—but I knew enough to be pissed.

Also unbeknownst to me at the time, that Q and A over heat-lamp hash browns marked the beginning of my new mission: teaching women to invest. Only a couple of years after that weekend, I started writing in my blog, *The Dumpster Dog Blog* (more on the name later), about topics like the high cost of beauty standards and how the finance industry exploits regular people. Then I started teaching classes about investing. What started as small, in-person gatherings with a few curious young women has grown over time into a full-fledged online business, called Invested Development. Nearly a decade later, I've taught over twenty-five thousand students, mostly women, to pursue financial independence through investing.

And to think! It all began with a few gals who realized the casino's real jackpot was in the advice being dispensed by Lisa and me. To this day, I'm profoundly grateful for their proactiveness and intuition. If they hadn't known to ask the questions, I might not have known to step up and answer.

If you're holding this book, I'm willing to bet you have questions, too—or maybe you're not even sure where to begin. Maybe you know you *should* open that Roth IRA, but a mystery casserole of shame, overwhelmedness, and low-key dread keeps getting in the way. Or maybe you're already investing but want to be dead sure you're doing it right. No matter what you're searching for, you've come to the right place. If you have ever felt left out of the conversation, this is your invitation to join it. Because I've been in enough closed-door rooms where power and wealth are discussed—and let me tell you, the guest list sucks. That's why I wrote this book: to fling those doors wide open.

Fighting Back Against a Rigged System

A few years into my work at the firm, I had a hunch it wasn't a big ol' coinkydink that all my rich clients were men, save the occasional widow. But now I know: Money is harder for women to accumulate, and this fact is the deliberate outcome of centuries of economic design.

As recently as the late 1980s, women were denied access to business loans and credit without a male signature. In the decades before that, women were frequently refused property ownership, work in certain professions, credit cards, and banking privileges. Some states even had "head and master" laws, which gave husbands total control over the finances. (So, yeah, next time someone waxes a tad too nostalgic about "the good ol' days" or about how marriages "used to last," feel free to remind them that Grandma didn't have a bank account.)

My own Grandma Betty, a sparkly, hardworking woman carrying the entire domestic load, ironed the shirts of men in jobs she could've done with her eyes closed, if she'd had the chance. My mom, brilliantly creative but shy, was told by a high school guidance counselor to "just be a secretary." I don't know if the counselor's suggestion reflected an inability to see my mom's talents or a world where those talents had a place. Probably both. And while both jobs represent dignified forms of labor, notably both exist in support of professional men—and come with low, built-in ceilings on income, mobility, and fulfillment. It's dizzying to think about how recently women were forced to structure their entire lives around the ambitions of men—and how many women still are.

To this day, men's careers are subsidized by women doing unpaid work at home—the cooking, cleaning, and caregiving—often *while* maintaining their own careers. Even when women are the primary breadwinners, they still do the majority of the household labor, for their own families *and* for their aging parents. A savagely titled study from the American Sociological Association, "Daughters Provide as Much Elderly Parent Care as They Can, Sons Do as Little as Possible," found that daughters take on far more caregiving than sons, with deeply uneven emotional, physical, and financial costs. Another study showed that women over fifty who are forced out of work to care for aging relatives lose an estimated $324,000 in wages and retirement savings.

If we know that the cost of caregiving can sink women, then motherhood is financial quicksand. Women lose half a million dollars in lifetime earnings, on average, just by becoming mothers. Because it's not only the hours they miss but the opportunity to compound raises and keep skills sharp and connections warm. It's accumulation, in reverse. But when a man shows up with khakis and a kid? He gets a salary bump and the benefit of the doubt. The exact same event that marks women as a professional liability is seen in men as a sign of reliability. Yes, the gender wage gap is real, and it's driven by the motherhood and caregiving penalties, workplace discrimination, and the systemic devaluation of anything considered "women's work."

Although I'm primarily using a gendered framework to look at structural economic inequities, it's not the only one, or even the most important. People born into wealth have astoundingly better outcomes than those born into poverty, no matter their gender. Wage gaps are far worse for Black, Latina, Native, trans, and disabled women. And these wage gaps transmute into gnarly wealth gaps. For every dollar a white man owns, women overall own just thirty-two cents. Black and Latina women own less than one penny.

Our big economy-wide problems—like wage stagnation, the cost of living crisis, and women making up the majority of the low-wage workforce—are best understood as the outcome of unchecked capitalism. In this politico-economic system, workers produce excess value, which is siphoned off to company owners and shareholders, rather than, say, being distributed to the workers themselves. Because the objective is corporate profit, not fairness or worker dignity, labor is seen as a cost to be minimized. And while all workers are vulnerable to exploitation by extraordinarily powerful corporations, the easiest people to exploit are the ones who are already vulnerable.

I, for one, think we should consider a different system entirely; one where the economic markets exist to serve workers, not one where workers exist to serve the economic markets. But until then, we need a few bare-minimum fixes: actual limits on corporate power, a revitalized labor movement, and a real social safety net—one that includes paid parental leave and subsidized childcare. Because right now, women are barked at to have children, then disproportionately left to drown in the financial consequences. Sociologist Jessica Calarco, author of *Holding It Together: How Women Became America's Safety Net*, argues that this reliance on women to fill systemic gaps comes at an enormous cost to their well-being, and yes, that includes their financial well-being. Instead of a functioning social safety net, the US has women.

It is downright diabolical, then, that the economic oppression of women is used as evidence that women are "bad at money." You've probably heard it before: the sexist personal finance propaganda that "women just don't invest!" because our tiny girl brains are filled with glitter or whatever. But even this assertion falls apart when we consider that investment risk-taking is largely a function of income, not gender. Said another way, women don't invest as much because women don't have as much money to invest. We know who gets to take the big dick swings in this world, and it's not a single mom of three kids working two jobs to scrape by.

But here's what they *won't* tell you: That when women do invest, the data shows they are better at it than men. Not because they take bigger risks, but because they don't take as many stupid ones.

Even something as seemingly simple as women's daily spending habits are scrutinized in ways that men's just aren't. Every woman I know has had what I call a "Brad Experience," wherein a walking, talking pair of boat shoes condescends to her about her spending. It's the guy with a sloppy DraftKings habit who thinks his wife spends too much when she's buying for the entire family. It's an entire aisle at the bookstore dedicated to the irresponsibility of her lattes but that makes no mention of his nine-dollar craft beer that tastes like a two-by-four. Apparently, as long as your choice of overpriced beverage could double as wood stain, it's an acceptable financial decision. Even though men splurge more, spend more, and have more credit card debt than women, despite earning more, the "women be shoppin'" narrative persists.

The story that women are compulsive spenders who can't be trusted with money serves a function: It keeps men in charge. Not just in politics or on payrolls, but at the kitchen table. We're taught to see this as normal, maybe even responsible. And while it's generally chalked up as a harmless hangover from a less enlightened time, this story has plenty of cosponsors. It is crafted and circulated by those who benefit from keeping women in their place. And right now, it's working. In just two and a half years—between May 2022 and November 2024—public opinion on traditional gender roles underwent a historic shift. The share of Republican men who said women should return to the home jumped from 28% to 48%. Among Republican women, it rose from 23% to 37%.

Even before the recent backslide, a 2021 survey revealed that in 69% of millennial heterosexual marriages, men report doing the long-term financial planning. Among the women who relinquish the duty, 82% say it's because they lack the same knowledge as their male partner. Seventy-eight percent are already overburdened by other responsibilities, like household chores and childcare. And I get it! Our refusal to build real support systems for women has left them improvising and adapting from within a hostile structure. When the opportunity to hand off a responsibility comes along, even a crucial one, it can feel like a small mercy.

And though I'd classify this as a failure of neoliberalism, not individual women, this dynamic has real-life consequences. Women are disconnected from critical financial decisions, leaving them even less informed and with even less power, further entrenching financial inequality. At the very least, women are left out of the decisions that will make or break their lives. Among men who handle the family finances, 68% say they do it so they'll have control in the event of a divorce. Don't believe me? Boogie on over to Reddit, where men are openly coaching each other on how to hide assets in crypto—so their ex-wives and children get less than they're legally owed.

If you feel unsure or underqualified when it comes to money, well, shit, *of course you do*! That feeling didn't come out of nowhere! It was grafted onto you, over and over, until it felt like your own skin. While this can seem grim, there is reason to be hopeful. Just because you're here today, doesn't mean you have to be in the same place tomorrow. I'm the first to admit that there are real limitations to personal finance advice; you can't compound returns you were never allowed to earn in the first place. But a lack of knowledge represents a problem we can solve together, and solve quickly.

Education becomes a survival tool in a capitalist economy that much prefers an overworked, under-informed populace and where entire monopolized industries operate like shakedown scams for consumers to navigate. This is especially true of consumer finance, an industry that preys on our lack of education. It's not an exaggeration to say that Wall Street dines out—steak, wine, and dessert—on the fees it quietly leeches from the retirement accounts of schoolteachers in the poorest school districts in America. And trust me: They want nothing more than for you to blame yourself for not understanding what was purposefully designed to confuse you.

I hope that, as you learn about how the system works, you will find ways to reclaim personal power from it. Or, as my friend Paco de Leon, author of *Finance for the People,* writes, this practice is about "finding your agency at any moment, despite existing within an unequal system." I have seen how quickly financial education can change the lives of the women who choose to engage with it. My investing students routinely tell me that it has allowed them to feel a confidence they never before thought possible. And I have found that oftentimes, you just need the right teacher. Someone who will honor your struggles and your intelligence. I hope to be that teacher for you.

For this task, I ask that you give me the space of this book. Although it will vary from person to person, I think it should take about twenty hours. That's right: twenty hours, just one time, to read the chapters and do the homework. That's not to say this is a complete education—no book is. But at the end of those twenty hours, you'll have everything you need to set up a smart, automated investing strategy for yourself. Because while the financial advice fire hose delivers an unrelenting flow of information, what you *truly* need to know isn't endless. My goal is to get you set up in a way that doesn't require constant fretting or monitoring because I only see investing as useful to the extent that it allows us to live beautiful lives.

And the sooner we find some stable financial ground for ourselves, the sooner we can look up and fight for the collective solutions we all deserve. Budgeting, personal discipline, and even investing can take us only so far in a system where individual security is fragile by design.

The journey ahead will be difficult, but it's also true that we have far better options than our mothers and grandmothers. Perhaps you will consider doing it for them. I know I do. For the remainder of this book, I ask that you channel their dreams and tenacity into your avatar for financial independence: your Rich Old Lady.

How to Be a Rich Old Lady

I want to be up-front in my goal for this book. I want you to achieve *financial independence*. But what do those two magic words really mean?

There are a few interpretations. For women, especially, it means not solely relying on a man or partner for money. This is a form of financial independence I ask you take seriously.

In the investing world, though, financial independence has a somewhat more specific definition: not needing to rely on a job for money. With this version of financial independence, you have enough money invested to live off the income those investments generate. Said another way, you have reached financial independence when your investments spit off income at a rate greater than your spending rate. And to be clear, reaching retirement with enough money in your 401(k) to comfortably live off the proceeds *is* financial independence in action!

Back in Grandpappy's day, retirement was tied to an age, like age sixty-five. But with the death of the company pension and the assaults on Social Security (the federal government's pension plan), retirement timing is now dictated by the amount of money you've saved—or more accurately, invested. As a result, retirement planning looks a bit different for us. You'll retire when you have enough money to retire—when you've reached financial independence. This may happen at sixty-five, or it could happen sooner, later, or not at all—it all depends on how much and how well you invest. Whether you call it *retirement* or *financial independence,* the fundamental premise is the same: having enough invested so you can, someday, live independent from a paycheck.

For now, here's what you need to know about reaching financial independence: Start investing early, stick with it, and with time, you can create a life where working for money becomes *optional.* If you *want* to work? Great! Me too! I am way too pale and haunted to spend the rest of my days relaxing by the pool. The goal, here, is options—*the power to choose the life you want.* And this life is not going to happen without investing. Saving money in the bank is good to a point but won't get your money growing the way you need it to become a Rich Old Lady.

Next, I will be asking you to summon your inner Rich Old Lady. Now, I know what you're picturing: a crusty old broad in a big hat being mean to the waiter at the country club. But that's not what it is. Well, except for the big hat. What I'm talking about is the freedom to imagine a future that is wild, weird, and uniquely you. Imagine, say, quitting your job in tech at age fifty to run a sanctuary for rescued farm animals with your three best friends. Or, becoming the grandma who's neighborhood famous for both her cheesecake and her right bicep—still beating the guys at arm wrestling at sixty-five. Maybe you're the woman who, for her eightieth birthday, goes naked Rollerblading down the Venice Beach Boardwalk. (I wanted to name this book *Naked Rollerblading When You're 80,* to which Simon & Schuster said absolutely the hell not.)

Before we get started on all the boring (but necessary) shit like asset allocation, I first want you to imagine your future self. I want you to envision your Rich Old Lady. No, really, do it. Picture this diva in all her glory. Where does she live? Who is she with? What does she spend her day doing? Go wild here. Write it down. Say it out loud. Don't be scared of what you want.

Maybe it will help to hear my vision for Rich Old Lady Amanda. My Rich Old Lady will be an artist, never without her statement cane (I have bad knees). Her financial independence allows her to remain in her beloved New York City while doing low-paid work that inspires her, like advocating for labor rights. She splits time in her native Pacific Northwest—she's even convinced a few of her friends to build sister cabins on a forest plot in the North Cascades. But on occasion, she'll throw on her most obnoxious jewels and jet off to Italy to meet up with her significantly younger lover to slurp down the business end of a spaghetti noodle, *Lady and the Tramp*–style. But mostly, you can find her laughing with her friends because that's the whole thing—*that's what it's all about.*

To be a Rich Old Lady is to be rich in life, options, experiences, and especially love. Nothing is more important in life than our relationships—and I want you to have plenty of time for yours. Your people won't be here forever, after all. Neither will you. To be a Rich Old Lady is to get so real about using your money to create a life of connection, not mindless consumption.

You don't have to be old, or a lady, to be a Rich Old Lady. Anyone can be a Rich Old Lady. More than anything, Rich Old Lady is a vibe. It's an essence. And being a Rich Old Lady is about more than just investing money for the (admittedly tenuous) long term. It is about gifting yourself the psychological relief of knowing you're doing everything you can, right now. You are engaging in Rich Old Lady behavior right this very moment, in reading this book.

Please, allow your Rich Old Lady to be the Werther's Originals sugar rush that will power you through the more technical material in the book. To navigate the work ahead, it will help to put a face on the process. And that face should be an adorable, wrinkly version of the face you have now.

If you follow the wisdom in this book, that Rich Old Lady dream—whatever it looks like for you—can become yours.

PART I

FINANCIAL FOUNDATION

The first step to investing in yourself
is building a strong financial foundation

1

HOW TO USE THIS BOOK

*How can I make the most of this *rich text*?*

How to Be a Rich Old Lady is not a typical personal finance book. It is not a primer on the basics. I will provide a few solid strategies for building a financial foundation in this section, but you won't find forty-page chapters on credit scores or building a budget. Not because this type of thing isn't valuable—it will be hard to reach financial independence without knowing how much you spend every month—but there are many resources (excellent books, YouTube videos, TikTok accounts) teaching these lessons over and over. This book is about investing: what you need to go from surviving to thriving.

But *How to Be a Rich Old Lady* is not your dad's investing book. You know, the fusty, dry investing tome written by a man with waves of silver hair and opinions on yachts. You may even already own that book! There it is, sitting on your nightstand, collecting dust. I have studied and learned from many of these books. But they often go so far into the ephemera that readers are left confused and frustrated.

I wanted to write a book on investing for regular people, maybe even people who aren't really that interested in finance at all. (For another possible book title, I threw out *The Hater's Guide to Investing*, but the thoughtful, reasonable people at Simon & Schuster suggested I maybe not lead with hatred.)

My hope is that reading this book will be like learning about an intimidating topic from your big sister's coolest friend. Think of me as the older girl from down the block who told you which teachers to avoid and what it means to 69. Because I want this book to feel like a chat between friends, I've structured it around the most frequently asked questions I hear from my smart, resourceful students. (You'll find these at the top of each chapter.) It's just you and me, and we're sipping fizzy drinks in some sidewalk-facing bistro chairs, talking through all your questions and concerns about investing while we people-watch through our dark sunglasses. I will be writing in my voice, which means I break down jargon using normal-people language, metaphor, and the occasional boner joke.

I designed this book to be read in order. Investing concepts are like building blocks: Advanced topics won't hold up if you don't first understand the basics. For example, if you jump straight to the chapter on ethical investing, you might find yourself lost without the foundation of basic investing principles and terminology to support it. I know our brains are all accustomed to the instant gratification of a thirty-second TikTok, and it may be tempting to skip ahead, but if you want to be a successful student of the material, take the time to work it through.

That said, I've very purposefully given the chapters super straightforward names, always in ALL CAPS, so you can easily navigate to chapters you want to revisit. Chapters are grouped into these six sections:

I. Financial Foundation

The first step to investing in yourself is building a strong financial foundation

II. Retirement Account Basics

Helping you understand and choose the retirement account that's right for you

III. How to Invest

Everything you need to know about investing so you can make confident decisions

IV. Building and Maintaining Your Strategy

Turning theory into action. This is where we go from "thinking about it" to "doing it"

V. Fine-Tuning Things

Optional ways to tweak your investment strategy

VI. Pearls of Wisdom

Big-picture and advanced topics from the perspective of a Rich Old Lady

At the end of each of the above six sections, you'll find **Homework** that pulls together the key lessons from that part of the book. Please don't skip it! This is how the real change happens, off the page and in your life. You'll also come across several **10-Minute Missions** sprinkled throughout the book: quick, meaningful actions I hope you'll take right away. They're small enough to knock out faster than your Rich Old Lady can do a lap around the mall. And last, to encourage you to slow down and take the occasional, necessary brain break, I've included interstitials between sections called **Rich Old Lady Reflections**.

If you follow the educational program laid forth in this book, you will be well on your way to your wild, beautiful life. Before you embark, one last reminder. When learning to invest, you are learning a whole new language: the language of money. And learning a language takes practice. Treat this book like it's Duolingo but for money, and instead of a deranged green owl threatening your family if you miss a lesson, it's just me, talking you through material that will feel totally foreign at times. Because it is! All of this finance stuff is completely made up, and no one is born with an innate knowledge of interest rates and index funds. Therefore, I encourage you to be patient with yourself, return to passages that made your eyes go dry, and practice explaining the material to a friend. These are not detours in the process; they are the process.

What do you say? Ready to learn how to speak Rich Old Lady?

2

WHAT FIRST

What should I work on first?

One reason why you might've put off creating a financial plan is simple: You have no idea where to start.

To say that there is noise in the financial advice space is perhaps the understatement of the century. For example, maybe you've considered investing for retirement, only to get scolded by financial "guru" Dave Ramsey, who implies that your debt is a moral failing and that paying it all off should be your first priority. (This, from a man who once filed for bankruptcy himself.*) Then, you scroll Instagram and hear the exact opposite—credit card debt is *actually* fine, says the contoured influencer encouraging you to use it to buy her course on making more money. "It proves your commitment to money manifestation," she claims. Or maybe you tried to open a high-yield savings account, only to find yourself fourteen clicks deep into Reddit, where CryptDad420 is making the case that fiat currency is dead and you should put everything into Ethereum *right now*.

No wonder you feel torn between opening a Roth IRA, paying off your debt, and ignoring your bank accounts while hiding beneath the covers eating cold pad Thai leftovers. Luckily, there's a pretty standard order of financial operations agreed upon by financial planners and experts. That's not to say that you're not a special snowflake with unique

* The problem isn't filing for bankruptcy—it's making people feel ashamed to even explore the option. The trade-offs are serious and real, but in some situations, bankruptcy can be the wisest path forward.

goals and needs, but that we're all humans tasked with being alive in this insane world, and we share a lot more in common than we don't. Everyone needs to pay their bills and clip their toenails, y'know?

And this is where we will begin our journey. Your first step is to build a *financial foundation*. I've specifically chosen this terminology because a foundation indicates a solid base for building. Using the term *financial security* works, too, but I like the picture the word *foundation* paints—a Rich Old Lady mustn't build her fabled lair atop sinking mire! Having a strong financial foundation will make you safer now, and down the line it will provide the firm ground from which you can take risks as an investor.

Building a financial foundation consists of these three steps:

1. Save an emergency fund
2. Pay off credit cards and other high-interest debt
3. Begin investing for retirement

Next, I am going to say something obvious. I understand if you need to throw the book across the room. Do it! That remains your right as this book's owner. Ready?

To save money, you need money to save. To actively pay down debt, you'll need extra money to pay down debt. To invest money, you need money to invest. It is only possible to build a financial foundation when you have a secure income that is higher than your expenses.

For example, if you're earning $70,000 per year after taxes and your expenses amount to $58,000, you've got an income surplus of $12,000. From here on out, this surplus is what I am going to refer to as *The Gap*. The Gap (and how you use it) represents your financial possibility. The Gap is where the magical shit happens! The Gap is what allows you to make progress on steps 1, 2, and 3 above. You better be careful because if your Gap gets too big, you might fuck off to Morocco to surf for the summer. The Gap buys the investments that will produce the income that will pay for the nipple tassels you'll need when you're eighty. Your Rich Old Lady life is made possible by The Gap. (I pitched the book title *How to Buy Nipple Tassels When You're 80*, and Simon & Schuster looked at me, their eyes full of quiet despair, reconsidering every choice that led them to this moment.)

The Gap is your best and most important financial tool.

If you find yourself overdrawing your checking account or falling further into credit card debt each month, you don't have a Gap. This tells us *exactly* where you should begin your journey. Your first step must be working to create a Gap.

To create (and expand) your Gap, you have three options:

1. Decrease expenses,
2. Increase your income, or
3. Both

Both strategies are good in different ways. Decreasing spending allows you to grow your Gap immediately. Quick wins are the best way to get started—and they're good for the soul. When you shimmy over to the income side of things, there's a potential for a bigger payoff. You can increase your income by more than you could ever cut back. But earning more money is a long game. We'll make a game plan for both, in chapters 5, BUDGET, and 7, INCOME.

Maybe you've already got a Gap. If you're easily making transfers to a savings account or 401(k) contributions, hell yeah, it sounds like you've got a Gap. If you've got money piling up in your checking account after paying all your bills—smells like a Gap! As you continue the work of expanding the Gap, simultaneously, let's put that Gap to work. I'll explain how in the next two chapters, 3, EMERGENCY FUND, and 4, DEBT VERSUS INVEST.

Before we go, I want us to take a beat. Listen to me closely when I say this. Get closer. Closer than that!! **forehead kiss** Building your financial foundation *is* an investment in your future. Building an emergency fund *is* an investment. Paying off credit cards *is* an investment. Strategizing how to grow your Gap is arguably the best investment of time and energy you'll ever make.

So, even though we aren't yet "investing" in stocks and bonds, don't worry, because financial independence isn't only about stocks and bonds. These are all valuable steps along the same journey of building wealth and creating your Rich Old Lady life. And for now your task is not to be overwhelmed by the noise, which often has more to do with the algorithm than with you. You must only take action on your one next step.

3

EMERGENCY FUND

How much emergency money do I need?

I had a student—who I will call Janet—whose grandmother had been married three times. None of the marriages was a happy one. On Janet's wedding day, Grandma gave her $2,000. "Just in case," she said. Janet's grandma knew exactly what it meant to lack the resources to leave a bad situation. Thankfully, Janet hasn't needed it, but it still sits in a separate account, ready and available. "When the time comes, I'll pass it on to my daughter," Janet said. "And frankly, we should all tell our daughters, sisters, and friends about the importance of having a Fuck Off Fund."

Emergencies happen: a major health crisis strikes; a boss pulls something shady; a relationship turns sour or, worse, dangerous; or you're laid off from a job. The only question is whether you're prepared. That's why every person needs an *emergency fund*. Or, as Janet described, a Fuck Off Fund—a term coined by Paulette Perhach in a viral essay of the same name. However you brand it, the idea is to have money set aside in an accessible savings account, ready for life's inevitable bullshit.

If you are a woman, especially, do not let anyone convince you there isn't value in keeping cash in a bank account. For as great and important as investment accounts are, it's often not easy to access that money quickly, or without considering tax implications, but cash in the bank is yours when you need it. Although you will never hear the finance bros talking about boring old cash in this way, for women there is an almost indescribable value that comes from being able to act from a position of power and not fear, subservience, or desperation. Any person who has ever been without cash doesn't take the value of cash for granted.

Start small, be consistent, and grow your emergency fund until you can cover **six months of expenses**. Six months because the biggest reason most people need this money is job loss, and it's common to be out of work for several months after a layoff. If you haven't already, take ten minutes and calculate your target number. When considering expenses, most people include only the necessities, like rent, utilities, and food, because if you're out of work, you're definitely cutting out all the fun spending until you are back to greener pastures. So, if your bare necessities total $4,000 per month, then a fully funded, six-month emergency fund is $24,000. Take a look at this number once more, considering any financial support you provide for your family. (For example, if you support your parents, you may want to save more.)

It's a big, intimidating number! Just because saving an emergency fund comes early in the process of building a financial foundation, it does not mean it's easy. But good news: You don't have to wait until your emergency fund is fully funded before you begin your work on other steps. If I were starting an emergency fund from scratch, I'd break it into phases, giving myself plenty of chances to take a breath, celebrate my progress, and integrate other goals. Below, I've written out a template to follow. *Please* tailor these numbers to your needs and cost of living. While making all necessary monthly payments on your existing debt:

1. Save $2,000 in an emergency fund to cover a small emergency. *(At this point, I would integrate actively paying off credit card debt.)*
2. Keep saving until you hit $5,000 in your emergency fund. *(Here, I would layer in investing for retirement.)*
3. Continue working on fully funding an emergency fund of six months of expenses.

Where Should Your Emergency Fund Go?

Although it is smart to keep a small amount of cold, hard cash stashed in your freezer or stuffed in a teddy bear, most emergency money should be kept in cash in a savings account.

As for the best savings account, well, the best account is the one that is getting used. (Get ready to hear me repeat that line a lot.) If you currently have a savings account and it works well within the financial system you've already built, that's fine. The most important variable will always be how much money you save (or invest)—*not* the account itself.

But, Amanda, I've heard you can get paid on your savings? Yes! And it ain't happening at Wells Fargo, Chase, or Bank of America. In addition to questionable business practices (just Google "Wells Fargo scandal" if you feel like punching a wall), the big-box banks pay very low interest rates on their savings accounts. Interest is the money the bank pays you for parking your moola in their care, and these banks are laughing in our faces with how little they offer.

Your emergency fund account can be at a different bank than your main bank, and that can be especially helpful if you tend to spend money you have easy access to. (Hi, it's me!) That little extra barrier can help keep this money out of impulse-purchasing hands. Instead, I keep my emergency fund in a *high-yield savings account (HYSA)*, which are typically online only. Because they don't have brick-and-mortar locations, they tend to pay much higher rates of interest. Look for the *annual percentage yield (APY)*, which is the interest rate, translated into the percentage you can expect to earn each year when you consider compounding. At the time of writing, Chase pays an insulting .01% APY on savings, whereas a HYSA is currently paying 4%. For a $10,000 savings account, this is a difference of $1 and $400 in interest per year.

I have personally used and liked HYSAs from Marcus and Ally, but there are many others. When you are comparing banks, you can use a resource like NerdWallet to look for a HYSA with free accounts (with no *maintenance fees*), no minimums, and *FDIC insurance*, which covers you if the bank fails. I also look for a competitive APY. It doesn't have to be the best APY, because rates can and will change. The United States' central bank, called the Federal Reserve, guides interest rates higher and lower to control the money flow across the economy. Banks are also in constant competition with one another. You might see one bank pump up its interest rate for a promotional period in an attempt to woo you, only to bring it back down in line with other banks after the period is over. The bank with the highest rate now won't be the bank with the highest rate next month.

Because HYSAs are generally free and have no minimums, you can open multiple accounts for different purposes. (Alternatively, yours may have a "buckets" feature. Each bucket stands in for a different category you want to save for.) I strongly encourage you to label each account (or bucket). Saving for something real and specific is much more inspiring than saving to account number 3829BEEPBOOP20448. Have fun with this! I've got a savings account for emergencies and a down payment, but also a trip to Japan. I even have a savings account labeled "Wild Woman Fund" because you never know when the mood will strike to buy something dumb. I don't deny that this side of me exists! Instead, I plan for her.

As an alternative, I love a *credit union*. Credit unions are local, not-for-profit, and often community-based banks. Think of a credit union as Wells Fargo's bra-burning, llama-owning hippie aunt from Portland. While Bank of America is busy squeezing its customers for the benefit of shareholders and executives, your local credit union uses fees and interest to serve its members. JPMorgan Chase bankrolls the fossil fuel industry; meanwhile, your credit union helps the family who owns the corner laundromat finally replace their busted dryers. Best of all, they are much easier to use than people think. Most credit unions are part of a nationwide ATM network, so you can still withdraw cash without hunting down some sketchy convenience store in the rain in a place you've never been. (Although I don't know. Could be fun.)

What about Certificates of Deposit (CDs)?

CDs are savings products that hold your money for a set period—anywhere from a few months to several years. In return for giving up access to your cash, you typically earn a slightly higher, locked-in interest rate. Withdrawing early usually comes with a penalty.

Because of this, a CD is not appropriate for your emergency fund, which you will want easily accessible. And frankly, I prefer most of my short-term money that way—and find the *interest rate spread* hardly worth it. That said, you might find CDs interesting for savings goals a few years out. If you had reason to believe that rates were going to come down in the future, CDs would allow you to lock in the current interest rate—although this can be difficult to predict.

Whatever you decide, do *not* confuse endlessly shopping around for bank accounts with the real work of saving money. The former is the personal finance equivalent of the "Look Busy, Jesus Is Coming" bumper sticker. The latter is actually getting ready. Pick an account and get moving! Because **the best account is the one that is getting used**.

10-MINUTE MISSION

My goal for my fully funded emergency fund is ____________________.

Open a savings account specifically for your emergency fund and make your first transfer.

4

DEBT VERSUS INVEST

Should I invest when I have debt?

You walk into Victoria's Secret at age nineteen for a Very Sexy Push-Up Bra and enough Love Spell fragrance to casually choke out an entire dorm floor. You leave with new cleavage and also debt. (And on a hilariously named Angel credit card, no less. Because c'mon, "The Devil's Plastic" was right there for the taking!) If you spend time thinking about it, this scenario is absurd. And yet it is such a typical American experience that I can write about it here and everyone will know exactly what I am talking about. Credit card debt is not just extremely common in the US but is actively pushed onto people (teenagers!) who probably can't afford it *and* who don't understand how fast it can spiral.

Forty-five percent of American adults are carrying a balance on their credit cards, with an average balance of nearly $6,100. For many, the total is even higher. Although having credit card debt is far from a personal failure—an indebted population is not a sign of a caring, functioning society—you won't regret taking radical responsibility and paying off your credit cards. Approach paying off your credit cards with urgency, as if they fund your biggest haters. Because, in a way, they do.

Despite what the beautiful, racially ambiguous family wearing matching Christmas pajamas in the Mastercard commercial wants you to think, credit cards are predatory, designed with outrageous interest rates, fees, and penalties (which I'll get to) that disproportionately affect folks who are already struggling, exacerbating any existing hardship. In 2022 alone, Americans paid over $130 billion in interest and fees to credit card companies, a figure that exceeds the value of Guatemala's entire economy. I can think of few other mechanisms as efficient at funneling the hard-earned money from the hands of working people and into the silk-lined pockets of the Big Bank executives.

I'm picking on credit cards because they are both ubiquitous and have criminal rates of interest, but really credit cards are just one type of debt. There are also loans, leverage, and lines of credit. American banks are a veritable Baskin-Robbins of different flavors of debt. Debt is defined as money borrowed by one party from another, usually to be paid back with interest over time. So-called *good debt* refers to the type of borrowing that could be considered an investment in your future, such as student loans, mortgages, or business loans, where the prospective, potential returns outweigh the costs. (I say *so-called* because it doesn't always work out this way. Ask anyone crushed under the boulder of their student loans.) *Bad debt* is borrowed for depreciating assets like a car or a Peloton bike turned laundry rack. Interest is usually high, and costs surpass any potential value gained. Although bad debt is not ideal, people may accrue it when they're otherwise out of options.

That said, let's address the question at the heart of this chapter: Should you invest or pay off your debt?

To begin, consider credit cards. In 2024, the average interest rate on a credit card balance—an *annual percentage rate* or *APR*—was 22%. (So, if you were to make a $1,000 purchase on a credit card with a rate of 22% and maintain a debt balance of $1,000 throughout the year, you would accrue approximately $220 in interest charges.) Further, rates can change and go higher. For example, if you miss payments, you can be charged a *penalty APR* as high as 29.99%.

You can't earn that kind of return with investing. Not with stocks, bonds, or real estate. Not even with Victoria's Secret push-up bras! (Although to my college mind, they were an investment, guaranteed to generate free Long Island iced teas at the bar.) With your investments, assume you'll earn between 5% and 10% per year, on average. With credit cards, you are *losing* double or triple that in interest. As long as we're talking about being nineteen again, you might think of investing while in credit card debt as the Cabo San Lucas spring break equivalent of wearing stilettos in the sand. Any height you may achieve is quickly swallowed up. Therefore, it makes mathematical sense to tackle high-interest debt *before* investing.

In an ideal world, you pay off your credit cards in full each month. If that's not your current world, and you have a balance at the end of each month, our first order of business is to get that balance down. Eventually, to zero. Do this by making more than the *minimum monthly payment*. Minimum monthly payments are designed for maximum pain: You pay only a sliver of the principal, while the majority goes to interest. This effectively drags out the repayment schedule, costing you a lot in the process. In addition to making higher payments, you'll want to stop adding to the balance. Let yourself get ahead. Get those stilettos to terra firma.

There is, possibly, one big exception here: if your 401(k) offers a *company match*. That's where your employer matches the money you *contribute* (save to) your plan. This is an instant doubling of your money—a 100% gain!—which trumps even a 22% interest rate. COOL, HUH? I can assure you that a retirement match is the only legal, reliable way to double your money instantly. (Trust me, I have researched the matter extensively. My God, the hours I've lost.) Unless you feel like you are drowning in it, having some credit card debt is not a reason to leave your match money on the table. Whatever your company matches, make that happen now.

And because it always comes up, I'll beat you to it: The points or miles you earn on a card do not make maintaining a credit card balance "worth it." Not a single card even gives bonus points for keeping a balance on it. In fact, the interest people pay on their credit cards is what subsidizes miles programs. Said another way, your interest payments fund Brayden's trip to Bali. (Not to mention, Bob the banker's bonus.) Poor people pay for rich people's vacations. Even when accounting for miles, the ideal way to use a credit card is still to never pay interest. So if you're scheming for miles, sure, get your points from what you charge, but only if you can then pay the balance right off.

But what about debt with a rate of interest that falls in the 5% to 10% range of expected investment returns? Well, if your debt causes you emotional pain—no matter the interest rate—you have my permission to aggressively work on it.

But please don't wait until you've paid off *all* debt to start retirement investing!

While it's clear that actively paying off high-interest debt is a top priority, things get a little murkier with lower-interest debt. For debts with rates below 10%, which includes many mortgages and federal student loans, you'll at least want to consider focusing your Gap on investing over proactive debt repayment beyond your current monthly payments.

Here's how that might look: Once you've tackled your high-interest and emotionally distressing debt, you swiftly integrate investing into your strategy—even if you've still got some debt. I know it sounds like a backtrack! But it's not. You do not need to be totally debt-free to start investing. No way.

For one, you deserve more than your debt. Don't let that hoebag Sallie Mae stop you from building your own thing. But this is especially true when considering the power of *compounding returns.* One of the more spectacular features of investing, compounding returns is when your money makes money, which then makes you even more money. On the surface, an interest rate comparison seems straightforward. After all, 7% interest is 7% interest, whether you are paying it or earning it, right? Well, compounding, especially over long periods like decades, tells a different story:

Consider a $10,000 student loan at a 7% rate of interest versus a $10,000 investment earning a 7% rate of compounding returns, over the same ten-year period:

$10,000 student loan with a 7% APR paid monthly over a ten-year period:

- Total amount paid over ten years: $13,933
- **Total interest paid: $3,933**

$10,000 invested earning a 7% compounding rate of return over ten years:

- Final value after ten years: $19,672
- **Total earned investing: $9,672**

So, if you had an extra $10,000 lying around, should you use it to proactively pay off your student loan or invest? If you were to pay off the student loan, you would save $3,933 in interest over ten years. If you were to invest the $10,000, you would earn $9,672 over the same period. At first blush, investing seems like the obvious choice! There is a catch, though: Investment returns aren't guaranteed, and there's always a chance that markets won't cooperate and your returns will fall short. Paying off the student loan, on the other hand, offers a guaranteed return in the form of interest savings. Plus, sometimes the sheer peace of mind of paying off debt can be worth the trade-off. So, either path might be the solid choice, depending on what feels right to you.

But that's not all. If you are investing for financial independence and have a long investing life ahead of you, it is *also* fair to consider what happens beyond the ten-year timeline. Because presumably, you're going to keep that $10,000 invested for years or even decades to come. Back to our example:

$10,000 invested earning a 7% compounding rate of growth over forty years:

- Final value: $149,745
- **Total earned investing: $139,745**

After forty years, that same 10,000 bucks continuously earning a 7% compounding rate of return creates $139,745 in profit! So, forty years from now, would you prefer to have an extra $139,745 or to have saved $3,933 in interest decades prior? I have a hunch you'll want the big money. I wasn't lying when I said that investing is how your money grows for real.

Now, you could also achieve nearly the same effect by (1) paying off the $10,000 student loan, and (2) after it's paid off, redirecting the money you'd been spending on monthly payments to investing. Either technique works great. The point is that you find ways to prioritize investing as you manage and make payments on any reasonable debts. Over the long, glorious arc of your life, you won't regret the money you invested. This is your case for getting started investing as soon as you're able—after you've saved up a solid start to your emergency fund and you've paid off high-interest debt.

The example above illustrates the power of COMPOUND RETURNS, which we will learn more about in chapter 23, but they aren't the only reason you'll want to consider investing now. Unfortunately, savings don't keep up with *inflation* (rising costs) and investing lets you end up with more than you put in—even after inflation is accounted for. Investing is what gives us a shot at having enough for retirement, which is likely to be the biggest expense of our lives.

Not convinced? Consider how much it costs to live for one year. Now multiply that by twenty or thirty years. Add your nipple tassels to that and let's just say the number is getting big. Many of us *will* live into our nineties, and I was sent here by your future self to remind you of this. Get started with whatever amount you can, and you'll thank yourself later.

The job of saving enough for retirement can be scary to consider. I don't deny that, but I also like to use a positive reframing: *Hopefully*, it is the biggest expense of my lifetime. Hopefully, we get to spend twenty-plus years off the clock and on the open road with our Rich Old Lady biker gang, wind in our grays!

10-MINUTE MISSION

While you make all necessary debt payments, make a plan to proactively pay off your high-interest debt. Begin by prioritizing your debt with the highest rate, working your way lower. Or you can pick off any cards with low balances, securing psychological wins. Don't overthink it. Make a list of your debts including their interest rates; choose one and attack.

Here's an example of what that might look like:

						INTEREST RATE	SMALLEST BALANCE
Debt	**Balance**	**Monthly Payment**	**Interest Rate**	**Payment Date**	**Time Remaining**	**Priority**	**Priority**
Visa Credit Card	$6,007	currently $200	22%	3rd of the month	45 months	1	2
Student Loan	$12,880	$571	6%	5th	24 months	3	3
Car Loan	$4,840	$148	8%	16th	37 months	2	1
Mortgage	$375,000	$2,270	4%	1st	20 years	4	4

Next, it's your turn!

						INTEREST RATE	SMALLEST BALANCE
Debt	Balance	Monthly Payment	Interest Rate	Payment Date	Time Remaining	Priority	Priority

If you'd prefer to do this work on a computer, I have created a digital debt repayment spreadsheet that you can access at richoldlady.com.

5

BUDGET

How do I build a budget that actually works?

It pains me to admit I'm an ex–finance bro. From the moment I wrestled my way into my first discounted poly-blend blazer from Ann Taylor Loft, I probably could have surmised that the career was a spiritual mismatch. Instead, it took about five years before I fully accepted how unhappy I was. It was also around that time that I realized I would always be a finance bro because my cycle of spending was keeping me locked into the job, without an ability to save.

It was in 2008 that I landed my first Big Girl Job as an associate at the finance firm. At the time, I was proud to be a young woman in a mostly male space, which I naively took as a sign of my exceptionalism, not that something was broken. Honestly, I wasn't really thinking that deeply about the work at all. I was just following the prescribed motions, doing what you're supposed to do after graduating from UCLA with degrees in economics and communications.

A year and a half in, a manager pulled me aside. "Hey," he said. "I notice you talk shit to your coworkers all day. Why don't you come upstairs and talk shit to our clients?" (True story.) You see, the stock market had just experienced the most spectacular crash of our lifetimes, and the firm was recruiting smooth talkers into client-facing roles. Thus I became an investment counselor, on the phone with high-net-worth clients, explaining portfolio strategy during a time of widespread financial terror. At twenty-five, my job was letting grown men scream at me about their money. Then, once I hung up, I was butting up against internal office politics shaped by inflated male egos and on more occasions than I care to count, fielding unwanted advances from coworkers.

My disdain for the work eventually curdled into full-blown disillusionment. But, there was a problem. I had spent my twenties honing just two skills: talking about the stock market and sucking up to rich men, neither of which I *ever* wanted to do again. I knew I needed to walk away from finance but I couldn't walk away without money.

At the time, I didn't have much. I had burned through paychecks because I was young and fun and stupid but also because I hated my job and was self-soothing, mostly at bars. I could not see what is now so obvious in retrospect: My reckless spending was keeping me tethered to the very thing that was making me spend recklessly. If I wanted out, I would need to break free from the work-consumption loop.

On January 1, 2013, I made a life-changing resolution: I was going to save enough money to quit, travel for a year, and figure out what was next. To do this, I immediately began to keep relentless track of every dollar. I cut all nonessential spending. I went from a person who regularly bought rounds of shots for strangers in bars, my favorite pastime, to someone who didn't set foot in a bar for months. My budget for daily splurges, clothing, socializing, and beauty was $0. My hair got so long that it gave itself a haircut by breaking off at the ends.

I also tried freeganism, where "what's for lunch?" depends on what is, well, free. We worked long days and ate at our desks, and I never hesitated to ask Chris or Rob or Manny, "Hey, you gonna eat the rest of that?" (It's fine; they all made more than me.) Every morning, I did a lap around the building for leftover team bagels. On Fridays, I raided the fridge before it was cleaned out, rescuing the abandoned leftovers and uneaten Chobani yogurts.

At the time, I rolled with a crew of guys who were in on my plan. When they hit up the Round Table Pizza buffet for lunch, they'd sneak a few breadsticks out for me. They fondly referred to the contraband, and eventually to me, as Trash Sticks, which morphed into Dumpster Dog and then Dumpster Doggy. (To this day, and despite the better advice of business coaches everywhere, I am still @dumpster.doggy on social media.)

Between some heavy metal budgeting and selling all my belongings, including my beloved Subaru, I had saved $30,000. By mid-August, I was in my boss's office, ready to put in my two-week notice. As I explained my plan to take time away from work, he cocked his head to the side and looked at me, putting the pieces together in real time. He had personally seen me pull a half-eaten burrito out of a trash can.

"Is this why you've been eating . . . trash?" he asked.

"Yes," I said. "This is why I've been eating trash."

I won't lie, the period of restriction was really hard. But no drink, drug, or material purchase could match the high of peeling out of that parking lot for the last time, windows down, Florence & the Machine blasting, office chair still spinning.

Two days later, I was on a flight to New Orleans, where I began my slow, meandering journey south, through Mexico, Central America, and South America. I traveled mostly by bus, though sometimes by more creative methods, like hitchhiking. One memorable leg found me hitching a ride in the Patagonia region of southern Chile, tucked away in the back of a sausage delivery van with a sausage delivery man. The road was bumpy and long, giving me plenty of time to reflect on how radical it felt to admit that I had made the wrong choice for myself—and then make a massive change. I wondered often whether it was an insane privilege or the most basic human right. Whatever it was, I wished everyone had access to it.

Cradled by the hum of the van and in my bed of Chilean hot dogs, I slowly began to walk back on my promise to leave finance behind for good. Helping rich men get richer had never been my life's true calling—but for the first time, I saw money not as something to collect for status but as a tool for second chances. And I wanted to talk to women about it.

Your story might not look like mine—unless you're also fleeing a finance bro past by literally disappearing into the Amazon jungle. That's okay. I'm not telling this story because I think you should quit your job to learn to play the pan flute at a backpacker's hostel in Costa Rica or even because extreme budgeting is necessary. (Or maybe your first climb is out from under the student debt society thought was fine to strap on an eighteen-year-old.) Whatever your starting point, I only hope it gives you a glimpse of what's possible when you question the default and explore whether there's another option.

Here are five essential principles of budgeting to help you find your own version of freedom.

1. Audit Your Spending

Many people begin budgeting by assigning dollars to categories without first auditing their spending. They may think they spend about $200 per month dining out, but they actually spend $400. To cut down, they randomly give themselves a $100 budget. They blast through it because they're budgeting based on vibes, baby, and that doesn't work.

Instead of this cycle of self-defeat, get serious about tracking your spending. You can do this manually or use an online money-tracking app like Copilot. Either way, spend three months getting intimate with your spending habits. Here's the energy I want you to bring to the investigation: Your best friend is dating someone new, and she's asked you to do some internet recon. *You're on it.* You crack your knuckles, get yourself a gigantic iced coffee, fire up your screens, and spend eight hours sleuthing every cobwebbed corner of the internet. By EOD, you have a detailed PowerPoint presentation complete with their Uber rating and ratio of positive-to-negative small-business reviews on Google. Yeah, *that* energy!

You won't have to do it forever, but for now, track every single purchase. Then categorize purchases in ways that make sense to you. (Can't figure out where to put your Target spending? Make up a category called "Target." There ain't no laws.) Study your spending habits as if you were reading from a textbook, free from shame or regret. It is simply an act of knowing. It is not saying, "Fuck me, I'm so bad at money," it is only noting, "Huh, I spend $30 a month on farmer's market specialty pickles! That is information I did not have before, and now I do."

2. Identify Areas for Improvement, Make Compromises

When possible, go for big wins. Find ways to save on transportation, food delivery, and dining out. Try to negotiate everything from your internet service to the interest rates on your credit card debt. Switch cell phone and car insurance carriers. I've seen too many people ruin their financial security because they bought a too-expensive car. (In my opinion, the best car is a reliable sedan that's paid off.) And yeah, do it: Go and cancel a subscription or two.

For discretionary spending, look back to your tracking from step 1. Identify every purchase that, a month or two later, felt totally forgettable. If you are like most people in the age of frictionless spending, you'll find these charges littered all over your transaction history. Be gentle with yourself—we live in a world that relentlessly pressures us to spend—but be ruthless about cutting those kinds of rascally purchases from your spending moving forward. If you cannot eliminate the category altogether, set a firm boundary (that's a budget!) for monthly spending.

3. Set Up Automations

If you currently have any Gap whatsoever, put it to work right away. Set up an automatic monthly transfer between your checking account and whatever goal you are currently working on, whether an emergency fund, debt repayment, or investing.

Or, if you have a W-2 job, it's often possible to split a paycheck so part of it goes straight into a savings account, an off-site emergency fund at a high-interest bank, even a separate investment account.

Timing is clutch because you don't miss money you never saw. If you consistently get paid on the same days of the month, try to set up automatic transfers on the next business day so you barely notice the money before it's gone again.

4. Increase Automations Every Three Months

Set yourself a quarterly calendar reminder to increase your saving and investing automations. (Put it in your calendar *now*.) Also, make a mental note to increase your automations anytime you get a raise at work or bag a bigger regular client.

If you are self-employed or have a sporadic income, you'll want to do a combination of automations *and* manual transfers. For automations, set up an amount that you feel comfortable clearing each month. Then, quarterly, do manual transfers with any additional funds.

5. Try Other Stuff

Try anything! My friend and former finance blogger Luxe would move money into her savings and investment accounts every time someone said something annoying at work. As you can probably imagine, she is a very rich person.

The "everything in moderation" contingent may come for my throat on this one, but I'm also a fan of the occasional no-spend or savings challenge. Personally, I operate in energetic seasons. In the winter, I'm curled away in my cave with my Netflix and blankie. Come summer, I'm swinging naked from a lamppost at a San Francisco street rave and getting into fistfights with strangers at the local dive. I go through sprints and periods of rest with my money management, too. Do not burn yourself out, please, but it's okay to try techniques that allow you to get excited about accomplishing a tangible and specific goal.

If you've tried the more fluid, DIY approach I've outlined above but feel like you're flailing like a wind sock at a used-car dealership, you should implement a regimented budgeting program. Plenty of people will find that they need or want a rigid structure to their spending. And that's okay! Know thyself! Budgeting apps seem to come and go, but currently I am using Copilot, the same app I recommend for tracking your spending.

For something more hands-on, try zero-based budgeting with the software (and app) You Need a Budget. Copilot and YNAB each cost around a hundred bucks a year. (Although I don't use YNAB, you'll find no shortage of evangelists who swear by its ability to pay for itself tens of times over.) Another highly recommended free budget app is Cashew (cashewtrack.com), or you can use the premade budgeting templates available in Microsoft Excel or Google Sheets. If you are a gel pen and notebook girly, try a physical budgeting workbook. I like the one by The Budget Mom.

No matter which strategy you pick, remember that trying stuff that doesn't work *is* part of the process! Experimenting *is* learning how to budget! This practice is not about perfection, it's about paying attention, knowing yourself, and adjusting as you go. As you do, continue to ask yourself what really matters. It's about learning to say no to what doesn't serve you, so you can say yes to what does. This is how you begin to use your money in a way that honors both who you are now and the Rich Old Lady you're becoming.

10-MINUTE MISSION

1. *Print out your last three months of statements and study them.*
2. *Find two immediate ways to increase your Gap via reduced spending.*
3. *Set up automations for savings, debt repayment, or investing.*

6

SPENDING

Okay, but for reals,
how can I stop spending so much money?

We can probably all agree that the first step to spending less is having a clear picture of where your money is going. But we also live in a world designed to drain us of our hard-earned dollars. To protect ourselves and our futures, we must confront the powerful profit-driven forces that compel us to spend money in the first place.

We're up against a goddamn machine, darling, and I want to talk about it.

I recently had a flashback: I was resting my head against an ironing board, a firm hand against a nearby wall, as my friend pressed a scalding-hot clothing iron over my thick, curly brown hair. We were doing hair and makeup together for our high school senior-year winter formal, and my eighteen-dollar Rite Aid flat iron couldn't deliver the firepower needed to obliterate all signs of frizzy imperfection—a feat of follicular mastery I had taken into my heart as a sacred feminine duty.

The memory was triggered as I flipped through a magazine at the airport, stumbling across an ad straight out of my youth. Apparently, L'Oréal models still have hair that comes down in one glossy wave, light refracting off its seemingly singular surface. I snapped the magazine shut, thinking of all the time and money I've wasted chasing that hair. Hair that, as a girl born with a mop more reminiscent of Richard Simmons's, was never mine to have.

After spending two decades in a physical and financial battle with my hair, it feels sweet to get compliments on it now, in its natural state. Sometimes, people on the internet even ask me for my hair routine. And sure, no secrets here. "I just scrunch it while soaking wet using some drugstore curl cream and let it air dry," I respond. But then I trip over myself to explain that "This is just the way my hair is!" and to really nail the point, I add, "If your mom didn't say, 'Damn, this bitch looks like Howard Stern!' when you slid out the womb, you probably can't achieve this particular look! And whatever you do, do not let any L'Oréal model, Sephora marketing executive, or curly girl with a TikTok shop convince you otherwise."

I now recognize that my past efforts to adhere to the beauty standards of the time were an attempt to fit in. Back then, I believed that straight, shiny hair would deliver me to a sort of social Shangri-la. And so much of our behavior can be explained this way: We all need love and to be loved. We need to feel accepted and worthy of attention and respect. And because true love and acceptance can be hard to obtain, well, crank that Black+Decker up to its highest heat.

Insecurity is the mechanism by which we are open to receiving feedback from those around us, allowing us to adjust our behavior to be a better, more harmonious member of the tribe, which was (and is) necessary for survival. But insecurity in a modern world isn't spontaneous, or an internal signal that arises out of nowhere—it is almost always shaped by the world we live in. At its most harmful, insecurity is cultivated to keep people compliant, spending money, and reaching for approval. And once that insecurity is firmly rooted, it's exploited to hell and back by extraordinarily powerful corporations looking to make a profit.

I read an essay in 2019 that changed how I think about beauty forever. In "In the Name of Beauty," Tressie McMillan Cottom describes beauty as a system that stratifies. Beauty is always relative, but that relativity isn't random; it creates hierarchies on purpose. Why? Because the people on top enjoy it that way. The more the dominant, Eurocentric, patriarchal beauty ideal is reinforced, generally by those it serves, the more status is stripped from those already excluded by it, like Black women and poor women. Because it exists to rank and exclude, beauty functions as an oppressive system.

Even gender itself is a performance we're disciplined into, and beauty standards are some of its strictest enforcers. Some days, I tell myself beauty is fun and not that serious. Other days—specifically, the day I get a particularly vengeful bikini wax—performing beauty feels like a malicious act of institutional compliance. I can feel myself reinforcing a system that uplifts those who conform, and quietly punishing those who don't.

Here is where it gets *really* uncomfy: We do live in a world where our safety, status, and prosperity are tied to the existence of someone *below* us. Our lives are propped up by people less rich, more vulnerable, less beautiful—less *valuable,* by capitalism's standards. I recently watched a Netflix comedy special by a very famous blonde comedian who said, with blunt honesty, that the first thing she does when she enters any room is look around to make sure she is the most beautiful person there. She finds this practice comforting.

All of this effort, all of these costs of maintenance imply another side to beauty's ledger: power and capital. McMillan Cottom writes that beauty is the only form of capital that women are allowed without challenge, and that they are encouraged to obtain. But she clarifies that "Beauty is not *good* capital. It compounds the oppression of gender. It constrains those who identify as women against their will. . . . It colonizes. It hurts. It is painful. It can never be fully satisfied. It is not useful for human flourishing. Beauty is, like all capital, merely valuable." That is, until it isn't.

There are undeniable benefits to "beautiful privilege" that I won't refute here. Beauty, especially the kind that signals proximity to whiteness and wealth, can open up options, and conversely, a lack of conventional beauty or "normality" in facial structures or body shape can take them away. As humans, we commonly exhibit a cognitive bias wherein we conflate morality with physical attractiveness. Every year on my birthday, I get to witness the *halo effect* in action, because I happen to share said birthday with Jennifer Aniston. Every year, on our special day, I watch as the internet trips all over Aniston, who is "aging in reverse" because she is "unproblematic" and "stays in her lane." Taps microphone: *People? She is extremely fucking rich?!*

I really, really feel for us! All of us. And trust me, I believe everyone is doing their best calculus in a world that indeed values beauty and, perhaps even more than beauty, compliance. But I have also worked with enough women to know that pursuing beauty at all costs can backfire. Because women are taught to see beauty as their primary form of value, they are left without the tangible resources they need to survive. That's the danger: Beauty is a form of wealth that women are encouraged to prioritize but that they never truly own—at least not for long. Worse still, the pursuit of one, an unstable currency at best, often comes at the direct cost of building more durable forms of power.

Further, there is no end to what beauty asks of us. This is what Katie Gatti Tassin of Money with Katie—who has done phenomenal writing on the subject of beauty and money—describes as the "Hot Girl Hamster Wheel," where every dollar you spend on beauty functions as a commitment to spend more in the future because each and every treatment must be maintained. And because the corporate profit motive is bottomless, there is no natural end to the game. Gatti Tassin writes, "This is the ambush of ceding an inch to aesthetic labor: It will always return for its due mile. In the industrialized west, beauty standards are just a very specific, powerful manifestation of capitalism, so of course we *must* keep inventing new gimmicks and increasing their demands. How else do LVMH's shareholders achieve 25% year-over-year growth?" The LVMH she references here is Moët Hennessy Louis Vuitton, the French mega-conglomerate that owns Fenty Beauty, Make Up For Ever, Benefit Cosmetics, Bite Beauty, and Sephora, to name a few brands.

Instead of making meaningful progress in dismantling beauty standards for the benefit of all women, capitalism dreams up new problems for us to fix. While the Tumblr-era obsession with extreme thinness is now less overtly acceptable (though, disturbingly, it seems to be making a comeback), it is completely culturally acceptable—encouraged, even—to talk about wrinkles like they're a problem to be solved. But believing that getting a wrinkle warrants alarm is profoundly damaging to the self-worth of all people, but especially girls. Girls, who can now be found at Sephora in droves, spending their hard-earned allowances on retinol creams, a practice they learned from the adults. No one benefits more from this than the beauty industry, which sees in every aging face not a representation of a life to be celebrated but a chance to exploit insecurity.

I'm picking on the Beauty Industrial Complex, I know. While I believe that there is no way to exaggerate the harm it does to women, it's also a perfect canvas for illustrating the broader issue at hand: **So much of our consumption was never really our idea in the first place.** It's the idea of a culture that teaches us to look or live a certain way to be loved.

That is why "'I just like what I like' is always a capitalist lie," writes McMillan Cottom. "If beauty matters at all to how people perceive you, how institutions treat you, which rules are applied to you, and what choices you can make, then beauty must also be a structure of patterns, institutions, and exchanges that eat your preferences for lunch." In the same way, we are coerced into believing that if we just get *this thing*—the next haul, the next phone, the next car, the diamond ring, the big suburban house—then our lives will have just a bit more meaning within the social contexts in which we exist.

We're not just up against a few catchy jingles and glossy billboards of the 1950s. How quaint! No, this is military-grade psychological warfare, with advertisers deploying every trick in the behavioral science playbook to infiltrate our brains and make us buy stuff we didn't even know we needed. Corporations, driven by the relentless pursuit of profit, hire advertisers. Governments prefer a pacified populace—exhausted workers self-soothing with little treats, just comfy enough with our online purchases and iced coffees to never demand a change.

And it would be one thing if the battlefield was just for your wallet, but it's for your sense of self-worth, shaped by forces that don't have your best interests at heart. The cumulative effect is the undermining of our self-love and ability to be in community with each other and the planet. It doesn't help our cause that spending money actually *feels good*—at least for a moment. Every time we shop, our brains give us a little splash of dopamine, the chemical that makes us feel rewarded and motivated. The system is rigged to exploit not only your insecurities but also your biology.

So, yeah. This is my chapter on reducing spending. I'm not here to tell you how to save a dollar on said iced coffee or to cut iced coffee from your budget—I don't think we need surface-level hacks. But this isn't an invitation to beat yourself up over how you spend your money, either. I'm not anti–spending money. Spending in ways that make your life genuinely better, more interesting, more joyful—that's money well spent. This is simply an offering of awareness; a chance to see the system we're operating within a little more clearly. And when you're ready, you can use that awareness like a blacklight over your budget—exposing the residue of expectations and conditioning, so you can wipe away all the crud that does not belong to you.

As my best friend Emma says, "we're all just animals with credit cards," and I think it's worth reflecting on what we're really trying to achieve: love. To achieve that love, we lose ourselves to acquiring signifiers of personal success, spending, beauty, and clout instead of taking the simpler, more direct route: practicing love itself. This is a practice that does not cost money, but it is deep work. It is one of lifelong persistence. It is work that may require dealing with the feelings of unworthiness created by the very system that wants you to keep spending.

What can cost you your happiness, though, is a lifetime of keeping up appearances. To strive endlessly—on social media, with strangers, with friends—to make it seem you have no discernible flaws or cracks or flaps. To believe that life is a journey to fix what was never broken in the first place.

Something that keeps me grounded is recognizing that my consumption doesn't just affect me; it ripples out to those around me. We are all connected. This is true in a literal sense; for example, when we buy fast fashion, we're bolstering a system that exploits other human beings with dreams and hopes just as big as ours. But it's not just about the literal impact; it's about the *tone* we set. When people meet me, I want them to feel no pressure to be anyone other than exactly who they are: evolving, aging, and utterly perfect because of their quirks, not in spite of them. In college, we used to have "Come as You Are" parties. It was really just an excuse to show up at the frats in our sweats and unwashed ponytails for a jovial evening of beer pong, and I think that's beautiful. The world is a party, and the theme is Come as You Are.

I achieve self-esteem by knowing that people can rely on me, and I genuinely believe that true fabulousness comes from creativity, resourcefulness, bravery, a sense of humor, and a willingness to embrace what is, not from trying to outrun time (or the women around me) with a credit card. And if I'm chasing admiration or respect through my consumption, the unintended consequence is that the people around me might feel like they need to keep up. And that's *not* the feeling I want to be transmitting to my fellow Rich Old Ladies. I want all of us to get wrinkly and solve problems and put on weird little plays together. Who's joining my commune?

Never forget it: The powers that be *want* you to believe love and worth can be bought. They'd be thrilled if you spent your entire life chasing validation through consumption, never pausing long enough to invest in yourself or your future. But that's not what I want for you. I want you to get old without fear, build financial security, and invest in the things that actually make life rich. Save your money, and if you're going to swim with great white sharks, let it be off the coast of Australia, not with the oligarchs who get richer every time you take their bait.

7

INCOME

How do I earn more money?

If there's one lesson about earning more money you need to know, it's this: Earning money is a skill completely separate from the job you do.

Me, personally? I took my sweet time learning this.

Ten years ago, I began my self-employment journey with a blog. It was 2016, right in the middle of the great stampede to social media, and I was out here blogging like it was 2003. I had a vague hopefulness that it might someday become a revenue stream, but mostly, I just wanted to share my ideas and be a writer. That was the extent of my business planning. In retrospect, no one could say that *The Dumpster Dog Blog* was an entrepreneurial masterstroke.

To stay afloat while I blogged, I took on side gigs writing freelance articles and copy for banks, mostly covering topics related to student loans and investing. And then, in a career twist that really confused my parents, I got my first-ever bartending job. I was thirty years old.

By then I knew my next mission was to help women who'd been left out of conversations about investing become a part of them. And at some point between scrubbing urinals and refreshing my blog's tragic page views, it started to dawn on me: The young women I most wanted to reach didn't even know to look for this information, let alone in a niche finance blog. So while I kept writing and freelancing, I knew I needed to find another way to connect.

One night, while pouring a beer at the tap, it hit me: *sororities.* If I could weasel my way into sororities, I could reach women a hundred at a time *before* they stepped into their first corporate training session.

Not long after my epiphany, I was knocking on the door of my first sorority house. A young woman with a greasy topknot opened the door, visibly puzzled by the clearly not-college-aged adult standing before her. "Hi, I'm Amanda and this is very random," I blurted all over her oversized LAMBDA CHI FORMAL T-shirt, "but I'd love to teach your members how to invest."

She took my business card, but I knew I would never hear from her again. Painful and embarrassing as the interaction was, I kept trying. I continued to knock on doors and tapped into my Greek connections. Eventually, I received a yes, and then another and another. This marked the beginning of both a West Coast sorority tour and the version of the business I still run today, which focuses primarily on live, educational experiences like workshops.

From a 120-woman dining room in Seattle to a basement in Corvallis to a packed living room in Berkeley, the women showed up in sweatpants and UGG boots, unsure of what they were getting into but still abuzz with the energy of a room full of close girlfriends.

To set the tone, I always kicked things off with a story of my own. While presenting at Alpha Phi at the University of Washington, I told them my sister used to be a member—until she got kicked out for smoking pot. During rush week. While she was rush chair. The gals *lost* it. Laughing at the delinquency of my (now-successful) sister—thank you, Madelaine—cut through any stiffness they expected from a finance presentation. And because they knew I wasn't there to judge or patronize, they opened up, unafraid to ask questions. Best of all, they had no shame that they "should have already known this by now."

And while those young women confirmed that I was indeed onto something, I wasn't making good money. I was still cobbling together income from, like, five or six different sources and barely scraping by. Tired of constantly chasing invoices for $200 articles I'd written months prior, I knew something had to change. I had experimented enough. It was time to pick a path and learn the skill of earning more money.

First, I decided to listen to my audience, who were clearly telling me they preferred learning from me in a classroom setting. Accepting this meant letting go of what I thought I wanted, which was to be a writer. With my ego in check, I cast my energy into building a bona fide business. That meant following the momentum of the workshops, turning my lessons into scalable online products, building a sales channel (goodbye, blog; hello, social media and email newsletter), and executing a marketing strategy. Now, when people ask what I do, I still say, "I teach women to invest." But as a business owner, I know that's a sliver of the work I do.

This is how I came to believe that each of us has two jobs: the job we do, and the job of marketing ourselves to make as much money as possible while doing it. When I began my career in corporate, I didn't know this. I only got a big pay bump at age twenty-five because I was poached by a higher-paying department, not because I strategized for it. It led me to believe that promotions and raises were assumed, and that "moving on up" was a product of time and hard work.

Entrepreneurship snapped me out of that fantasy real quick. You can offer the best service or product on the planet, but if you can't get people to pay you for it, you're cooked. And I believe this to be just as true for people with paycheck jobs. If your job is all you do, no matter how well you do it, you're missing half the game.

My dears, I don't say this because I like it. Telling people to "just make more money" is rude and wildly out of touch. We live in an extraordinarily powerful system designed to keep people, especially women, financially repressed. But then again, what option do we have but to develop the skills that protect our time and labor from exploitation? To ensure that we get our fair share?

Which, by the way, *the guys are doing*. I've personally known many men who spend as much time strategizing their next raise as they do actually working. So yeah, that's why every single one of us needs to be in this conversation—even you, bitch (compliment) making $300,000 a year! Because you know that man sitting next to you is pulling $350K for doing less!

A study on gendered language in money media found that 65% of articles in women's magazines characterized women as excessive spenders. Nearly 90% focused on how to save. Meanwhile, 70% of money-related articles for men emphasized building, growing, investing, and making money. Men are conditioned to claim their financial power. Women are taught to shrink from it. And while we can all agree that some practical strategies for saving money are helpful in this ridiculously expensive world, the frugality discourse reinforces the idea that women should play small.

I want to give you permission, maybe for the first time in your life, to shift your financial focus away from budgetary restriction and toward expansion. Specifically, toward growing your income. Especially if you feel like there's no more hacking away at your budget to be done, this is a much better use of your limited energy. Saving and investing are a function of earning, and more money invested means more money returned.

That this book devotes only a few pages to increasing your income isn't a reflection of how important it is; only that this is a book about investing, the process of turning income into wealth. So instead of diving into specifics, providing scripts, or telling you to sacrifice your Saturday to a side hustle, I want to offer five big ideas that I hope will shift the way you think about earning. Pick what feels useful to you and your situation and leave the rest.

1. Reckon with the Economic System

If you are trying to navigate a corn maze, the first step is to know that you're in a corn maze. By addressing broader systems, we can be more savvy participants of that system.

Businesses under the current capitalist model are typically designed to benefit owners, not individual workers. The primary function of a worker in this system (you) is to create value in excess of your cost (your pay). That excess value then becomes wealth for the people who own the business, whether executives or shareholders. Your boss's boss's boss wants to make a profit, not make room for you and all your unique glory. There are few exceptions to this.

Therefore, your value to your company must be measurable and obvious in terms of the business's profitability. No need to rise, grind, and tithe at the altar of Shareholder Value, but I am asking you to see labor under a capitalist model for exactly what it is. The best way to increase your income is to increase your value to the company, to be integral to the initiatives that propel the company toward profitability.

And just as important, to be seen as integral. Although it can be difficult, find thoughtful ways to talk openly about your contributions on a regular, ongoing basis. Remember, your second job is to make visible how good you are at your first.

2. Understand Your Industry's Quirks for Advancement

If you've been within five feet of LinkedIn in the last decade, you've probably heard the millennial *job-hop* gospel. And there is some truth to the advice to switch employers often. You often have the most leverage to negotiate when you're being hired. (And you must negotiate. They want to hire you, *and* they're expecting you to counter their offer. I promise.) Once you're strapped in, it's much harder to grow beyond a company's predetermined *pay bands*.

However, this advice may be effective only in corporate America and within specific industries and market environments. For example, this approach worked well during the Silicon Valley hiring heydays of the mid-to-late 2010s, when low interest rates and a venture capital boom meant money flowed more freely than the nitro cold brew on tap. But layoffs swept the industry in 2024, and with many companies slashing salaries, it appears that the era of fat raises, LEGO rooms, and in-office back rubs is on pause. At least, for now.

This is not to say you shouldn't look around and see what else is out there. You should! Relatedly, you may have heard of the strategic magic of an *outside offer.* Even if you're not looking to leave, a second offer can theoretically give you serious leverage. You can take the new job and negotiate up front, or you can use the offer to trigger a conversation about compensation with your current manager. That said, this is ground on which women must tread lightly. Women are at particular risk of being seen as combative—see the next section on negotiating while female.

But perhaps the *best* strategy for advancement is this: Know your industry's quirks. Identifying realistic paths for advancement in your line of work beats taking career advice at face value any day. Some fields reward loyalty and internal promotion. Others penalize it. Some value credentials, others connections. The only way to find out is to study it. Creep LinkedIn job histories. Lurk in industry forums. Talk to people two, three levels above you and ask what actually helped them increase their income over time.

Job-hopping can be great when it is great, but understanding both the skills you need to make it to the next level of pay and the route you can take to get there is even better.

3. Negotiating While Female

For years, women were told the reason they earned less was because they didn't negotiate. I won't blame this entirely on the 2010s-ass, girl-boss-style career advice many of us came of age hearing, but it certainly had a hand in reinforcing the story that if women could just act more like men—ask for more, talk louder, beat them at their own game—we'd close the wage gap ourselves.

That's not how this works.

A recent study found that women *do* negotiate nearly as often as men. The problem isn't that women don't ask; it's that when they do, they're more likely to hear a no. Another study, published in 2024, found that women actually negotiate *more* than men. And yet another observed that while women aren't more demanding than men, they are frequently perceived as such. Whereas men need only display competence, women must balance their dual spinning plates of competence *and* niceness.

Worst of all, the belief that "women just don't ask" isn't just wrong, but is shown to actively undermine the support of the policies that may actually fix the wage gap.

Because gender bias often drives negotiation outcomes, stomping up to the table like a dude can backfire. To negotiate successfully, women may want to take extra care to be collaborative, not combative, always highlighting the benefit to all parties involved. For example, "I exceeded my sales target by 20% over the last four quarters, and believe that I can continue to exceed these targets by 20%. This will be integral in assuring the department reaches its sales goals."

Only once you've made your value to the "team" clear should you bring up whether you're being paid below market rate. Don't lead with this; it's hard to appeal to fairness in a system shaped by unconscious bias. What feels "fair" to your manager might still be influenced by outdated ideas about who deserves to be paid more. Come armed with salary data for your role in your geographic area and frame your request as alignment, not as a complaint. For example: "I recently came across industry research showing that the average pay for my role in the Chicago metropolitan area is 10% higher than what I'm currently earning. Considering I'm a top performer and committed to the success of our team, I'd love to discuss how we might close that gap." Find these salary figures on LinkedIn, Glassdoor, The Salary Project, industry spreadsheets, or Facebook groups. Thanks to salary transparency laws, some states now require employers to include salary ranges in job listings.

So, you've got this. Go in ready and practiced but with your shoulders relaxed. Believe in yourself and believe in them. Know that "no" is not a final answer; it is the beginning of a conversation about what is needed to achieve more pay. If your manager or company isn't open to a conversation, this, too, is good information to have! It is time to take your talent elsewhere. And if you'll allow me to round out this hype sesh on a slightly petty note: Please know that if they can't pay you and pay you well, that's embarrassing for their business, not for you.

Part of what is so frustrating about writing about the gender wage gap is that it is framed as a "Women's Problem" in the same way that sexual assault is framed as a "Women's Problem." It is not. It is a problem of bias against women by those in positions of power. A biased person can be any gender, but most often, it is men. Therefore, it is a "Men's Problem."

So, allow me to address the fellas for a minute. First, if you are reading this, hi! I am so happy you're here, and I bet you're wonderful. It is your duty to ensure that all women in your sphere of influence are compensated fairly. Share your salary and speak up on behalf of your colleagues. Examine your own desire to work with and for other men, because it's not harmless. It is a form of golf course discrimination that keeps women locked out of opportunities. And when you hit the voting booth, remember: We're on the same team. The policies that support women at work, like parental leave and worker protections, will make your life undeniably better, too. Don't fall for the lie that when she gets more, you get less. And please, call bullshit on any political narrative that pits us against each other in the name of scarcity, *especially* when it's coming from people who have more money than they could ever spend in multiple lifetimes.

4. Collective Bargaining

For all the ink spilled on women in the workplace over the last two decades, three of the most commercially successful books on the topic—*Lean In, Nice Girls Don't Get the Corner Office,* and *#GIRLBOSS*—share one glaring omission: Not a single one of them mentions labor unions.

Which is odd, considering that unions were basically invented to fix bias and exploitation in the workplace. Labor unions are worker-led organizations that use *collective bargaining* to negotiate fair pay and conditions for everyone they represent. That collective approach levels the playing field in ways that individualized strategies can't: Women in unions in the US earn 23% more than women in nonunion workplaces. The gender wage gap between unionized men and women narrows to 94%, compared with the 78% for nonunion women and nonunion men. The racial pay gap narrows, too: Black union workers earn 17% more than their nonunionized peers; Latino union workers earn 23% more. Because unions help to standardize wages, it's a lot harder for employers to quietly discriminate on the basis of race or gender.

If you have access to union work, take it seriously! It's one of the most reliable ways to protect your pay, your time, and your future.

Unions also fight for what allows women to stay in the workforce: paid family leave, job protections, and flexible schedules. The benefits don't stop there: Union members are also three and a half times more likely to have retirement pensions than nonunion workers. And the wins they secure don't just benefit union members; they ripple outward, raising standards across industries. We have unions to thank for weekends, eight-hour workdays, and child labor laws, to name a few. Which is why supporting union efforts, even if you're not in one, matters. That means no crossing picket lines, darlings! That is *not* Rich Old Lady behavior.

And if you're wondering why unions get left out of corporate feminist narratives, look no further than who benefits from keeping wages low. Meta, the company *Lean In* author Sheryl Sandberg helped lead for over a decade, has been found to actively resist unionization efforts. While empowering individual women was good for optics, empowering all workers would have been bad for business.

Let's hope the next era brings truly inclusive thinking, a kind that doesn't train women, or any workers, to play a rigged game, but to melt down the Monopoly board and build something better. If you are American, this'll take unlearning. You may even be experiencing defensiveness inside you as you read this right now. It's okay, very powerful forces condition us to believe that wealth can only be an individual achievement, not a collective possibility. But what if this is wrong? We know we're at our best when we look out for one another. What if the way to get rich is to band together and use our collective power to take back what we built in the first place?

5. Community

As you move up and along your career arc, your network is, without a doubt, one of your most valuable assets.

From inside a job, moving up the career ladder without someone advocating for you is almost impossible. Keep that in mind as you interact with the people in your orbit; those above you, of course, but also your coworkers. Being good at your job is important, but it's rarely enough on its own. Now, don't go baking everybody cakes for their birthdays like I did, *sigh.* (I tell myself I was fueled by nothing but a passion for Funfetti, but who knows, there may have been some implicit gender role fulfillment happening there.) Instead, find ways to make your manager's job noticeably easier. One simple example? Don't just flag a problem—fix it, and then let them know it's handled.

If you have a boss who, for whatever reason, will not be your advocate, I'm really sorry, but you should consider moving to a different department or looking for a new opportunity immediately.

Not that getting a new job is easy. I'm writing this from the middle of one of the most competitive job markets in recent memory, where it's not unusual to be up against a thousand other applicants for a single role. And the truth is, the odds aren't improving. Entire professions are evaporating as AI eats its way through industries that once felt solid. In this environment, a well-placed connection—someone who can nudge your résumé to the top of the pile—can mean the difference between an interview and nothing at all. (I know, I know. Cool meritocracy, bro.)

To stay sane while networking, which can feel forced and superficial, try to see it for what it can be: community building. When you approach networking with a mindset of reciprocity—helping others and receiving support in return—it feels more like an ecosystem than a transaction. Work is so oddly defining, isn't it? In many ways, our work will shape our lives. Do your best to fill it with beautiful people and maybe even try to have some fun.

And hold on for dear life to the creativity I know you were born with. Get out into the world! Inconvenience yourself for the sake of art! Keep your weird hobbies! Not because I want you to monetize your weird hobby, but because your life will be fuller for it. As a bonus, yeah, you'll be a more interesting person with cooler connections. Our life paths are ever evolving, but they can evolve in interesting and unexpected directions only so long as we keep those pathways open. And when the time comes, give back. Share what you've learned, lift others up, and create the opportunities you once needed. Them's the Rich Old Lady rules!

PART I HOMEWORK: Your Financial Order of Operations

It is time to build your own financial *order of operations*, where you make a list of what you want to work on next (and then after that). Assign each of your financial to-do items to one of two categories. The first is "Working the Gap," or how you'll grow your Gap. The second is "Putting the Gap to Work," which is how you plan to use your Gap.

To get your juices flowing, I've provided a detailed example. This is not to say that your list will look like this one, but to illustrate different directions you might explore in both categories. Feel free to build on this example for your own list. Use the space here, or make a big ol' checklist and hang it up somewhere visible.

Example Financial Order of Operations

Working the Gap

1. *Find three immediate ways to cut spending*
2. *Track spending for three months*
3. *Schedule a conversation with manager about pay*
4. *Design a plan to acquire skills necessary for promotion*
5. *Build a budget using information from spend tracking*
6. *Interview two people in my line of work about how they increased their income*

Putting the Gap to Work

1. *Begin an emergency fund (goal: $2,000)*
2. *Invest enough to secure retirement match*
3. *Pay off credit cards*
4. *Save one month of expenses for emergency fund*
5. *Increase retirement contributions*
6. *Save full emergency fund*

My Financial Order of Operations

Working the Gap	Putting the Gap to Work
1. ______________	1. ______________
______________	______________
2. ______________	2. ______________
______________	______________
3. ______________	3. ______________
______________	______________
4. ______________	4. ______________
______________	______________
5. ______________	5. ______________
______________	______________
6. ______________	6. ______________
______________	______________

RICH OLD LADY REFLECTION

One of the best things any young woman can do is surround herself with older women. Both in real life and online. Not just because older women have the best stories, give the best hugs, and make for our finest character actresses, but because they expand our understanding of womanhood beyond the narrow confines of youth. It's a tragedy, really, that our culture worships women's youth so intensely that we're conditioned to see it as our most valuable currency—when in reality, it's one of the least interesting things about us.

For me, the Golden Girls are front and center on my Rich Old Lady vision board. (Now, not everyone will want to model themselves after a quartet of cranky old white ladies, and I encourage you to find your own muses.) They remind me that the real secret to life isn't about chasing youth; it's about roasting your friends. Take, for instance, when Blanche proclaims that "flirting is part of my heritage!" and Rose innocently asks what that means, only for Dorothy to deadpan, "Her mother was a slut, too."

Let's leave it to the old ladies to show us what really matters: our relationships, the joy we allow ourselves to experience, and how to laugh our way through it all. In the words of Sophia Petrillo, "Move the coffee table, I wanna do a cartwheel."

PART II

RETIREMENT ACCOUNT BASICS

Helping you understand and choose
the retirement account that's right for you

8

RETIREMENT ACCOUNTS

What is a retirement account?

Retirement accounts are the new investor's greatest stumbling block, and even seasoned investors can misunderstand them. Online educators frequently spread misinformation about retirement accounts, and rarely are we taught this critical financial literacy in school. When I was fifteen, I had to write a paper about the Franco-Prussian War, but I did not get a single lesson on credit card interest or filing taxes, let alone setting up a retirement account. (Don't get me wrong, I'm all for learning history and trigonometry and, yes, even square dancing. I just wish I'd also learned how to square my finances. The only "capital" I knew was state capitals—I can name all fifty.)

There is, if I am being real, good reason for the confusion. Retirement accounts are legitimately complicated. It sucks that choosing a retirement account is often the first step in the investing process, because it's frustrating and people quit before they even begin. Let's change that. In the next three chapters, I am going to break down investment accounts like we're in the eleventh-grade personal finance class we all wish we had. And if you can make it through this section, I swear, you can do anything. Ready? Let's go.

A retirement account (sometimes called a *retirement plan*) is just that—an account. It is an account that holds cash and/or investments. Here's what a retirement account is *not*: A retirement account is *not* itself an investment. Do you have a 401(k) through work? It is not an investment—**it's a bank account that *holds* investments.** Have a Roth

IRA? Same idea. A Roth IRA is *not* an investment—**it's a bank account that *holds* investments!** To be even more precise, retirement accounts (all of them!) are **bank accounts that hold investments *and* that get special tax treatment when you invest.**

This is true for retirement accounts opened by your employer, like a 401(k) or 403(b). (I'll be calling these *workplace retirement accounts.*) This is also true for retirement accounts you open independently, like a self-employed 401(k), Roth IRA, or Traditional IRA. (IRA stands for *individual retirement arrangement*—emphasis on the *individual.*)

Referring to retirement accounts as investments (and not a separate thing entirely) blurs the distinction. We can blame a lack of financial literacy for the confusion, but I also suspect automation is partially to blame. Automated investing, like the kind that happens in a workplace retirement account, conceals the fact that there are several processes at play. Money is taken from your paycheck and deposited into the account. (That is your *contribution.*) Then that cash automatically purchases investments, typically mutual funds that include stocks, bonds, or both. You will see your retirement account grow in size, but the growth comes from your cash contributions and, later, investment growth, *not* from the retirement account itself.

To give you a visual, I like to think of retirement accounts as if they're a Caboodles. For anyone who is not a millennial woman or gay man, a Caboodles is a plastic organizer for your girlhood treasures. Mine was hot purple and teal. There was also a sophisticated light-pink-and-blue version. While a Caboodles is totally fabulous in its own right, at the end of the day, it is still just a glorified storage unit. Same with your retirement account. Think of the treasures you collect inside your Caboodles as if they are your investments. Your Lisa Frank stickers, stick-on earrings, Dr Pepper Lip Smackers, butterfly clips, and miniature novelty eraser collection—these are your stocks, bonds, and funds. (And what we'll cover in part III.)

My friend—let's call her Layla—made a very common mistake at the beginning of her career. No, I am not talking about sleeping with a coworker (or two) because Layla wants you to know she regrets nothing!! But as for handling her retirement account, well, she missed out on tens of thousands of dollars of investment returns. Each month, she contributed money to her Roth IRA, but she had no idea that she *also* needed to purchase investments; a separate step entirely. Because she thought that her Roth IRA *was* the investment, those contributions sat in her Roth IRA in cash, earning nothing.

The Point of a Retirement Account

Our next most common misconception is that a *company match* is what makes a retirement account. When your employer matches all or part of what you contribute to your retirement account, that's a company match. For example, with a 6% match, your employer will contribute an amount equal to 6% of your salary—but only if you contribute 6% of your salary first. (And no, it is not "free money." Your employer does not give you free money; they compensate you for your labor. But if you don't take advantage of the match, you are turning down compensation, effectively giving your employer FREE labor!)

While it is true that a company match is a fantastic incentive, it is *not* what makes a retirement account a retirement account. *Nope!* A retirement account is a *tax shelter* for investment growth; a kind of container (Caboodles!) where your money can grow, shielded from taxes while it does.

Before we get into exactly how a tax shelter works, let's take a big step back and talk about how we even got here. Because you see, retirement accounts are a relatively new invention. If you, like me, grew up in the country that Ronald Reagan built, you might not know that retiring didn't always require every single person be their own master of investing strategy.

In the decades after World War II, many workers had pensions: big pools of money funded by employers, which sent out monthly checks in retirement. Professionals managed it, and if you worked long enough, you were taken care of. Best of all, you didn't need to know shit about investing.

Then, in the late 1970s, some accountant man discovered paragraph 401(k) in the tax code. That's right: A 401(k) is sadly not named after the amount of money in the account but the tax code that describes it.

Unlike pensions, which were entirely funded by employers, 401(k)s put the responsibility on workers to save and invest for themselves, offering a tax benefit as an incentive to do so. Slowly, companies caught on—the new 401(k) model was way cheaper and easier for *them* to maintain. Did you catch that? Not better for you. Not better for workers. Better for corporations.

Throughout the 1980s, '90s, and 2000s, corporations moved away from pensions to the 401(k) model, shifting the burden of saving and retirement planning to individuals along with it. Today, unless you're a government employee or in a strong union, you probably don't have a pension. You're on your own, left to Google, "What in the super heck is a 401(k)?"

Instead of a functioning system of social benefits, we are incentivized to save for our own retirements through tax breaks. (I swear, I have owned fishnet tights that work harder than the US's social safety net.) If you've ever wondered why these accounts have so many complicated rules, like income thresholds and contribution caps, this is it: Uncle Sam doesn't want you sheltering *too much* income from taxes.

The key thing to know is this: The difference between a retirement account and a non-retirement account isn't *what* you invest in but *how* the money is taxed. In fact, you could hold the exact same investments in both. For example, I have a Solo 401(k), a Roth IRA, and a non-retirement account. (You'll hear these more casually referred to as *regular investment accounts* or *brokerage accounts.*) Each one holds the same three index funds. The investments are identical, but the tax treatment is not.

All Retirement Accounts Are Tax Shelters

The primary benefit of every single retirement account—401(k), Roth IRA, Traditional IRA, all of them—is that you get to grow your investments *without* paying taxes on the profits while they're growing.

Because—surprise!—investing introduces a whole new category of taxes: on *dividends, interest,* and *capital gains.* If you make money from your investments, yep, our buddy Uncle Sam aka the Tax Man aka Colonel Corn Subsidy wants to hear about it.

You will always need to report and pay a tax on any profit you've made investing, UNLESS YOU MADE THAT PROFIT IN A RETIREMENT ACCOUNT!!

And this is what we mean when we say retirement accounts are tax shelters. Retirement accounts allow for *tax-free investment growth*.

Contrast this to how taxation works on all other types of investment profit. When you earn money investing in a brokerage account, you must report certain investment profits and pay taxes on that profit each year. This is the baseline rule. But retirement accounts are the exception to tax law—*not* the baseline. This is easy to miss because many of us will have no experience with the baseline, because we get our start with the exception—retirement accounts!

Take the example I mentioned earlier. Inside each of my accounts—Solo 401(k), Roth IRA, and brokerage—I hold index funds that pay dividends. But I only report and pay taxes on the dividends paid to me in the brokerage account. The dividends inside the retirement accounts? No one needs to know about it; no tax reporting required.

Want to know what rich people love? *Tax shelters.* Rich people simply love a tax shelter. And, they know how to use one. They know that the more profit you have to protect, the more valuable that shelter becomes. A retirement account is not a retirement account just because the IRS "says so." They function as retirement accounts because the benefit only reveals itself over time and with successful, long-term investing. Instead of slicing off a chunk of your profit every year to pay taxes, you get to keep all that money growing, compounding, and working for you.

If you have many years ahead to let your investments grow, it's ideal for that growth to happen *inside* a tax shelter. And any retirement account will do, because this core tax benefit is shared by all of them. (Even then, retirement accounts aren't the end-all, be-all of investing! Investing in a regular brokerage account is still a good thing. Great, even. It's certainly better than not investing at all. You just won't get the tax break.)

If you've never heard of a retirement account described as a tax shelter before, I wouldn't be surprised. Again, hardly anyone talks about these things with clarity, or they focus entirely on the Roth versus

Traditional debate, which, yes, we will settle once and for all in the next chapter. Before we do, I want us to take a beat and consider what we've just learned. First, that all retirement accounts are just that, accounts. Second, that all retirement accounts are tax shelters, and third, that all retirement accounts are good. Remember in chapter 3, EMERGENCY FUND, when I said that the best bank account is the one that is getting used? That goes for retirement accounts, too. Whether you go with the purple-and-teal Caboodles or the light pink and blue, the real work lies in stuffing it full of treasures.

9

ROTH VERSUS TRADITIONAL

What's better, a Roth IRA or 401(k)?

"I have a 401(k) through work, but I've heard it's better to do a Roth IRA," said Rosie, a student of mine. "Is that right?"

Rosie is all of us. She represents every person who has ever had "learn the difference between a 401(k) and a Roth IRA" perpetually carried over their last 150 to-do lists.

And not just the 401(k) and Roth IRA but the Traditional IRA, the 457(b), the SEP IRA, the 403(b)—I could go on. This number-and-letter alphabet soup has half of America asking "4-0-1 K BUT Y? Why all the rules? Why *this*? How could a loving God cause such agony?"

As you may have picked up on by now, the answer to these questions is: tax code.

Before we get into the nitty-gritty of it, I want to point out that the retirement account you use will largely be determined by what you have access to. For example, if you have a workplace retirement account, you will want to start there. Especially if you have a match. If you don't have an employer account, your options will largely depend on your level and source of income.

Your Employer Opens	
401(k)	Employees of private corporations
403(b)	Employees of public schools, nonprofits, churches

continued

457(b)	Employees of state and local governments and some nonprofits
Thrift Savings Plan	Federal employees and uniformed service members
SIMPLE IRA	Employees of small businesses with 100 or fewer employees
SEP IRA	Employees of small businesses

You Open as an Individual	
Roth IRA	Individuals who qualify
Traditional IRA	Individuals who qualify

You Open as a Business Owner	
Solo 401(k)	Self-employed individuals or business owners with no employees (except a spouse)
SEP IRA	Self-employed people and small business owners

I'll provide more specifics in the next chapter, RULES.

Two Retirement Account Taxations

Once you've sussed out what you qualify for, you may find yourself needing to make a choice between Roth and Traditional taxation. Because tax law loves to be complex for no reason, there are not one but *two* different types of retirement account taxation. Rosie's 401(k) has *Traditional* taxation, which I will also call *tax-deferred.* (It is *also* sometimes referred to as *pre-tax.*) Her Roth IRA has, yep, *Roth* taxation.

We talk about these accounts like they're epic rivals; Katniss and Peeta, pitted against each other in the Hunger Games, forced to fight to the death. But they weren't truly enemies. It was a manufactured rivalry, and both were just trying to survive the same brutal system. Same with retirement taxation. Roth and Traditional accounts are allies.

But they are different. Ready to know how? The difference lies in WHEN you pay income taxes on the money you put into them: now or later.

When Do I Pay Income Taxes?

Traditional/tax-deferred	Roth
Traditional IRA	Roth IRA
401(k)	Roth 401(k)
403(b)	Roth 403(b)
457(b)	Roth 457(b)
Thrift Savings Plan (TSP)	Roth Thrift Savings Plan (TSP
SIMPLE IRA	Roth SIMPLE IRA*
SEP IRA	Roth SEP IRA*
later	now

But Amanda, you'd be right to wonder, *what do my income taxes have to do with anything? I thought we were talking about investing.* We are! But most of us will be investing money that we earn through work. And when we earn money through work, we owe income taxes. While retirement accounts do not present us with an opportunity to avoid income taxes altogether, they do give us an option to choose WHEN we pay income taxes.

You can pay income taxes NOW, in the year you contribute. That's a Roth retirement account, like a Roth IRA or a Roth 401(k).

Or you can pay income taxes LATER, on the money you withdraw in retirement. That's a Traditional/tax-deferred retirement account. (Get it? You are *deferring* your income taxes until later.) Any retirement account without Roth in the name is Traditional/tax-deferred.

This stuff can get kinda heady, but stick with me because this will have a huge impact on your tax bill come April 15 *and* on your

---

* SIMPLE IRA and SEP IRA plans are now allowed to include a Roth option. But as of this writing, none of the major banks have actually rolled out this offering. Similarly, all workplace retirement accounts can now offer a Roth option, but not all banks and platforms do.

long-term returns. Follow along with the visuals of the money flow; from when you earn it to when you spend it, along with all the potential taxes in between.

To get us oriented, let's start with baseline taxation: the flow of money and taxation when you invest in a non-retirement brokerage account.

Brokerage Account Taxation

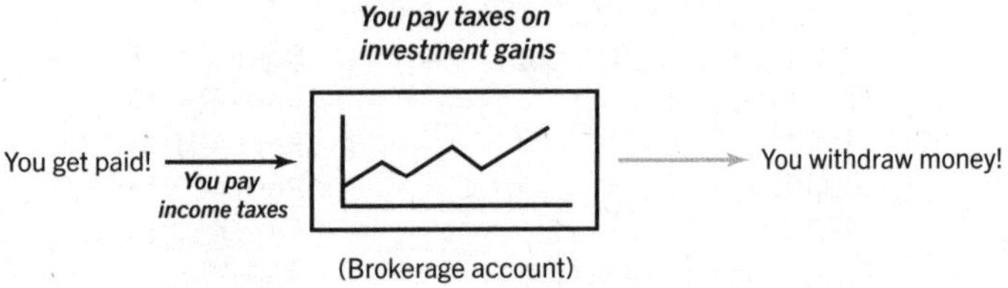

Notice that **you pay taxes twice, in two ways**: First, you fund the account with income you have already or will pay income taxes on. Second, you pay taxes on investment gains.

Next, compare that to a Traditional/tax-deferred retirement account, like a 401(k).

Traditional/Tax-Deferred Account Taxation

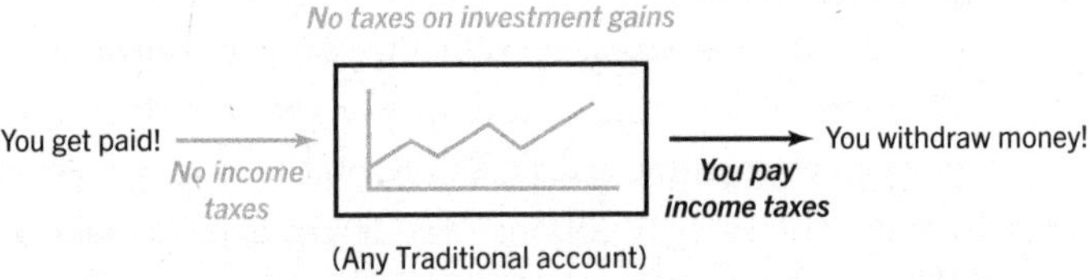

Here, you will see that **you pay taxes once, in one way**. You do not pay income taxes on the money you contribute to the retirement account, and you do not pay taxes on investment gains. You only pay income taxes on the money you withdraw from the account in retirement.

To avoid taxes in the year you contribute, you *deduct* the contribution amount from your taxable income for the year. Say Rosie earns $80,000 and contributes $10,000 to her 401(k). After subtracting the $10,000 *deduction,* she has reduced her taxable income base to $70,000. She will have other deductions, like the standard deduction, but let's keep it simple for now. Just envision that she chops that $10,000 off the top of her taxable income. The trade-off is that later, in retirement, money she withdraws from her 401(k) will count as income, and she will pay income taxes at the time of withdrawal. For example, if Rosie withdraws $10,000 from her 401(k) in 2060, she will pay income taxes on that amount, at that time.

The idea is that you will likely pay a lower overall income tax rate if you defer them until later, when your income is much lower as a retired person. This is thanks to our marginal income-tax-rate system, which taxes us more at higher levels of income earned. (See box on page 63.)

Again, some context may help! The 401(k) was initially interpreted to be (yet another) tax break for rich people. With a 401(k), a person could stash away extra money for retirement in addition to their pensions. When they did, not only did they lower their tax bill by their highest marginal income tax rate in that year but they also deferred their income taxes until retirement—a time when their overall income tax rate is likely to be substantially lower.

For anyone using a Traditional/tax-deferred account through work, you'll notice that those automatic contributions don't make as much of a dent in your paycheck as you might have thought. That's because a big chunk of those contributions would have otherwise gone toward your tax withholding. Therefore, you should be able to contribute about 25% more than whatever your budget tells you.

Next, let's peer into the taxation of a Roth account:

Roth Account Taxation

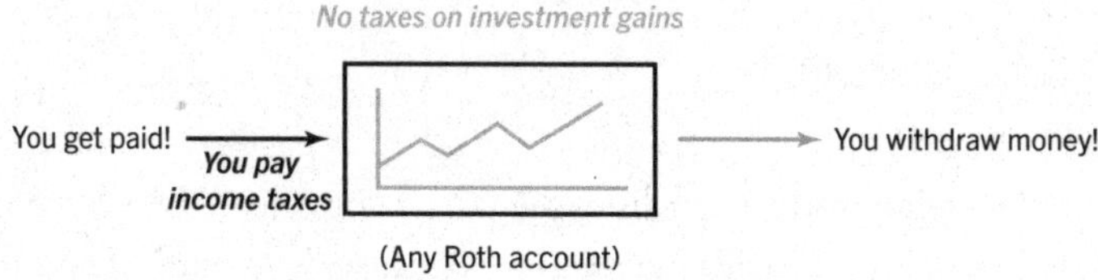

With Roth accounts, **you pay taxes once, in one way**: You pay income taxes on the money you contribute. You do not pay taxes on investment gains, and you do not pay income taxes on withdrawals.

How that actually works in practice: You do not deduct Roth contributions. So, if Rosie contributed $10,000 to a Roth 401(k), that amount *is* included in her taxable income for the year. There is no income tax break in the year you contribute to a Roth account. The trade-off is that Rosie won't pay income taxes on money she withdraws from her Roth in retirement.

Roth accounts were initially designed for lower earners. The idea is, "Hey, you're already paying a relatively low income tax rate, might as well just pay 'em now and get 'em over with!" Then you won't have to worry about taxes ever again. I like Roth taxation because I like taking care of the taxes now as a gift to my Rich Old Lady so she can spend those future tax-free withdrawals on faux fur and platform orthopedic lifts—even if it is not technically the most tax-advantageous thing.

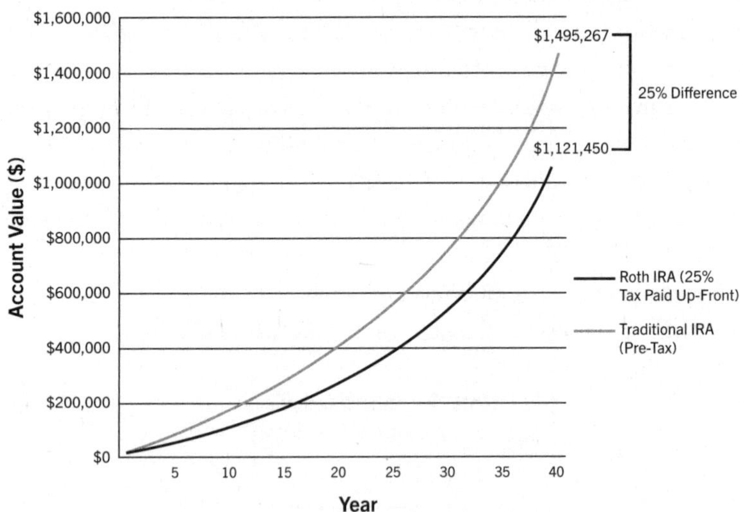

In explaining this to Rosie, she wasn't convinced that she might actually save money with her 401(k). "Because," she said, "if you have to pay income taxes on any money you take out of your 401(k), that means you're paying that tax on contributions *and* investment gains. With a Roth IRA, you only pay on contributions." And this is true. She will be paying income tax on *any* money she withdraws from her 401(k). But if more taxes up-front = less investing overall, you'll have less gains to tax in the first place. (You should be able to invest approximately 25% more if you use a tax-deferred account.)

To visualize this, imagine we had a flat tax rate of 25% (we don't) and Rosie has ONLY $7,000 she can commit to retirement each year. With a Traditional IRA, she can contribute the full $7,000 because there are no taxes. With a Roth IRA, though, her contributions come from after-tax income. If Rosie were a super-careful budgeter, she'd have to account for that 25% tax hit first—leaving only $5,250 to invest. Because of this, the Traditional IRA looks 25% ahead, but that advantage vanishes at withdrawal—she'll pay the same 25% then. If tax rates matched going in and coming out, the result would be identical even when considering compounding growth! But here's the thing: We don't pay the same rate of tax on the way in as we do on the way out!

Rosie Does the Tax Math!

Allow me to introduce you to our marginal tax rate system. Because it's much easier to understand by looking at some concrete numbers, here's how the math shakes out if you used 2025's actual income tax rates, using Rosie, who earned $80,000, as our example.

2025 Marginal Income Tax Brackets				
Tax Rate	**Single**	**Married Filing Jointly or Surviving Spouse**	**Head of Household**	**Married Filing Separately**
10%	$0 to $11,925	$0 to $23,850	$0 to $17,000	$0 to $11,925

continued

12%	$11,926 to $48,475	$23,851 to $96,950	$17,001 to $64,850	$11,926 to $48,475
22%	$48,476 to $103,350	$96,951 to $206,700	$64,851 to $103,350	$48,476 to $103,350
24%	$103,351 to $197,300	$206,701 to $394,600	$103,351 to $197,300	$103,351 to $197,300
32%	$197,301 to $250,525	$394,601 to $501,050	$197,301 to $250,500	$197,301 to $250,525
35%	$250,526 to $626,350	$501,051 to $751,600	$250,501 to $626,350	$250,526 to $375,800
37%	$626,351 or more	$751,601 or more	$626,351 or more	$375,801 or more

First, let's assume that Rosie gets only the *standard deduction,* the tax deduction available to everyone who does not itemize deductions on their taxes. In 2025, that's $15,000. Therefore, the IRS will assess Rosie's federal taxes on a base of $65,000.

Instead of paying one flat rate of income tax, the rate steps up at certain levels of income earned. Rosie pays a 10% tax rate on amounts earned between $0 and $11,925. (So do the rest of us.) On amounts between $11,926 and $48,475, Rosie pays a 12% tax. (Us, too!) For amounts earned between $48,476 and through the remainder of her taxable income ($65,000), she pays a 22% tax rate.

Therefore, Rosie does not pay her highest *marginal rate* of 22% on her entire income. She pays an average of these rates, called her *effective rate.* (So, no, you do not flip your entire income into a higher tax bracket because you got a raise. You, I, Rosie, and yes even the world's richest mofos pay the same lower rates of tax on lower levels of income earned.)

If Rosie were to contribute $10,000 to her 401(k), she would deduct it from her taxes and not pay income taxes on that amount. Again, imagine chopping that $10,000 right off the top of her income, leaving her with $55,000 that's considered taxable. Because she would have otherwise paid her top 22% rate on most of that $10,000 contribution—some of it dips into her 12% bracket—let's estimate that she saves approximately $2,000 in federal income taxes.

That's not all! Rosie lives in California, which also has a marginal tax rate system. (Know your state's!) Her $10,000 contribution would have been taxed at her highest marginal rates of 9.3% and 8%. That's another approximately $850 in savings, bringing her combined savings to a total of about $2,850—a fun little kickback when tax time rolls around!

But Rosie *will* have to pay income taxes later, on any money she withdraws from her 401(k) in retirement. Fast-forward a few decades. Rosie's "income" now comes from her 401(k). If Rosie were to withdraw only that same $10,000, she'd pay nothing in federal income taxes, thanks to the standard deduction. But let's assume her money has grown and she takes $36,000 from her 401(k)—and is collecting $24,000 from Social Security. Between the two sources, she receives $60,000.

For Rosie, the IRS counts 85% of her Social Security benefits as taxable. That means $20,400 of her Social Security is added to her $36,000 in 401(k) withdrawals, for a total of $56,400 before subtracting the $15,000 standard deduction. $41,400 of Rosie's retirement income is considered taxable income. Rosie pays 10% on the first chunk of that income and 12% on the rest. Her top federal marginal rate in retirement is 12%. But her effective rate—the average across the entire $60,000 she receives—is only about 8%.

Again, these contributions would've otherwise been taxed at her highest marginal rate (22%). By kicking the income tax can down the road, Rosie pays a substantially lower rate overall (8%). Same idea for her state taxes. In California, she pays a roughly 9% marginal rate on the contribution compared to a 1% effective rate in retirement. Combining federal and state, Rosie will pay about 9% instead of 30% by deferring her income taxes.

High earners may especially be enticed by the chance to avoid paying taxes at their highest marginal rate. Rosie's friend Jasmine is an executive who earns $500,000 per year. When she contributes $10,000 to her 401(k), she avoids paying taxes at her highest federal marginal rate of 35%, plus about 10% in California.

And what happens when Rosie and Jasmine contribute that money to a Roth 401(k)? If Rosie contributes $10,000 to a Roth 401(k), she does not deduct that amount and therefore pays her highest rates on those dollars. Jasmine pays hers. But when they withdraw money from their Roth 401(k) accounts in retirement, they will not pay any taxes at all.

Note: We pay a third type of tax on our income—the FICA taxes that fund Social Security and Medicare. You can't get out of these! You do not avoid FICA taxes on any Traditional/tax-deferred deductions, but you also won't pay them later when you withdraw from a 401(k).

I bet you'd like a hard-and-fast rule on Roth versus Traditional, and I'm apprehensive to give one. That said, the biggest relative jump is between the 24% and 32% tax rates; and represents an 8% increase in your tax rate. For amounts under $197,301 earned (as a single filer), you pay a 24% rate of tax. For amounts over, a 32% rate of tax. So, if you are earning in the $200,000 range and above, you'd almost certainly benefit from a tax deferral, as most retirees will not be paying a 32% federal income tax rate in retirement. For what it's worth, barring major changes, most retirees won't pay 22% or 24%, either.

Then again, if you're planning to invest the same amount either way, taxes be damned, then a Roth is the better choice. Say a person decides they're going to put $7,000 into an IRA no matter what. If that money goes into a Traditional IRA, they will get a kickback this year. If it goes into a Roth IRA, their tax bill stays the same—no kickback. Presumably, a person getting tax savings this year could invest more because of those savings. But if that tax difference doesn't *actually* change your behavior—you won't invest more or less either way—then eat the taxes now. Dollar for dollar, Roth money is more valuable, because you won't owe any taxes on the money later.

To play the Rich Old Lady game on expert mode, utilize a Traditional/tax-deferred account AND invest the tax savings. In Rosie's case, by investing her $2,850 in tax savings into a Roth IRA. It's the financial equivalent of tricking out your cruising golf cart with fireworks that shoot off the back and a subwoofer so loud it rattles the neighbors' mailboxes.

Here's what the tax optimization fanatics will never admit: The Roth versus Traditional decision largely boils down to a matter of preference. Really, we can't know for sure which will turn out better, because we don't know what future tax rates will be. Even the tax pros can't predict the future, so we're all making this decision with an unknown variable. So yes, take advantage of the tax breaks available to you, absolutely. But also, let's not spiral into obsessive optimization mode over something we can't ultimately control.

And so instead of spending even a single minute more on this, I will conclude right back where we began. Both Traditional and Roth are fine. Just know when you'll owe the income taxes. Have some of both for tax diversification. Know that this is not the difference-maker; how much you invest and your investing choices will have far greater impact. Fortunately, regardless of your choice, you'll benefit from the key feature common to all retirement accounts: They provide a tax shelter for your investment growth.

10

RULES

How much can I contribute to a retirement account?

Because the government throws us a tax bone when we invest for our own retirements, the flip side is that they write the rules. And those rules are convoluted. They do not always make sense. No, the US tax code is a haunted patchwork doll, stitched together and amended over time by generations of lawmakers. And retirement accounts? Just one cursed limb of the whole creation.

If it were up to me, we'd cast that freaky little fuck into the flames and forge something better. Something like one simple, generous retirement account for all, like a universal 401(k). Or better yet, scrap the DIY model entirely and bring back pensions. But until that revolution comes, our job is to learn the IRS rule book.

I cannot and will not list every tax rule here. Instead, here are eight rules or ideas to know as you're navigating the retirement account system. Keep in mind that every number in this section will change—and probably already has. You'll want to keep up with changes, but what matters most right now is understanding the concepts.

1. Knowing what you qualify for is half the battle. If you are opening your own account, a Roth IRA is a great, popular first option. You can also do a Traditional IRA, although be careful if you're already covered by a workplace retirement plan—those two don't always play nice. Not everyone qualifies to contribute to a Roth IRA or a Traditional IRA.

Do I Qualify to Contribute to an IRA?

Roth IRA

You can open and contribute to a Roth IRA if you don't have a workplace retirement account, and if you do! But here's the catch: You can't earn too much money to actively contribute.

In 2025, Roth IRA contribution limits for single filers begin to phase out at $150,000 of income and are completely phased out at $165,000. Here, income is measured as *modified adjusted gross income* (MAGI). For married couples filing jointly, the income phase-out range is between $236,000 and $246,000. Married couples filing separately will have difficulty with a Roth IRA—you cannot earn more than $10,000 and contribute if you lived together during the year.

Heads up: These income rules do not apply to a Roth account you access through work or self-employment, like a Roth 401(k) or Roth Solo 401(k). Utilizing these options is the easiest way to access Roth "room" even when you earn too much to use a Roth IRA.

If you are over the income limit but determined to contribute to a Roth IRA, you can consider a Backdoor Roth IRA. More on that in chapter 36, WHAT NEXT.

Traditional IRA

If you **aren't** already covered by a workplace retirement account, like a 401(k), but have earned income, you can use a Traditional IRA, no problem. Have at it!

But if you **are** already covered by a workplace plan and earn over a certain threshold, tread lightly. Basically, if you've already got a workplace retirement account, the Feds think you've already got plenty of tax-deferred space you can use. Especially if you are a higher earner, they can't have you tax-deferring all that delicious income!

For single taxpayers already covered by a workplace retirement plan, the phase-out range to contribute to a Traditional IRA is between $79,000 and $89,000. For married couples filing jointly, if the spouse making the Traditional IRA contribution is covered by a workplace retirement plan, the phase-out range is between $126,000 and

$146,000. For a Traditional IRA contributor who is not covered by a workplace retirement plan and is married to someone who is covered, the phase-out range is between $236,000 and $246,000.

Just so you know, the Tax Man isn't going to come flying out of the IRS locker room and tackle you for contributing to a Traditional IRA while you've got a workplace plan. You *can* put money in—the catch is you might not be able to deduct it if you earn too much. And that deduction is the whole point! Without it, your contribution goes in after-tax, and later the IRS will tax every dollar you take out, so you pay income taxes twice.

You can actively contribute to multiple accounts, so long as you qualify. A workplace retirement account pairs nicely with a Roth IRA. If you're self-employed, you could do a SEP IRA or Solo 401(k) along with a Roth IRA. If you are both traditionally employed and have side income, you could feasibly be contributing to your workplace retirement account, a SEP IRA, and a Roth IRA. (This isn't to say that you need to, just that it's possible.)

2. Know your *annual contribution limits,* also known as the *max.* In 2025, you can contribute up to $7,000 to a Roth IRA or Traditional IRA. Seven thousand dollars is the max. You will *max out* your 401(k) at $23,500. Why is the 401(k) max so much higher? I don't know. Ask your senator. It's not as if someone who only has access to a Roth IRA needs to invest any less money for retirement than someone with access to a 401(k).

Account Type	2025 Standard Contribution Limit (the "max")	Catch-Up
401(k), 403(b), 457(b), TSP	$23,500	$7,500 (Age 50–59 or 64+), $11,250 (Age 60–63)
Traditional IRA, Roth IRA	$7,000 (total across both)	$1,000 (Age 50+)
SIMPLE IRA	$16,500	$3,500 (Age 50–59 or 64+), $5,250 (Age 60–63)
SEP IRA	Up to 25% of comp., max $69,000	N/A
Solo 401(k)	$23,500 employee + up to 25% of comp. employer (max $69,000)	$7,500 (Age 50–59 or 64+), $11,250 (Age 60–63)

3. Self-employed people have some of the best options for retirement accounts. Both a SEP IRA and a Solo 401(k) offer a ton of contribution room. If you are looking for an account that is easy to set up, a SEP IRA is better. If you want more contribution room up front and the option to go Roth, choose a Solo 401(k).

Both accounts share the same upper contribution limit of $69,000 in 2025. With a Solo 401(k), you can contribute in two ways. As the "employee," you can put in up to $23,500 of your earnings. As the "employer," about 20% of the business's net profit. (That's if you're a self-employed sole proprietor. If you pay yourself a W-2 wage, it may be closer to 25%.) With a SEP IRA, you only get the employer side: the 20% or 25% of your earnings, depending on how your business is structured.

If your business profits are modest, the Solo 401(k) lets you hit the $23,500 employee limit right away, while a SEP leaves you with less room because of the 20–25% cap. Either way, you may want to work with a tax professional or use an online Solo 401(k) or SEP IRA contribution calculator, like the one provided by Fidelity (calculators.ssnc.cloud/FidelitySEP/SEP).

Although I am generally agnostic between the low-cost brokerage banks, opening a Solo 401(k) is a tad more specific. As of this writing, I recommend Charles Schwab, which has a Roth option. For more on choosing a bank, see chapter 24, BANKS.

4. All retirement accounts require that you have *earned income* in the year you contribute. For example, if you contribute $7,000 to a Roth IRA, you must report at least $7,000 in earned income (that's income from work, not from investments or other "unearned" sources) that same year.

5. Having emergency money is important, but it should not be held in your retirement accounts. Same with any other near-term goals. Use retirement accounts for the purpose for which they were designed. That way, you'll actually reap their tax benefit *and* stay mostly clear of the IRS's most complicated rules and penalties. If you do find yourself in a situation where you need to access retirement money before the IRS retirement age of fifty-nine and a half, look to your Roth accounts first. You've already paid taxes on contributions, so you can remove those contributions without taxes or penalties at any time.

6. As your career and life evolve, you might find yourself with a graveyard of old retirement accounts from former employers or past savings efforts. While it's not always possible to consolidate these accounts, you may want to do so when you can, as it simplifies managing your investments.

What can be consolidated depends largely on the type of account and how it's taxed. Traditional accounts, such as a 401(k) or Traditional IRA, can usually be combined with other Traditional accounts. Roth accounts, like a Roth 401(k) or Roth IRA, can generally be smooshed with other Roth accounts. Google "IRS Rollover Chart" to double-check before making any big moves.

The term *rollover* means something specific: rolling one account into another of the same tax status. Technically, you can move money from, say, a 401(k) into a Roth IRA, but you'll have to pay income taxes on that amount. This is not a rollover; it is a *Roth conversion*. A Roth conversion is something you might consider if you happened to have a very low tax rate for the year—for example, if you didn't work during that year.

To initiate a rollover, have your new account information ready and call your workplace retirement account provider. Or you can use Capitalize, which helps streamline the process.

Just keep in mind that workplace retirement accounts tend to have stronger legal protections in their original form—something to consider if you're facing bankruptcy or work in a profession with higher legal risk, like medicine or law. Check with a lawyer in your state if this might apply to you.

7. Your *company match* is not the max, nor does it count toward your max.

For this, I need to tell you a story. I met Molly at an event I was speaking at in San Francisco. A first-generation college graduate and engineer with a shaved head that I found intimidatingly cool, Molly had worked hard to achieve a senior position at a great company with a 401(k). This was two decades ago, when the 401(k) concept itself was still relatively new. When she contributed 6%, her company matched half of that, so 3%, for a total of 9%. For the next twenty years, Molly *also* believed that 6% was the limit to how much she could contribute to her 401(k). She thought the match *was* the max. In reality, she could have contributed much more, allowing her to take even more advantage of the tax shelter that is a 401(k).

I like to think of a match as a mushroom boost on your Mario Kart ride to financial independence. It gives you a substantial advantage but it doesn't mean you automatically win the race. A match (and a max, for that matter) have nothing to do with how much a person actually needs to reach financial independence. Molly, now fifty-seven, has a solid 401(k) but she still may need to leave her high-cost-of-living hometown to make it last. "I'd give anything to go back in time and tell myself to do *more* than the match," she told me.

The same applies if you don't have a company match—it doesn't mean you can skip investing in a retirement account. In fact, it means you need to go even *harder* to make up for the lack of employer help.

Oh, and one last thing about company matches: Often, the match piece is not legally yours to walk away with until you've proven your loyalty on a timeline called a *vesting schedule*. No, I am not talking about wearing a puffy vest on a Monday, a tuxedo vest on a Tuesday, and so on. Not *that* vesting schedule. Instead, your match will either become "yours" all at once at some date in the future (*cliff vesting*) or over the course of several years (*graduated vesting*). Something to keep in mind especially if you are planning on quitting. I'd hate for you to miss your match by a week or two.

8. If you cannot figure out what retirement account you qualify for, use a brokerage account! No, you don't get the tax benefits of a retirement account, but it is certainly better to invest in a brokerage account than to hem and haw because you don't know which retirement account to use. I invest within a brokerage account with the exact same purpose (and strategy) as my retirement accounts. Even more on brokerage accounts in chapter 36, WHAT NEXT.

Woosh! You did it! That's a lot of tax law! With that, it's time to put everything you've learned from the last three chapters together. I encourage you to complete Section One in the Homework, even if you've already got a retirement account that you're happy with. It's good practice.

If you are seeking more guidance, Homework Section Two offers step-by-step instructions for choosing a retirement account.

What you won't find in this homework, however, are instructions to rush out and open a new retirement account. I know, I know—that would be a satisfying grand finale to this part of the book. But the financial institution where you open your account depends on the investing strategy you want to pursue. (For example, an automated investing service would lead you to one provider, while a DIY strategy might point you to another.) We're not there yet!

For now I want you to reflect on what you've learned and take pride in making it through one of the most technically challenging topics in investing. Seriously, this is no small feat.

PART II HOMEWORK: Picking a Retirement Account

Section One

If you have investment accounts already, the first step is wrapping your head around what they are, how they're taxed, what you're contributing, and what the limits are.

Fill in the following. What I need to know about my retirement account:

Account 1:

Type of account: ______________________________
Type of taxation (Traditional, Roth, regular brokerage): __________
This means I will pay income taxes: ____________________
(choose: "now," in the year I contribute, or "later," in the year I withdraw)
Is there a match? ______________________________
How much am I contributing? ____________________
Contribution limit: ____________________________

Account 2:

Type of account: ______________________________
Type of taxation (Traditional, Roth, regular brokerage): __________
This means I will pay income taxes: ____________________
(choose: "now," in the year I contribute, or "later," in the year I withdraw)
Is there a match? ______________________________
How much am I contributing? ____________________
Contribution limit: ____________________________

Account 3:

Type of account: ______________________________
Type of taxation (Traditional, Roth, regular brokerage): __________
This means I will pay income taxes: ____________________
(choose: "now," in the year I contribute, or "later," in the year I withdraw)
Is there a match? ______________________________
How much am I contributing? ____________________
Contribution limit: ____________________________

Section Two

If you don't yet have any investment accounts, don't fret! Here's an exercise to help you determine which one is right for you.

1. What do you qualify for, given your employment situation?

Some accounts can be accessed only through your employer. This is a good place to start.

Q: *Do you have access to a workplace retirement account?*

___

Next, consider whether you can open an account separate from work.

Q: *Do you qualify to contribute to a Roth or a Traditional IRA? (See page 69.)*

___

If you are self-employed, a contactor or freelancer, or run a single-person* small business, you have two great options: a SEP IRA or Solo 401(k). A SEP IRA is easier to open, but depending on your income, a Solo 401(k) may give you more contribution room.

Q: *If you are self-employed, write all the accounts you qualify for here.*

___

2. Do you have a company match?

If you get a match through your company, that's amazing. Start there. Do not leave any match money on the table.

Q: *What is your company match? Are you currently capturing the full match?*

___

* If the business's only other employee is your spouse, you can use a Solo 401(k). If you have employees, you must set up a plan that covers them, too, like a SEP IRA, SIMPLE IRA, or 401(k).

3. What type of taxation do you prefer, Roth or Traditional?

Here, apply what we discussed in chapter 9, ROTH VERSUS TRADITIONAL:

Q: *Of the accounts you have access to, what type of taxation do they have?*

____

Q: *If you have access to both, will you prioritize a type of taxation?*

____

Heads up! If you have both a Traditional/tax-deferred and Roth option for your workplace retirement plan (for example, both a 401(k) and Roth 401(k)), you may have to contribute to the Traditional/tax-deferred "side" to capture your match. Check with your plan to be sure!

And that brings us to our final criteria for choosing a retirement account.

4. Do you like the investment options (especially if using an account through work)?

The quality of investing options also matters. With a workplace retirement account, especially, you must choose from a limited set of investment options. Sometimes these options are great. Sometimes they aren't. In that case, you might instead choose to use an account that you open up yourself, like a Roth IRA, because you have total control over all the investing decisions.

Don't worry if this doesn't make sense yet! Just make a note to revisit this point after you've read the chapters on investing.

RICH OLD LADY REFLECTION

As you reach milestones throughout your financial journey, celebrating your progress is not optional.

No one is solving their entire financial life in a day, a month, or even a year, so instead of spiraling into an existential crisis about how there's always more to do, break it up into manageable, celebrate-able chunks. Acknowledge when there's nothing more to do right now.

Paid off a credit card? Terrific! Snuffed out a student loan? Goodbye! Saved your first $5,000? Atta baby! Now, maybe stop checking your bank account like it's a curling iron you can't remember if you turned off. Instead, do something thoughtful for yourself.

Speaking of right now, right now also happens to be the perfect time to celebrate. Seriously, you've survived the crustiest, most soul-sucking, brain-draining, jargon-filled section of the book—retirement accounts—and for that, I insist you treat yourself to a burrito. Make it the size of your calf. You've earned it. The tax code will still be here when you get back.

PART III

HOW TO INVEST

Everything you need to know about investing so you can make confident decisions

11

STOCKS & BONDS

How can money make us money?

Let's play a game: Imagine it's December 1997 and you're eleven years old. Your grandma gives you a limited-edition Princess Diana Beanie Baby. Sure, you'd love to snuggle this precious gift, but instead, you keep her in the factory plastic. Why? Because Granny tells you she's more than just a purple teddy bear plushy with a stitched white rose detailing. She's an *asset*. And someday, she is gonna pay for your college. Although you may not have realized it at the time, you and Grandma made an investment! Not a good one—the market never recovered from the Beanie Bubble of '99—but an investment nonetheless.

When we buy something that we think may increase in price over time—a piece of art, a share of Microsoft stock, or toast that looks like Jesus (I call him Grilled Cheesus)—that's investing! Alternatively, an investment may pay us, in some way, over time, like a bond or that loan to Cousin Rick that he swears he'll pay back in monthly installments (he won't) including interest (he definitely won't). To reiterate: An investment is just a thing we think will grow in value or pay us over time.

The term *investment* gets thrown around a lot, but most things don't actually qualify. Like a car, an expensive TV, really anything that loses value the second you buy it. Yes, even that pricey, trendy blazer you've nearly convinced yourself is an "investment piece."

Therefore, investing is the practice of identifying an asset that may produce value and then putting money toward that asset in the hopes the extra value materializes. Ideally, this becomes a practice you do over and over. But in order to do it at all, we need to start with the basics.

Right now you might feel like you're standing on the edge of a high dive. You've strapped on your swim cap and goggles, ready to take the plunge. But there's a grumble in your gut. The investing world is vast, overflowing with products, strategies, and an endless stream of opinions. There are index mutual funds, bond ladders, shitcoins, lean hog futures, and—dingleberry swaps? Okay, that last one isn't real, but I wouldn't blame you for thinking it was. You might also have been led to believe that being an investor required spending your life learning every last detail and nuance of the market. Well, I've got extremely good news for you: You don't!

What if, instead, I told you that you only need to start with **two** investment types? That's right, only two! Every single one of us must begin our journeys with *stocks* and *bonds.*

Now, I will admit that stocks and bonds might not be the only *asset classes* you invest in. (By the way, *asset class* just means "a broad category of investments that share similar characteristics.") You'll have *cash,* which is also considered an asset class. You may also choose to invest in real estate—don't worry, we'll cover that later! There are also cryptocurrencies, collectibles, and commodities like gold, oil, and agricultural products. But for now I want us to focus on the iconic duo that will make up the majority of your investing strategy: stocks and bonds. Let's dive in.

Asset Class	Historical Annualized Returns
US Stocks	10%
International Stocks	7–8%
Bonds	5%
Cash earning interest	3%
Cash not earning interest	0%

Stocks

A stock is a sliver of ownership in a company. A piece of their pie, if you will. That piece is known as a share, and once you have one, you are a shareholder. The very basic idea behind owning a stock is this: As the pie grows, so does your proportional piece of it. Stocks are a type of *equity*, and therefore we sometimes use the terms *stocks* and *equities* interchangeably. Think of it like this: When you own stock, you own equity in a company!

Therefore, the *stock market* is just that—a marketplace for buying and selling stocks. To purchase a stock, your *stockbroker* will place an order through the stock store, called an *exchange*, like the *New York Stock Exchange*. (These days, your stockbroker isn't a real person, it's just your *brokerage bank.*)

With stocks, you can make money in two ways: *price appreciation* and *dividends*. Price appreciation is when your shares grow in value; the *price* of that stock *appreciates* over time. You'd be right to be jealous of the person who, on a whim one day in 1980 bought 1,000 bucks worth of Apple shares, because those shares are now worth $2.5 million. That's price appreciation. Okay, you might be thinking, but why? How? What is the mysterious occult magic that converts $1,000 into millions? It's the company's *profit*. The more profitable a company is, the more people want to buy the stock, and that increase in demand pushes up the stock's value. (This is a bit of an oversimplification. We'll dig into this more later, I promise.)

While price appreciation is one way a company rewards investors, it's a bit indirect. There's also a more straightforward way: dividend payments. These are periodic cash payouts to all shareholders. But why would a company hand out cash when it could just *not*? Think of it as a "thanks for sticking around" payment—like a loyalty card, but instead of a free matcha after ten matcha purchases, you get actual money. Companies pay dividends to keep existing investors happy and attract new ones. Another way to think about owning a stock? You're basically buying the rights to a future stream of dividend payouts funded by a company's earnings.

Your profit is proportional to ownership, meaning that the more shares you own, the more price appreciation and dividends you'll enjoy.

Bonds

A bond is a loan, packaged as an investment. But this time, you are the one lending. That's right, you lend your money to a corporation or government, and they pay you a fixed rate of *interest* for the pleasure of borrowing your money. You're the bank now!

Unlike stocks, whose dividends can fluctuate, bonds fall into a category called *fixed income* because (you guessed it!) you are paid a *fixed* rate of *income* on your investment.

Because it's a wonky concept and hard to wrap our heads around, let's think through it without using the jargon. Imagine Delta Air Lines comes to you like, "Hey girl, can I borrow some cash?" And you're like, "Why in the super hell would I give YOU money?!" And they're like, "Okay, I know this sounds goofy, but we want to replace all our seats with massage chairs. We will pay you back and with interest, pinky promise!" And you're like, "Damn that is off-the-rails goofy but shit I'm in."

So, you lend Delta $1,000 for ten years, and they pay you a 5% rate of interest each year. That's $50 per year for ten years, or $500 in total profit. Then Delta will return your $1,000 *principal* at the end of the ten years. That's a bond. In this example, a *corporate bond.* Federal government bonds are called *treasuries,* and bonds with local governments are called *municipal bonds.*

Bonds are less volatile than stocks, thanks to their more predictable, fixed rate of return. But they also have less potential for gains. We'll get into the specifics of this risk-reward dynamic soon, but for now I want you to take a beat and really consider your role in each of the stock and bond arrangements. With a bond, you're in the position of the lender, owed a straightforward rate of interest. With a stock, you're the owner of a thing, one that you hope will become more valuable with time. Can you see how ownership requires taking a bigger risk but has more growth potential?

Cash

Cash is also an asset class—and it's one that you are already using. Cash, in this sense, means both physical cash and cash held in a bank account.

Because cash in the bank is the default, it doesn't always feel like an asset class. But it is! Cash provides a simple means of exchange, and its easy availability (we call this *liquidity*) serves a purpose in any financial strategy. Cash's value is considered to be relatively stable, though this is dependent on the country issuing that cash.

Oh, and just because it's the default doesn't mean that it's not a choice! As with any investment decision, cash holds both benefits and *opportunity costs*. We'll talk more about this in chapter 13, RISK.

If you've begun saving up an emergency fund, you've already integrated cash into your financial strategy. Good! It is there for a reason. As for stocks and bonds, well, *surprise*! You might already have those, too. For example, if you've got a workplace retirement plan, you are in a committed throuple with investing's favorite duo, stocks and bonds.

In fact, no matter where you do your investing thing, stocks and bonds are surely your core units of investment. (Alas, this is where we bid adieu to Beanie Babies.) And so, while I know it may seem a tad abstract to kick off with stocks and bonds—especially since you may never buy an individual stock or bond yourself—it'll make more sense as we go. Stick with me, okay? Everything builds from here.

What Are Annualized Returns?

Here's one of those funky little language things that's actually a big difference-maker: *annualized returns*. At first glance, they sound a lot like *average returns*. But they're not the same, and only annualized returns give us a true picture of how much money our investments are really making (or losing) over time.

With average returns, you just add up each year's gain or loss and divide by the number of years held. But that number can be misleading when your returns go up and down from year to year.

Annualized returns are more useful because they show how much your investment actually grew per year once you factor in the way gains (or losses) build on each other over time.

Say you invest $100. In the first year, it grows by 50%, so now you have $150. In the second year, it drops by 50%, leaving you with $75. The average return calculation gives us 0%—a gain and a loss that cancel each other out. But your investment didn't stay flat; ya lost money! The annualized return tells the real story: It works out to about -13.4% per year when using the *compound annual growth rate* formula. This is a truer representation of reality.

12

FUNDS

How do I invest in stocks and bonds?

Right about now you might be thinking, *Pshhh, this lady doesn't know what she's talking about. I don't invest in stocks and bonds: I invest in funds!*

And we are both right! You may indeed use funds to invest. But a fund is just a big ol' collection of *some other* investment type. It could be a collection of stocks, a collection of bonds, or a collection of any other asset class, whether cash, real estate holdings, or some combination.

You certainly wouldn't be the only person to think that funds represent their own asset class; something separate from stocks and bonds entirely. But they don't! Instead, they are just a way to buy a bunch of investments at once, usually for *diversification* purposes. Funds make investing easy, and—not to get ahead of myself—most of us will use funds to invest. I do! For example, it is possible to buy a fund that holds every single stock in the US. When you buy that fund, what you are *actually* buying is the US stock market.

By now you know I love to create a visual for you, and get ready for a new one here. You can think of an investment fund—*any* investment fund at all—like a suitcase. The suitcase, we can all agree, is essential in getting our belongings from point A to point B. (Traveling without a suitcase would be utter chaos, wouldn't it?) But the suitcase itself does not tell us very much about the trip you're about to have. If I were to ask you, "What are you invested in?" and you responded, "Mutual funds," it would be like me asking, "What are you packing for your trip?" and you replying, "A suitcase." While it's not incorrect, it does feel like you are kind of fucking with me, *and* it doesn't provide the crucial information we need—what's actually packed inside.

Imagine two different women, each packing to go on a trip. Again, we could not guess where they are headed simply by looking at their closed suitcases. To know what type of trip each woman is about to have, we need to know the contents of the luggage.

What is inside our first traveler's bag? She has packed some hiking boots, a trail map, a sensible fleece from L.L.Bean, and a gently loved copy of *Braiding Sweetgrass,* bookmarked with a pressed fern. All right, very illuminating: We know what type of trip our first traveler is about to have. (Pacific Northwest gang, rise up!)

Let's see what our second traveler has going on. The second traveler packed a pair of six-inch platform heels, a skirt that is legally a belt, a rhinestone bikini, fake lashes, backup fake lashes, and some party drugs she melted into an eyeshadow palette to sneak through TSA. (Viva, Las Vegas!)

So, yeah, our two gals are clearly about to have very different trips! And it's the same idea with funds. The contents of your investment fund, called the *holdings,* tell us the type of investing road you're about to travel on. If you buy a fund that holds stocks, you own stocks. You are invested in the stock market. Therefore, your investing journey is about to be very, very different than if you buy a fund that holds bonds. The two are not interchangeable just because they are both funds, in the same way our two travelers' suitcases may look the same but are not interchangeable. Like, let's hope they don't accidentally swap bags at the carousel. (Although hiking the Pacific Crest Trail on party drugs while wearing six-inch heels could be its own special adventure.)

Maybe you've heard that one type of fund is better than another. Mutual funds, ETFs, and index funds are the focus of endless chatter. I've definitely got my preferences, but we'll unpack that later. First, it's important to know that these funds are just containers (suitcases!). Therefore, picking the "right" one begins with really understanding what's inside: stocks, bonds, or cash.

13

RISK

What are we even talking about when we talk about risk?

"Apparently, it's normal to have a twenty-one-year-old with zero financial knowledge pick an investing strategy," said Imani, my student, as she recounted filling out her 401(k) paperwork on her first day of work a decade ago. "When I got to the 'What's your risk tolerance?' question, I remember thinking, 'Huh? What are we even talking about here?'"

Ultimately, Imani picked "moderate." Choosing "risky" with her precious retirement money didn't feel right, nor did "conservative." (Is my 401(k) trying to take away my right to a safe and legal abortion?) Nothing like making life-altering financial decisions on an already nerve-racking first day on the job. Like, hey, please find thirty seconds to choose an investing strategy that will determine your entire financial future in between meeting your new boss and pitting out your silk blouse!

Here's what I explained to Imani: Terms like *risky* have nothing to do with a willingness to eat the expired but okay-looking cottage cheese in the back of the fridge or wear a napkin top in public. The scale of investing *risk tolerance* is mostly a matter of one decision: how much of your portfolio is invested in stocks versus bonds. Here's a cheat sheet on words you hear used in reference to risk tolerance:

Conservative, income = more bonds
Moderate, blended = a mix of stocks and bonds
Risky = more stocks

That's it. That's the game!

Oh, and just so you know, these terms aren't universal. They're subjective in the same way that calling someone politically moderate can mean different things. For Imani's 401(k), *moderate* meant a strategy composed of 70% stocks and 30% bonds. Only after a proper lesson on risk in this context did she realize that, for someone in their twenties with decades of investing ahead, this was more conservative than she would have chosen had she understood the trade-offs. And had she taken on more risk, she likely would have earned tens of thousands more in returns. Because on the other side of risk isn't just uncertainty—it's opportunity.

Knowing that misunderstanding risk tolerance can cost someone tens of thousands of dollars—just ask Imani—I hate that it is often presented in a vacuum. Sure, making 401(k) investing a two-click process can be great, but it also strips away crucial context and education. At a bare minimum, we should be taught about risk *before* we sign anything. Like, are we talking about walking alone in the dark? Bungee jumping? Cutting your own bangs while in a post-breakup fugue state? Why don't you tell me the risk, and then I'll tell you if I can tolerate it.

Value of $100 Invested in 1928

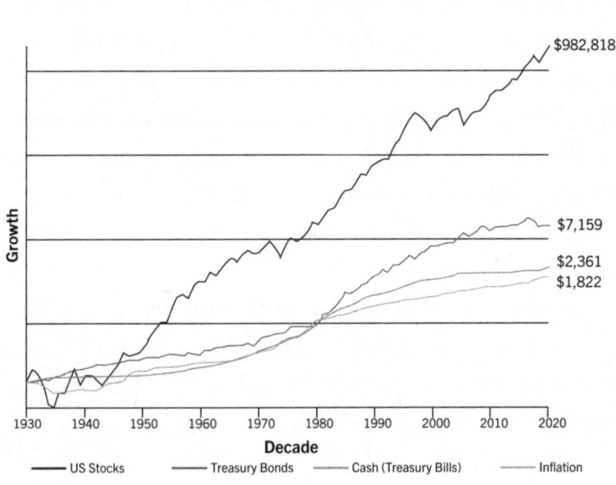

The Risks of Stocks

Running a business is a risky endeavor. Profit—that's the engine driving stock returns—is not promised. (Anyone who has ever run their own business understands this in their bones!) Because a stock is just a share of ownership in a company, all the risks of running a company are present in this kind of investment, along with the risks of existing in an economic system over which there is never total control. For this reason, stocks are considered risky.

When we look at all stocks taken together, two primary sources of risk emerge.

First, the stock market is *volatile*. Stocks experience major swings in price, in both directions, often by the minute. A wide variety of unpredictable factors can shift a company's stock price—hello, spike in demand for sweatpants during the pandemic! Those individual companies' stocks, in turn, create a larger climate in which the stock market experiences booms and busts. It is not unusual for the stock market to gain 20% in value in one year, nor is it unusual to have a year where stocks lose 20% of their value (although this is much less common). For as long as the stock market exists it will be volatile. That is a promise.

Second, stock returns are not guaranteed. Any company could go bankrupt and its stock could become worthless. Therefore, it is possible to lose 100% of your money in a stock. Enron, Lehman Brothers, and Sears are examples of major bankrupt corporations with stocks that went to $0. Funds mitigate that risk by investing you in hundreds or even thousands of stocks. And so while it is theoretically possible that one day all stocks will lose all value, it is highly unlikely. Barring an asteroid-level event where markets collapse and it's every pizza rat for themselves, a more reasonable concern is that stocks will perform worse in the future than they have in the past. That's why a lot of financial planners suggest using a more conservative returns estimate, like 6% or 7%, when running your own numbers.

The Risks of Bonds

In general, bonds are considered to be safer than stocks, but that doesn't make bonds free from risk.

First, a bond is a loan, and loans don't always get repaid. The company or government that issued the bond could default. This is called *credit* or *default risk*. That said, most high-quality bonds, like those offered by the US government, won't default.* *Creditworthy* companies like Disney historically don't default, either. A bond's default risk is measured using a *credit rating system*, where *investment-grade* bonds have less likelihood of default than *non-investment-grade bonds*, also known as *junk bonds*. And if a company does go under, bondholders get priority over stockholders with whatever is salvaged from the collapse.

Second is *interest rate risk*. When interest rates go up, bond prices tend to drop. (And when rates go down, bond prices go up.) Sounds weird, right? Let's break it down. But before we do, know that bond pricing is a brain pretzel, and the following might take a few rereads.

If you buy a bond and hold it to *maturity*, you'll get back its full value, plus all the interest it pays. Pretty drama-free stuff! But alas, humans are impatient creatures and don't always hold until maturity. As long as there is a buyer, you can sell any bond that you own. But why would you do that? Well, one reason is because you felt your money could be better invested elsewhere. Say you own a ten-year, $1,000 bond paying 4% interest. Five years in, interest rates go up, and new bonds are now being issued at 5%. Well, crap on a cracker! Your 4% bond suddenly looks way less attractive compared to all those new, shiny, 5% paying bonds. If you want the new bonds, and try to bail on your "old" bond before maturity, you would likely have to sell it for less than you paid for it; maybe something like $925 instead of the full $1,000. (And because most bonds are "old" bonds, many of which lose relative value when interest rates go up, this is what I mean when I say that interest rates and underlying prices move in opposite directions.)

If you owned a bond directly, you wouldn't even be aware of these up and down swings of the underlying value of each bond. Like with a house, you would only become aware if you were actively trying to sell it. But when you invest in bond funds, as many of us will, you will

---

* If the US ever failed to pay its debts, it could shatter global trust in Treasury bonds and shake financial markets everywhere. The global financial system runs on the belief that these bonds are the safest place to invest money. But with US debt levels climbing fast, and the One Big Beautiful Bill Act adding another $3 trillion on top, people are starting to wonder how long that can last. The government may not miss payments, but it could print more dollars to keep up, which makes those dollars worth less. At the very least, we need leaders who take this risk seriously.

experience the underlying price changes. Bond funds are required to reflect today's market value of the bonds they hold via a process called *mark to market*. Some years, especially when interest rates go up, all the old, lower-rate bonds in your funds may lose some market appeal and be priced down, which can create negative returns. This is despite the uninterrupted, ongoing interest payments. (And though higher interest rates sting at first, over time they should help bond funds earn more.)

Still, bonds, unlike stocks, generally take their Wellbutrin and tend to operate within a much tighter emotional range. A negative year or two isn't necessarily cause for concern. It's just part of the cycle.

Finally, there is a risk in not taking enough risk. Bonds, though more stable, risk underperforming against the stock market and lagging behind inflation over time. It's hard to know how bonds will perform moving forward, but it is politically popular to keep interest rates low, which means bonds pay less. Moving forward, you may want to assume bond returns are closer to 3% or 4%.

The Risks of Cash

Keeping your money in cash might feel comforting, but there are risks.

The primary risk of cash is that it loses value over time, thanks to the invisible tax that is *inflation*. Inflation is prices rising over time. As a result, each dollar buys you less with each passing year. We are coming out of a difficult few years of rising prices, so I bet you understand this intuitively. It sure does get harder and harder to stretch that same dollar.

The rate of inflation varies over time due to different factors, including corporations raising their prices because they can, but it can also be understood as a policy decision where governments create inflation by creating more money. Increasing the supply of a good devalues it. (One text from your crush is exciting. Thirty-two texts from your crush in seven minutes is criminal.) The historical inflation rate is about 3%. So, if the stuff you buy gets more expensive at a rate of 3% (or more) per year, your cash earning 0% in your Bank of America checking account can't keep up.

To be fair, inflation doesn't just affect cash; it takes a chomp out of all growth in all investment types. And you should account for that. To estimate the *real returns*—a measure of true growth that accounts for inflation—take the historical data on the returns of each of the major asset classes and subtract out average inflation of approximately 3%.

	Nominal Returns	Subtract Inflation	Real Returns
US Stocks	10%	-3%	7%
International Stocks	7–8%	-3%	4–5%
Bonds	5%	-3%	2%
Cash Earning Interest	3%	-3%	0%
Cash Not Earning Interest	0%	-3%	-3%

Or you might decide to subtract inflation from a more conservative estimate of future returns. For example, if you are predicting a 7% rate of growth in the US stock market, you are left with approximately 4% after inflation. This can feel deflating when compared to the 10% returns you were promised by the #finfluencers, but it still represents growth beyond what you've put in—something cash cannot and will not do.

Are you beginning to see it? That risk is actually subjective and something you should consider against the time horizon in which you're investing? Although the stock market may have won the label of "risky" with its occasionally screams-in-your-face volatility, over decades you've been more likely to lose money by holding on to cash.

Remember, dear friend, we aren't just taking risk for no reason. Opportunity and potential return are what exist on the other side of risk. And with that, there's an investing truism I want you to carry with you until the end of time. Ready?

Investment risk and reward are two sides of the same coin.

Where there is less risk, there will be less potential for reward. To earn a higher rate of return, you must take more risk. Imagine an investment that is extremely risky but pays a low rate of interest. Who would buy this investment? No one! Any investment must carry at least the possibility of compensating the investor for their bravery, or else it will cease to exist. Therefore, designing your investment strategy isn't about avoiding risk but managing it. We'll talk about how to do that—next!

14

ASSET ALLOCATION

What should my mix of stocks and bonds be?

Almost all investing strategies begin with a mix of stocks and bonds. Commonly, the stock portion will be split between domestic (US) and international.

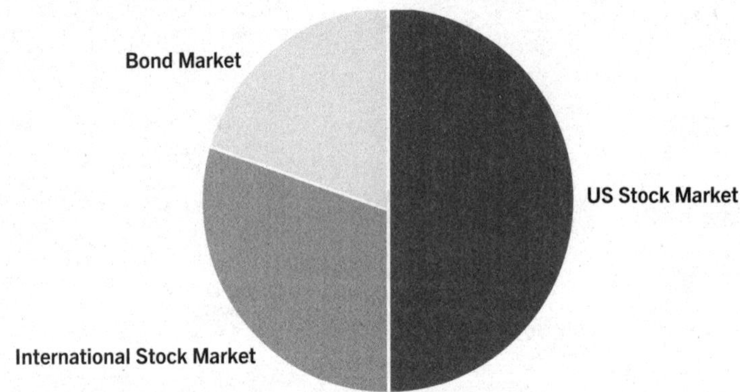

Because this is the core of your strategy, the decision that'll drive the majority of your returns is your breakdown between stocks and bonds. This decision even has a fancy name: *asset allocation*. How will you *allocate* your money to the different *asset* types?

If you've never heard about asset allocation and its supreme reign over your financial future, that's probably because it's, well, boring as hell. Carefully weighing the merits of stocks and bonds, as I've now spent several chapters doing, does not make for good content. In fact,

I wouldn't be surprised if the current online culture around money led you to believe that investing is all about identifying the next explosive stock or placing the one right trade. Investing, it seems, is about hitting it big or going bust.

That's not to say there's no difference between Apple stock and Microsoft stock. But in the grand scheme of your diversified investment strategy, weighing specific stocks remains a small-picture decision. It is not where we start. We need to take a fat step back. Before we debate single stocks, we need to decide whether to invest in stocks *at all.*

Think of it like this: Choosing your asset allocation is like dating. That's right, it's time for another analogy. This time, using my hypothetical love life. Now obviously, not everyone lives in a prison of heterosexuality like I do. (I wish better for you than straightness.) But alas, I date men, so for my next example, I ask that you pretend I am dating the following two men:

First is Guy #1. His name is Steve, and let me tell you, Steve is a nice guy. He's an accountant! Steve is always there when I get home from work, ready to settle in for some evening television. Most likely, the nine-part Ken Burns baseball documentary. (Again.) He's steady. Predictable. Dependable. A human Honda Accord. He tucks his sweater into his jeans. So, no, you won't catch us sailing around the Mediterranean for our anniversary, and we aren't exactly leaving footprints on the wall every night. We are, however, in bed by nine thirty and my skin's never looked better.

Next is Guy #2. This guy's name is . . . well, Guy. He's the lead singer of an up-and-coming band. Maybe his band turns out to be the next Rolling Stones. Maybe he's destined for an eternity playing the sad-bar circuit. Dating him is a roller coaster. The chemistry is electric. He writes songs about me. I am also living off gas station hot dogs and selling bootleg T-shirts out of his flame-painted tour van, occasionally wondering if I've made a horrible mistake. But at the end of the day, there's a chance I could be riding an albino tiger through the courtyard of my Miami Beach mansion, lighting my Newport Slims with hundred-dollar bills, sipping Dom Pérignon while Guy accepts his third Grammy and thanks me in his speech.

So, how do I choose?

I don't. I keep 'em both around because *sometimes*, I want Guy #1. *Sometimes*, Guy #2 is better. Babe, that's just called keeping your options open! It's not like anyone is forcing me to get married to either one of these jabronis! In this way, investment diversification is a lot like playing the field in dating. While I'm certainly welcome to lock it down with either Steve or Guy, it is worth asking whether there will be times I regret this decision. There will be long stretches where Steve's quiet consistency makes me itch. Or times when Guy gets a gig in Milan and poof! He's disappeared for months, leaving me to wonder why I put up with his shit.

One type of investment is not always simply, unilaterally better than the other. They are just different. And each of them is a worthwhile consideration. For working people with lots of time to invest, stocks are certainly the more popular choice. Rightfully so, as they have consistently produced a higher rate of return than bonds over long periods, like twenty years or more. That said, the stock market goes through volatile patches. Bonds have limited upside, yes, but tend to hold up better during scary economic times, providing both a psychological and financial cushion to investors. (A stability that may even help us to be better, more calm stock market investors!)

To determine your mix of Steve (bonds) and Guy (stocks), begin with this asset allocation formula:

120 - your age = your stock allocation

So, if you are thirty years old, 120 - 30 = 90% stock allocation (and a 10% bond allocation).

This formula attempts to simplify a widely held principle of investment management that generally recommends a riskier, stock-heavy allocation for younger people, who have the time necessary to allow the stock market to move higher, and a more stable, bond-heavy allocation for people as they age. But please know that this formula is merely a starting place. It may yield results too aggressive for some and too conservative for others.

For example, I'm forty, and I will personally keep 90% of my portfolio in the stock market until I am at least fifty years old. But that's easy for me to say, because I am *completely* comfortable with the risks of the stock market. My dear friend Sarah, on the other hand, harbors skepticism about the stock market, and I would strongly oppose any advice that dismissed her concerns. She must build a strategy to reflect her comfort level because over the long haul, **the discipline to stick with your chosen strategy is far more important than your precise asset allocation target**.

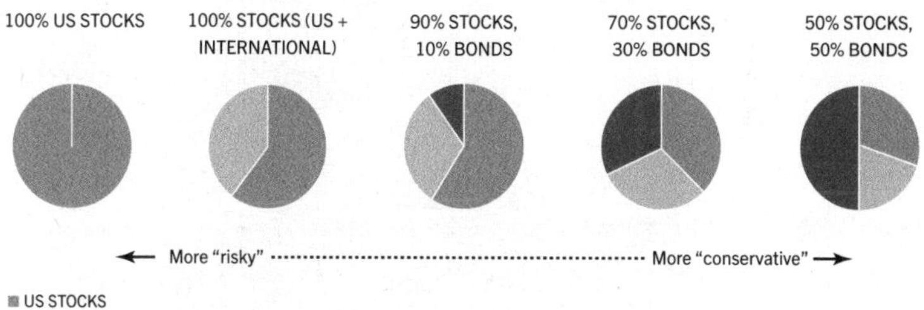

A more advanced approach to determining your asset allocation involves studying long-term patterns in investment markets. Because we assume that these patterns tend to repeat themselves, you can decide whether they make sense for you, your goals, and your timeline. And to be clear, we are talking decades of patterns. No making decisions based on honeymoon phases or after big, messy market breakups. More on this in chapter 19, EXPECTATIONS.

I want to leave you with one final thought. We cannot make the markets do anything they weren't already planning to do. There is no "but I can change him!" here. Investing, like dating, requires honesty with yourself. You don't control the markets, only whether you show up in the first place. Therefore, the right ratio of Steve to Guy will always be the one that feels good and makes sense to you.

10-MINUTE MISSION

What is your current asset allocation? Draw it out here.

Hint: Your bank likely provides you this breakdown in pie graph format. Stocks are sometimes called "equities," and bonds fall under the category "fixed income."

Example Asset Allocation

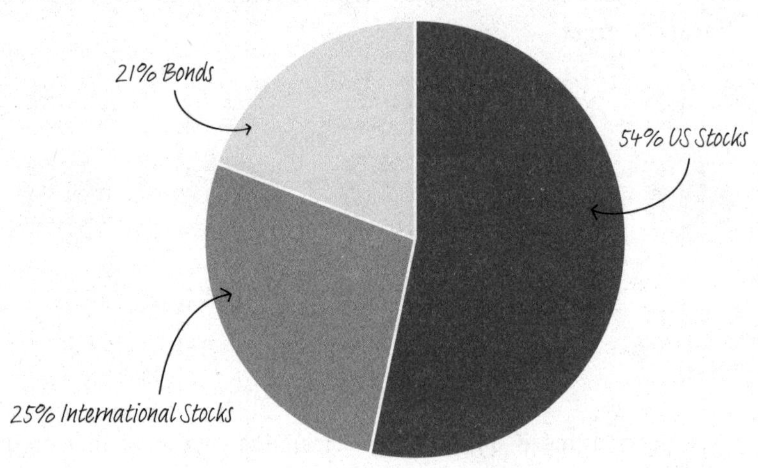

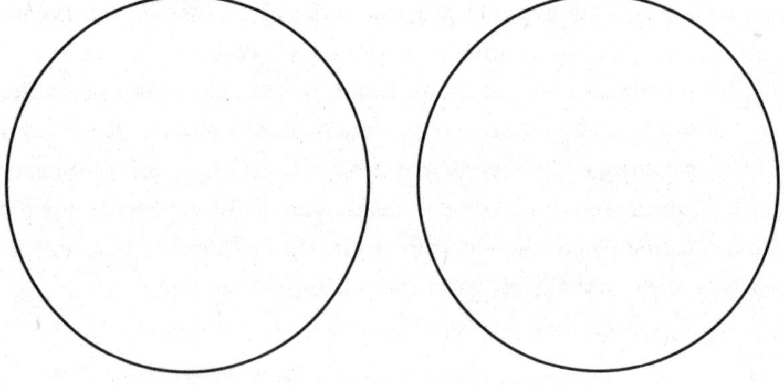

15

INDEX

How do we measure investment performance?

All right, kiddos, gather round, it's story time!

At some point, you've probably heard of this thing called "the Dow Jones," and you know it's somehow related to money. You're getting in a car to run some errands and turn on the radio to see what your friends over at NPR have to say. *Marketplace* is on, and once again, Kai Ryssdal is popping off about the Dow Jones. The Dow did this, the Dow did that. Kai, I love you, buddy, but what is the Dow Jones and why should I care?!

Contrary to what one might assume, Charles Dow and Edward Jones of Dow Jones fame were *not* the original finance bros. They were journalists: muckrakers covering business and the burgeoning investment industry in the late 1800s.

In addition to standard business reporting, our buddies began using their daily paper to publish the prices of every stock, mostly railroad companies at the time. The transparency into the often-dubious business practices on Wall Street became an invaluable resource to investors—and was good entertainment. Their "Customer's Afternoon Letter" grew far and wide, gained mad street cred, and ultimately became *The Wall Street Journal.*

But that's not all! Our boys wanted to find a way to measure how *all* stocks were doing, as a collective force. They created the first stock market *index*: the Dow Jones Railroad Average. Follow the index, and you'd have a general sense of how the entire market of (railroad) stocks was performing. As the economy industrialized and companies like Tennessee Coal, Iron and Railroad Company and American Tobacco began to flourish, Chuck and Ed added a second index, called the Dow Jones Industrial Average. This is "the Dow" we still use today.

Of the twelve industrial stocks originally included in the Dow, only one company remains: General Electric. Currently, the index measures more than just industrial companies, ranging from Disney to Visa to Nike. But because it includes only thirty stocks (selected by a committee of *Wall Street Journal* editors and financial experts), other broader measures of stock market performance, such as the S&P 500 index—which tracks five hundred US stocks—are considered more accurate and less subjective. Still, because of its history as the longest living stock market index, the Dow remains a media darling.

Although the Dow measures the US stock market, we use indices to measure all sorts of stuff. The Case-Shiller Home Price Index measures the prices of single-family homes in the US. The Consumer Price Index measures inflation. There are thousands of indices measuring investment markets all over the world. Some indices are broad, measuring an entire market, like the total global stock market. Some are narrow, measuring just one part. Each country or region has its most popular measure of stocks. In Brazil, they have the Bovespa; in Japan it's the Nikkei; and the Brits keep an eye on the FTSE (pronounced "footsie").

Every index is, first and foremost, a mathematical vibe check—a way to measure economic phenomena as it changes over time. Any stock market index shows us whether the stocks it measures are collectively growing in value, losing value, or just chilling. It is a measuring stick.

So, when Kai Ryssdal goes on about "the market," he could be referring to a few different things, but he's probably talking about the US stock market as measured by one of the big indices, likely the Dow or the S&P 500. Not that you need to be paying close attention to any of this. Truly, you don't. Sorry, Kai, not trying to put you out of a job. Although hey, there's always room for you at Rich Old Lady HQ!

My parasocial relationships with NPR hosts aside, these indices matter not because you need daily updates, but because they'll become central to how we build our investing strategies. Later on, they'll also help us monitor whether our investments are performing at least as well as the markets themselves.

Market-Weighting Versus Price-Weighting

Because it tracks five hundred of the leading US companies across all industries—called *sectors*—the S&P 500 offers a more comprehensive market view than the Dow. But that's not its only advantage. The S&P 500 uses *market-weighting* to calculate performance. This means larger companies (by market value) have more influence on the index. For example, Microsoft makes up 6.8% of the index, while Chipotle accounts for just .15%. So, a price swing in Microsoft moves the index far more than the same swing in Chipotle.

By contrast, the Dow uses *price-weighting.* Stocks trading at higher prices have more influence, regardless of the company's size. But here's the thing—the cost of one share isn't an indication of whether a company is big or small (or good or bad). It's simply a function of how many shares that company has made available for purchase. Two companies of equal size could have very different share prices based on their share count.

For example, Apple is much bigger than Goldman Sachs. But because Apple's stock trades at a lower price, it actually has *less* influence on the Dow. This highlights how the index can give more weight to smaller companies just because they happen to have a higher per-share price.

Beyond the Dow, here are a few good, broad indices to know:

US Stock Index	
S&P 500 Index	500 "leading" (largest) US companies
Russell 3000	3,000 US stocks (98% of US stock market)
Wilshire 5000	All US stocks (currently 3,326)

International Stock Index	
MSCI World ex USA	Developed economy stocks
MSCI ACWI ex USA (ACWI = All Country World Index)	Developed economy stocks *and* emerging economy stocks

Global Stock Index	
MSCI World	US and developed international stocks
MSCI ACWI	US, developed, and emerging international stocks

Bond Index	
S&P US Treasury Bond Index	US federal government treasury bonds
Bloomberg US Aggregate Bond Index	Treasury, corporate, and asset-backed bonds
Bloomberg Global Aggregate Bond Index	US and developed international bonds

16

INDEX FUNDS

What investing strategy gives me the best chance of success?

Now is a big moment. We are beginning the shift from talking about investing to actually learning how to do it. There are lots of strategies out there but let me cut to the chase and introduce you to my favorite: *index funds*. Index funds not only provide us with one of the easiest ways to invest but also they are historically the most successful. I'm going to say that again: Index funds are the *easiest* and *most successful* way to invest. *Rejoice!*

This simple method of investing is not a dumbed-down strategy for n00bs but is often recommended by the experts and even for wealthy people. Take LeBron James, who sought investing advice from legendary investor Warren Buffett—likely aware of the hard lessons learned by athletes like Mike Tyson, John Daly, and Allen Iverson, who lost tens of millions to risky ventures, poor financial advice, and spending that got too big. (I'm pretty sure Mike Tyson was, indeed, riding a Siberian tiger around his Miami Beach courtyard, or something like this.) "Athletes generally tend to get promoted by people with restaurants and real estate," Buffett noted. "Everybody's got an idea for him, and usually, the simplest is the best." Buffett's advice to James, who could afford any investment opportunity in the world? "Keep it simple. Making monthly investments in a low-cost index fund makes sense."

It's the same recommendation Buffett has been giving for a while now, even for us plebes without shoe contracts: If you want a reliable strategy for building wealth over time, invest in low-cost index funds, particularly those tracking the S&P 500. As you may be picking up, an S&P 500 index fund is a basket of five hundred large company stocks in the US. It is designed in the image of the S&P 500 index, discussed last chapter. Instead of trying to get clever and pick the best stocks (or paying an "expert" to do it for you, like someone in LeBron's tax bracket might), buying the index guarantees your investments will perform at least as well as the market it measures, because it is that market. Or at least, it's pretty dang close.

Remember, any investment fund is basically a basket, or, if you like my earlier analogy, a suitcase, filled with a specific array of investments, like stocks or bonds. An *index fund* is just a suitcase packed in a particular way; it is packed to mimic a particular market index, such as the S&P 500.

Let's consider another example: A total US stock market index fund mirrors one of the indices that measures every (or nearly every) stock in the US stock market, like the Russell 3000 or Wilshire 5000. Such a fund holds every single stock in the United States in proportion to the size of each stock in the actual marketplace. Even a puny investor like me can scoop up shares of over three thousand companies with a single fund. And because I own *all* US stocks, I own all the best US stocks, even though I don't know what the best stocks are yet.

Truly *passive* investing means using an index fund that reflects the entire market as it is, like a total US stock market index fund does for the US stock market. (This is my choice.) For some folks, the S&P 500 index fund is close enough. Both are considered "broad." But again, not all indices are broad. Remember, there are indices to measure every odd corner of the market—Australian stocks, small stocks, healthcare stocks—and you can buy index funds that mirror those indices as well. Most investors should focus on keeping it broad and passive.

Think back to our two traveling gals and their suitcase funds. What if it were possible for them to pack *everything* in their closets for a trip? In every possible travel scenario, whether they received an unexpected invite to the opera or a monster truck rally, whether they encountered a heat wave or a sub-zero freeze, they'd be ready. Now, I know this absurd hypothetical isn't technically possible! But this some-of-everything, ready-for-anything suitcase pack job is the idea behind a broad index fund.

Not all funds are created this way. Indexing is just one way to pack a suitcase. The stylistic opposite of indexing, a passive approach, is an active approach. This is called *active management.* Many funds have a manager who is trying to pick the best stocks or bonds in an attempt to "beat the market"—aka the market's average as measured by a broad market index. Fortunately for the fund manager and unfortunately for us, it doesn't matter if the manager beats the market or fails. They charge a fee for this service regardless. This means we pay even when they underperform the index average. Which they do frequently.

Basically, active management is the equivalent of having some button-down-wearing, middle-aged finance dude (or lady!) pack your suitcase for you. He is going to charge you a hefty fee even if he neglects to pack you a swimsuit for your beach vacation to Malibu, or if he packs your 2009 knockoff Jessica McClintock strapless zebra-print homecoming dress for your best friend's black-tie chateau wedding. It only matters that he did the packing.

Therefore, broad index funds have two benefits as compared to their actively managed counterparts: They have much lower fees and you don't run the risk of underperforming due to active management.

For these reasons, it's not just Buffett who recommends index funds. Index funds are also the choice strategy of Charles Schwab, as in *The Man*! The man behind the brokerage bank and who made his Scrooge McDuck vault of money by, among other things, selling high-fee actively managed funds to investors over the years.

A dogpile of the country's most credentialed economists recommends them, too. Economists rarely get along about anything, but 93% "strongly agree" or "agree" that, absent insider information, investors are best served by a well-diversified, low-fee passive index fund. (The other 7% did not respond.) "Almost everyone should be investing in this way and ignoring tips from friends and experts on particular stocks," commented Anil Kashyap, professor of finance and economics at the University of Chicago's Booth School of Business.

Next chapter, I'll show you how to build a strategy of broad, low-cost index funds. But before we go, take a minute to celebrate what might be the best personal financial news you'll hear, maybe ever: With investing, the best strategies are also the easiest. That's not usually the case with money, which can feel like a constant struggle. Budgeting, for example, is simple in theory but can be a total slog in practice. Good investing, on the other hand, is more difficult conceptually, but in practice it's surprisingly easy, and index funds are what make it so. Say it with me now: *Hallelujah!!*

Heads up! In this book, I'll use "index funds" as a blanket term that includes both index mutual funds and index exchange-traded funds (ETFs). For our purposes, an S&P 500 index mutual fund is the same investment as an S&P 500 index ETF.

What Is the Difference Between Mutual Funds and ETFs?

A lot goes into creating baskets of investments that investors across the globe can access at any time. And there just happens to be more than one way to structure these baskets: as a *mutual fund* or an *exchange-traded fund* (ETF). For now think of this as the "wrapper" for the fund—the technical, back-end way in which a fund maker wraps the investments together.

The main difference lies in how these funds are traded. Mutual funds trade only once per day, at the end of the trading day. In contrast, exchange-traded funds trade like stocks on an exchange (it's right there in the name!), meaning we can see their prices fluctuate throughout the day. Mutual funds came first, but traders seeking real-time pricing for things like S&P 500 index funds spurred the creation of a new, zippier type of fund: the ETF.

So, what's it to you? Not a lot. I suspect that you are not a trader. The choice between a mutual fund or an ETF is one of the least critical decisions when choosing a fund. If they are suitcases, a mutual fund is like a duffel bag, and an ETF is like a hard-bodied Away bag with wheels. You might prefer one over the other, but both will get your belongings (investments) from point A to point B. What's far more important is:

- What's inside the fund (the holdings: whether stocks, bonds, or a mix)
- How it's packed (index vs. actively managed)
- Whether there are costs involved (fees)

A common misconception is that all mutual funds are actively managed, and all ETFs are index funds. This isn't true. Both mutual funds and ETFs can be either index or actively managed. To identify whether your mutual fund or ETF is of the index variety, it should have INDEX or IDX in the name of the fund. This isn't foolproof, though, and sometimes it requires more detective work. We'll talk more about how in chapter 25, RESEARCH.

Whether you use mutual funds or ETFs may depend on what's available to you. For example:

- Workplace retirement accounts typically only offer mutual funds.
- If you're investing independently through a brokerage bank, you'll have access to both mutual funds and ETFs.
- If you're investing independently through a trading platform like Robinhood, you'll likely only have access to ETFs.

There are other differences, but I don't want to slow you down with an exhaustive list. For now, here's what you should know:

- Mutual funds are often easier for beginners because you can always buy in with a specific dollar amount (as opposed to needing to purchase a full share). This means you can invest with all the money you have to invest, no matter how much.
- Therefore, automated investing is generally easier with mutual funds than with ETFs.
- ETFs are more tax-efficient, which can make them a better option in non-retirement brokerage accounts where taxes are a concern.

17

DIVERSIFICATION & THE THREE-FUND PORTFOLIO

How do I use index funds to build a diversified strategy?

Cue a violently patriotic Toby Keith song, set off the illegal fireworks, and crack open a few Bud Lights in the bed of a 'roided-up F-150 (that, let's be honest, only gets used for commuting to a desk job), because nothing beats being American. Right? *Right?!*

American exceptionalism is an ideology that bleeds into how many US investors build their portfolios, developing 'MURICA-only strategies, convinced it's the superior way to invest. In fact, some of the country's most successful investors, like Warren Buffett, have long championed using a single US stock market index fund to invest.

But I don't!

You are certainly welcome to listen to Buffett—he is vastly richer than me, in case you hadn't noticed—and he has some valid points. First, it is absolutely true that a broad US stock market index fund, which invests across hundreds of companies and every industry imaginable, achieves a degree of diversification unfathomable to investors even a few decades ago. Second, most investors would be served best by extremely simple strategies. When the strategy is simple, there is less room for self-doubt and error to creep in.

It's also true that US stocks have whupped international stocks over the past nearly two decades, reinforcing the "US is best" belief that Americans have been mainlining since birth. But there's also no guarantee this will always be the case. Markets shift over time. South Korea and Japan dominated in the 1970s and into the '80s, the US surged in the '90s, Europe performed well in the 2000s, and the US took the lead again in the 2010s. Betting entirely on one country is to assume it will always stay on top. History suggests otherwise.

Decade	Best-Performing Stock Markets
1940s	Spain, Australia
1950s	Germany, Japan
1960s	Spain, Australia
1970s	South Korea, Japan
1980s	Sweden, South Korea
1990s	Switzerland, United States
2000s	Norway, Brazil
2010s	United States, New Zealand

I am writing to you in April 2025. Currently, the president appears to be hell-bent on making enemies of our global trade partners, privatizing public services, and selling off the economy to his rich friends. Confronted with the real-time fallibility of the United States of America, international diversification feels especially urgent.

But this isn't about predicting some imminent collapse. It's about recognizing that investing in just one country, any country, is a risk. You can't have it both ways. You don't get to enjoy the returns of only the best-performing category *and* have protection if the worst happens within that category.

That's where the three-fund portfolio comes in.

The three-fund portfolio is a simple, powerful way to spread your risk while keeping investing low-cost and easy to manage. It's a strategy popularized by the Bogleheads, a community inspired by John Bogle, the founder of Vanguard and the pioneer of index investing.

Here's how it works:

You invest using just three broad index funds, covering:

US stocks
International stocks
Bonds

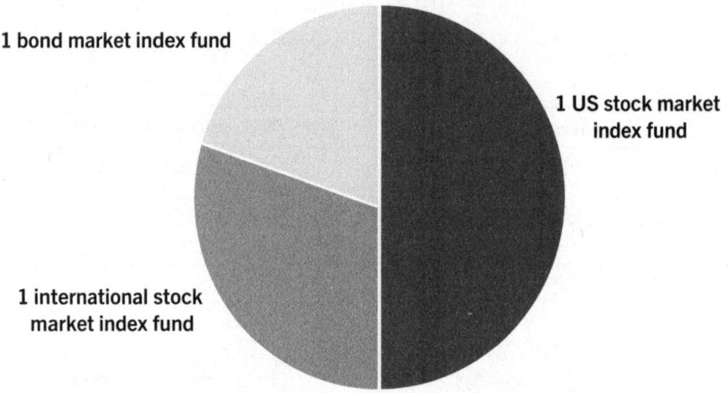

You'll adjust the mix depending on your desired asset allocation.

Two of my closest friends read an early draft of this book, and they both had the same reaction: "Wait. But you don't *actually* invest in anything besides the S&P 500, do you?"

Their sentiment reflects a common mindset among American investors, many of whom have only ever known strong returns from the US stock market in their investing lifetime. And I get it. Why would anyone willingly invest in worse-performing categories?

And still, my answer is, emphatically, yes. It is true that if the US continues to kick international ass, my diversified portfolio will do worse than if I kept an all-US strategy. But I am willing to give up potential returns to protect myself in the event that this does not happen. That said, you do you. I only need you to be clear on the risks you feel are worth taking.

As you diversify, remember this: The rewards of diversification come slowly. Along the way, you'll be constantly tempted by the siren song of the best-performing fund, and you may even resent the ones that lag. Different markets shift in and out of favor over years, sometimes decades. To see it through, you'll have to be patient. Like, maybe more patient than you have ever been in your whole life. And that's coming from me—Little Miss Tapping Her Toes if she has to wait more than four minutes for her Taco Bell bean burrito. We got this!!

US Stock Market Index Funds

When choosing a US stock market index fund, look for one that tracks the whole US stock market, like a total US stock market index fund. You may also choose to use an S&P 500 index fund, which invests across the 500 largest stocks. Because the 500 largest stocks are so proportionally large, even in a total market index, these two funds will perform similarly over time.

International Stock Market Index Funds

There are lots of ways to slice and dice the international markets. The big decision when picking an international stock fund is whether to use a fund that invests across *developed markets, emerging markets,* or both.

- **Developed markets** are economically stable countries like Japan, Germany, and the UK
- **Emerging markets** are growing economies like China, Brazil, and India

Some of these definitions are blurring. China, for example, might argue that the US is the *less* "developed" of the two giants. We will see if any changes are made to these classifications in the coming decade.

If you look at performance over the past 100-plus years, developed international markets come out just barely ahead. What long-term annualized returns don't show, however, is that emerging market countries have also gone through stretches of remarkable outperformance—only to suffer significant losses during downturns like the Great Depression. Returns depend heavily on the measurement window. What happens in the future? It's nearly impossible to say. That uncertainty is the very essence of risk.

	Historical Annualized Returns
Developed International	7–8%
Emerging Markets	7%

I think it makes sense to start with developed international stocks because they tend to be less volatile. Then, if you're comfortable, you can add emerging markets for additional growth potential. You can do this by choosing an international index fund that includes both developed and emerging markets, or by owning them in separate index funds.

Something to keep in mind: China dominates market-weighted emerging market index funds, as it is the largest emerging market by a lot. This isn't necessarily good or bad, just something to be aware of as you design your allocation. While China has been an extraordinary engine of economic growth, its government intervenes in markets in ways that can surprise investors.

Bond Index Funds

Diversification outside the stock market is, in my opinion, also essential. You can do this with bonds. As discussed in chapters 13, RISK and 14, ASSET ALLOCATION, bonds can provide protection if the stock market takes a serious, prolonged downturn. They are especially worth your consideration as you get closer to retirement and need more stability.

For simplicity, broad funds like a total US bond market index fund are a great starting point, as they typically include both federal government and corporate bonds. If choosing between the two, corporate bonds may have slightly higher returns, but US treasuries may be a better hedge during downturns.

When you see a bond fund labeled with a range of years, that tells you the average lifespan of the bonds within. Shorter ranges, like 1–3 years, generally mean lower, steadier performance, while longer ranges, like 7–10 years (or more), will swing more but can offer higher returns. This average length is what investors call a fund's *duration,* a quick shorthand for how sensitive the fund is to interest rates. Your choice depends on what you value more: stability or growth. I like shorter durations for folks wading into bond funds for the first time.

Types of Bonds

Government Bonds: Issued by national governments to fund public spending.

- Example: US Treasury bonds, Treasury notes, and Treasury bills.
- Considered low-risk since they're backed by the federal government.

Corporate Bonds: Issued by companies to raise capital for business operations, expansion, or debt refinancing.

- Example: Investment-grade bonds (safer, lower yield) and junk bonds (riskier, higher yield).
- Risk and returns vary depending on the company's creditworthiness.

Municipal Bonds (Munis): Issued by state and local governments to fund infrastructure projects like schools, roads, and hospitals.

- Example: General obligation bonds (backed by taxes) and revenue bonds (backed by specific projects like toll roads).
- Often tax-exempt, making them attractive to high-income investors. (This is a moot point in your retirement account, which is a tax shelter for interest paid on bonds.)

Asset-Backed & Mortgage-Backed Bonds: Bonds backed by pools of loans or other financial assets.

- Example: Mortgage-backed securities (MBS) (backed by home loans) and asset-backed securities (ABS) (backed by things like auto loans, credit card debt, or student loans).

Treasury Inflation-Protected Securities (TIPS): Issued by the US government and designed to protect against inflation.

- TIPS adjust the underlying principal value (and therefore interest payments) based on changes to the Consumer Price Index (CPI).
- TIPS offer lower yields than regular treasuries, but because the value is adjusted upward over time, they are considered a conservative hedge against inflation.

Without further ado, the resource that makes this book worth way more than its weight in gold, literally: the names and *tickers* (identifiers) for an array of excellent index fund options. To build your strategy, choose one that represents each category you'd like to invest in.

But let's not get ahead of ourselves. I'd like you to read the rest of parts III and IV before you make any big moves. Also, if you are interested in using the "ethical" version of these funds, check out chapter 30 on ETHICAL INVESTING *before* buying anything. For now, I ask that you simply begin visualizing how to use index funds as tools to build your strategy.

Index Mutual Funds			
Index Mutual Funds	**Charles Schwab**	**Fidelity**	**Vanguard**
S&P 500 Index Fund	SWPPX	FNILX	VFIAX
Total US Stock Market Index Fund	SWTSX	FZROX	VTSAX
International Stock Market Index Fund (developed only)	SWISX	FSPSX	VTMGX

International Stock Market Index Fund (developed and emerging)		FZILX	VTIAX
US Bond Market Index Fund (mix)	SWAGX	FXNAX	VBTLX
US Intermediate-Term Treasury Index Fund		FUAMX	VSIGX

Index ETFs			
Index ETFs	**Charles Schwab**	**iShares**	**Vanguard**
S&P 500 Index Fund	SCHX	IVV	VOO
Total US Stock Market Index Fund	SCHB	ITOT	VTI
International Stock Market Index Fund (developed only)	SCHF	IDEV	VEA
International Stock Market Index Fund (developed and emerging)		IXUS	VXUS
US Bond Market Index Fund (mix)	SCHZ	AGG	BND
US Intermediate-Term Treasury Index Fund	SCHR	IEI	VGIT

18

TARGET-DATE FUNDS

Should I use an all-in-one fund?

"It feels too easy," said my friend Mariam over our favorite afternoon treat: French fries and a tub of soda. "My 401(k) automatically invests in a *target-date fund.* Is that okay?"

"Well, it depends," I responded, two and a half knuckles into a side of ranch dressing because I'm nasty like that. "Target-date funds can be a great, easy, one-stop option for investing. But just as not all funds are created equal, not all target-date funds are created equal. I need more information!" And because I'm *also* not afraid to ruin a nice time, I had Mariam log into her 401(k) right there at the restaurant.

Retirement target-date funds—a real mouthful, if we are being honest—are also called *lifecycle funds.* From here on out, I'll refer to them as *TDFs.*

These funds are commonly the default option in workplace retirement accounts, designed for folks who don't know how (or don't want) to build a diversified portfolio from scratch. Instead of requiring each participant to choose individual funds, a TDF offers an all-in-one strategy that bundles together each of the major market categories: US stocks, international stocks, and bonds. Not every plan uses them by default, but they're becoming more common. (Fun! You can now buy them in regular investment accounts, too.)

Whereas a fund holds investments like stocks and bonds directly, a TDF is a fund that holds funds. Now, those funds may be low-cost index funds, or they could be high-cost, actively managed funds. This is what I mean when I say not all TDF products are created equal. Personally, I'd only use an *index TDF*. If my 401(k)'s TDF offering had high fees and held actively managed funds, I would not use it, instead seeking out individual index funds to build my strategy. Luckily, Mariam had an index TDF offering available in her 401(k).

Speaking of French fries, Jeremy Schneider, creator of the wonderful Personal Finance Club, compares buying an index TDF to ordering a fast food combo meal. "You can buy the burger, fries, and Coke separately, and that's like buying the individual index funds," he says. "Or you can buy the combo meal. That's an index target-date fund." I'd add that while the value of a combo meal is generally in some small financial discount, the value in an index TDF fund is its simplicity. All the work of building a portfolio is done for you.

You'll know you are looking at one of these funds because of the super-futuristic date in the name. The idea is to pick a fund with your general retirement year, like 2030 or 2060. I asked Mariam, who is twenty-eight, why she chose the fund with a target retirement date of 2035. That would place her retirement age at thirty-eight, much sooner than the usual retirement age. "Because I don't want to work until I'm freaking sixty-five," she responded. Fair enough! 2035 is her *aspirational* retirement date. Her *spiritual* retirement date, if you will.

Unfortunately, the date on the TDF has nothing to do with when Mariam gets to walk away from work. If only it were so easy. Instead, the date on the fund tells us only one thing.

Knowing what we've covered so far, this could be a fun moment to pause, take a big sip of soda, and channel that buzz into your best guess. What might that "one thing" be?

Answer? A TDF's date has *everything* to do with the asset allocation; the proportion of stocks to bonds held inside the fund. As of this writing, a 2035 TDF is designed for someone a decade away from retirement, and holds something like 70% stocks and 30% bonds. Depending on the twenty-eight-year-old, this may be too conservative. Compare that to a 2070 TDF, which will have an allocation closer to

90% stocks and 10% bonds because it assumes its users to be young, have long investing time horizons, and able to handle stock market risk. Therefore, Mariam is choosing an investment strategy that is relatively conservative and may have the opposite effect of turbocharging her retirement timeline.

Instead of picking the fund that corresponds to your fantasy retirement date, pick the fund that corresponds to your desired asset allocation. Do you want a strategy that is more stable but offers less potential growth? Stick with the 2035 fund. Or do you want a higher-growth strategy that, yes, will be more volatile? If so, use a later-dated fund.

Once you buy a fund, you never need to change it, because the fund is designed to grow older with you, including through and after the date on the fund. It does this by shifting into more bonds over time, as well as keeping your strategy in balance from year to year, making sure no part of your portfolio is getting overgrown. (Without a TDF, these are your responsibilities. More on that in chapter 28, UPKEEP.) To see the journey that your fund's strategy will take over time, look for its *glide path*. (Which would be a funny nickname for a vagina. *Sorry!!*)

Target-Date Fund Glide Path

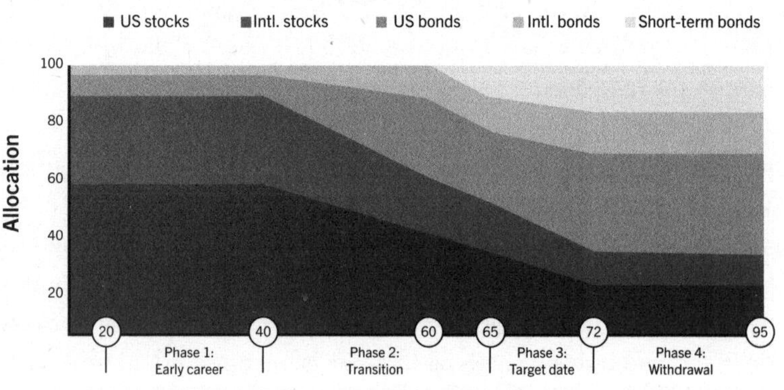

All TDFs will be a little bit different depending on who makes it. Like funds, TDFs are banking products, and lots of different banks (Vanguard, Fidelity, BlackRock, and so on) make their own versions. Each will make its own asset allocation and glide path decisions; a 2050 fund made by one brand might be different from a 2050 fund by another brand. But even then, it's not enough to make sure you've got the right asset allocation. What types of funds does the TDF use internally to build out that asset allocation?

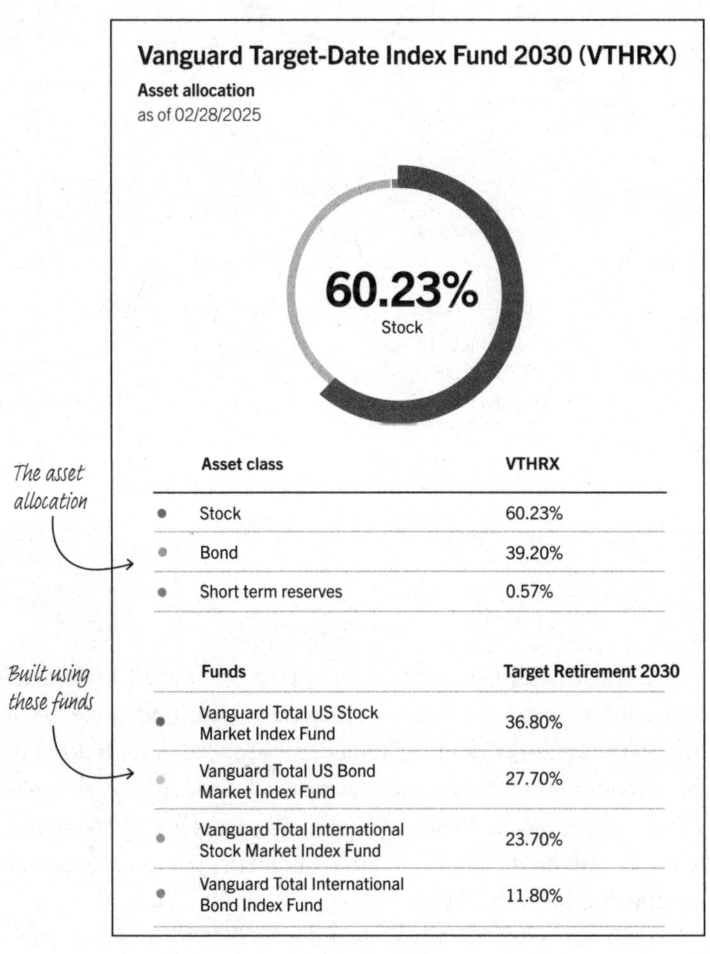

Asset class	VTHRX
Stock	60.23%
Bond	39.20%
Short term reserves	0.57%

Funds	Target Retirement 2030
Vanguard Total US Stock Market Index Fund	36.80%
Vanguard Total US Bond Market Index Fund	27.70%
Vanguard Total International Stock Market Index Fund	23.70%
Vanguard Total International Bond Index Fund	11.80%

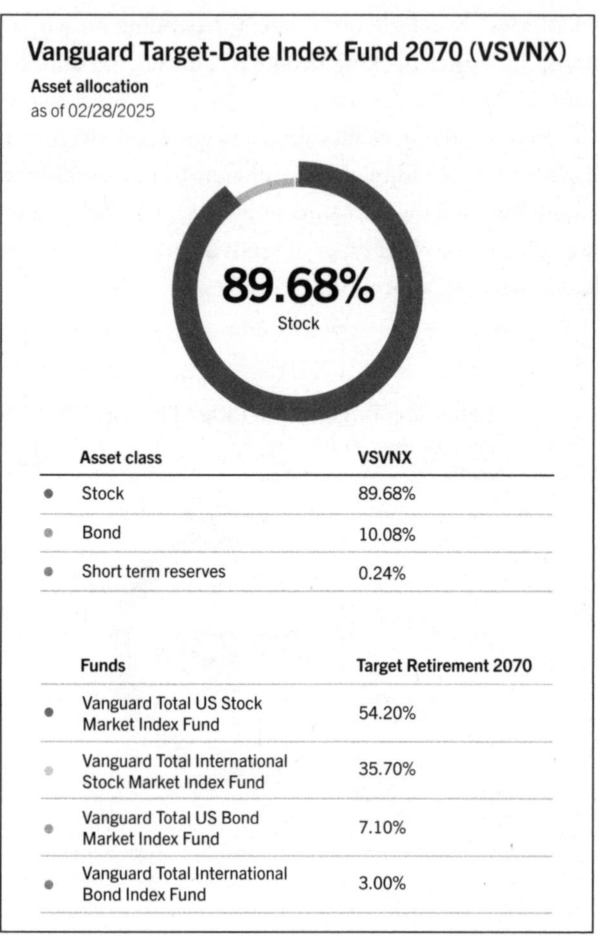

Vanguard Target-Date Index Fund 2070 (VSVNX)

Asset allocation

as of 02/28/2025

Asset class	VSVNX
Stock	89.68%
Bond	10.08%
Short term reserves	0.24%

Funds	Target Retirement 2070
Vanguard Total US Stock Market Index Fund	54.20%
Vanguard Total International Stock Market Index Fund	35.70%
Vanguard Total US Bond Market Index Fund	7.10%
Vanguard Total International Bond Index Fund	3.00%

Let's start with a good example. At least for now, all TDFs made by Vanguard are great and made of just four index funds: one US stock market index fund, one international stock market index fund, and two bond index funds. This is similar to the three-fund strategy detailed last chapter. The only difference is that it is all done for you. (Note the difference between the 2030 and 2070 funds isn't the funds used but the proportions held.)

Unfortunately, for every sleek index TDF like Vanguard's version, there are many more sloppy ones. Compare Fidelity's two different

2060 TDF products. There's the index version, called the Fidelity Freedom® Index 2060 Fund (ticker FDKLX). Then, there's the actively managed version, called the Fidelity Freedom® 2060 Fund (ticker FDKVX). They look crazily, suspiciously similar despite being very different. The former is low-cost, with an expense ratio of 0.12%, while the latter is more expensive, with an expense ratio of 0.75%. FDKLX holds just a handful of index funds, achieving simple, straightforward access to the major markets, while FDKVX is packed full of all sorts of unnecessary, high-cost, duplicative funds. With something like thirty funds, you're paying something like eight or nine different fund managers to get you invested in the US stock market alone. And by the way, it is not as if these managers are strategizing with one another. One could be selling McDonald's stock, while another is buying, all netting out at a cost to you.

I would gladly use Fidelity's index TDF but not their actively managed version. Sneaky, huh?! It's a good reminder that we must always, always take a closer look! Don't worry, I'll teach you how in chapter 25, RESEARCH.

Ultimately, Mariam was happy with the Vanguard index TDFs she had available in her 401(k). She only needed to move herself out of the 2035 fund and into a later-dated fund. She chose 2060. She preferred this to building her own strategy of index funds, which would require a bit more work on her part. It's true that index TDFs may have slightly higher costs than investing directly in index funds. That's because TDFs do the "extra" work of managing and rebalancing across multiple funds. Still, they're a screamin' deal and Rich Old Lady–approved for building a smart, diversified strategy with almost no effort.

As I told Mariam, perhaps the best thing about the simplicity of an index TDF is that it allows her to focus every bit of her energy on shoveling money in so that maybe—just maybe—she *can* retire by 2035.

Index Funds Versus Index Target-Date Funds

Whether you opt for a fully automated index TDF or take the wheel and build your own portfolio with index funds, these are two routes to the same destination. One's hands-off, the other's a bit more DIY, but both can get you where you want to go.

Two Paths to the Same Place

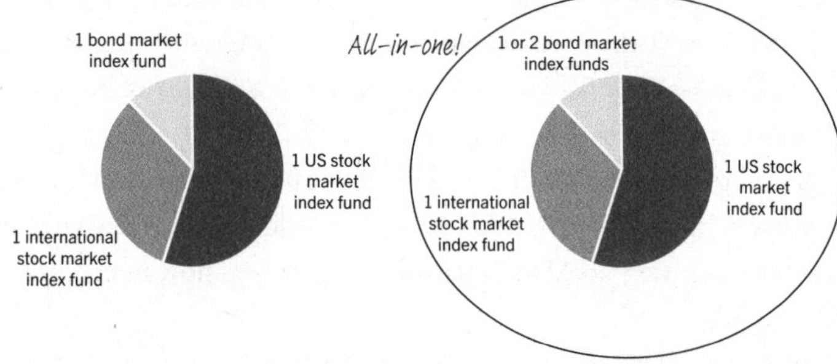

Which you choose is a matter of preference. If you were to build your own strategy using index funds, below is a quick summary of your responsibilities:

1. Determine your asset allocation—your mix of stocks and bonds
2. Buy the corresponding index funds
3. Rebalance once a year as funds grow unevenly
4. Shift into a more conservative (bond-heavy) strategy over time

Meanwhile, an index TDF handles all these aspects for you, a key part of its appeal. However, the trade-off for the convenience is reduced control. With any TDF, you don't dictate the funds (or their holdings), the asset allocation, or the glide path. All you can do is choose the one most closely aligned with your preferred strategy.

Index Target-Date Funds			
Retirement Year	**Charles Schwab**	**Fidelity**	**Vanguard**
2030	SWYEX	FXIFX	VTHRX
2035	SWYFX	FIHFX	VTTHX
2040	SWYGX	FBIFX	VFORX
2045	SWYHX	FIOFX	VTIVX
2050	SWYMX	FIPFX	VFIFX
2055	SWYJX	FDEWX	VFFVX
2060	SWYNX	FDKLX	VTTSX
2065	SWYOX	FFIJX	VLXVX
2070		FRBVX	VSVNX

19

EXPECTATIONS

What's the secret to being a good stock market investor?

To be a good stock market investor, you need to know how to protect yourself. But protection may not mean what you think. It's not about staying hypervigilant, ready to make the perfect defensive move at any moment. Your best protection is to know what to expect.

Consider the year 2022, when the US stock market returned a negative 18%. If you started the year with $10,000 invested in a US stock market index fund, you ended with $8,200. If you experienced this, you already know—it felt terrible! It was not good times! But being down 18% in 2022 wasn't a sign that you were "doing it wrong." In fact, it was the opposite: You were doing exactly what passive investing is designed to do—mirror the market's performance. Passive investing works because we know most years aren't like 2022, and because rough periods give way to better ones. But experiencing a year like 2022 can be a mindfuck, especially if you were never given clear and realistic expectations about stock market investing.

Raise your hand if you were led to believe that you'd get 10% returns from the stock market each and every year! The 10% historical returns figure is constantly bandied about in oversimplified personal finance TikToks, where it is rarely disclosed that this is the average when stretched across very, very long periods. In reality, it is unusual to get a neat and tidy 10% return dropped off on your doorstep on December 31, tied up with a bow. Generally, returns are much higher or much lower. Some years, you're getting a shiny new Jet Ski left at your doorstep. Other years, you're getting a bag of burning hair.

Have a look at the year-by-year returns of the stock and bond markets, below. You can see that the stock market can be up 28% one year, down 18% the next, and up 26% a year after that. But even when accounting for the bummer years *and* all the stinker stocks, the US stock market has still managed to pull off annualized returns of 10% per year.

Stocks and Bonds Performance by Year, 1990–2024		
	S&P 500 Index	**US 10-Year Treasury Bonds**
1990	-3.06%	6.24%
1991	30.23%	15.00%
1992	7.49%	9.36%
1993	9.97%	14.21%
1994	1.33%	-8.04%
1995	37.20%	23.48%
1996	22.68%	1.43%
1997	33.10%	9.94%
1998	28.34%	14.92%
1999	20.89%	-8.25%
2000	-9.03%	16.66%
2001	-11.85%	5.57%
2002	-21.97%	15.12%
2003	28.36%	0.38%
2004	10.74%	4.49%
2005	4.83%	2.87%
2006	15.61%	1.96%
2007	5.48%	10.21%
2008	-36.55%	20.10%
2009	25.94%	-11.12%

continued

Stocks and Bonds Performance by Year, 1990–2024		
	S&P 500 Index	**US 10-Year Treasury Bonds**
2010	14.82%	8.46%
2011	2.10%	16.04%
2012	15.89%	2.97%
2013	32.15%	-9.10%
2014	13.52%	10.75%
2015	1.38%	1.28%
2016	11.77%	0.69%
2017	21.61%	2.80%
2018	-4.23%	-0.02%
2019	31.21%	9.64%
2020	18.02%	11.33%
2021	28.47%	-4.42%
2022	-18.04%	-17.83%
2023	26.06%	3.88%
2024	24.88%	-1.64%

What you will notice, here, is that not every year can be a banner year! The stock market is negative about three out of every ten years. It is positive seven out of every ten years. (Honestly, this is goals? I'd take a seven-for-ten hit rate.) The barren years get a lot of attention, but the stock market is a story of more up than down.

Have you ever noticed how much humans love measuring in increments of years? From progressing across grades in school to resolutions, we are suckers for trying to fit broader experiences of growth or evolution into a progressive annual framework. But I assure you, the stock market does not give a shit about our precious Gregorian calendar. Instead, it tends to move in much larger sweeping cycles that include both positive and negative growth, cycles that we call *bull* and *bear markets*.

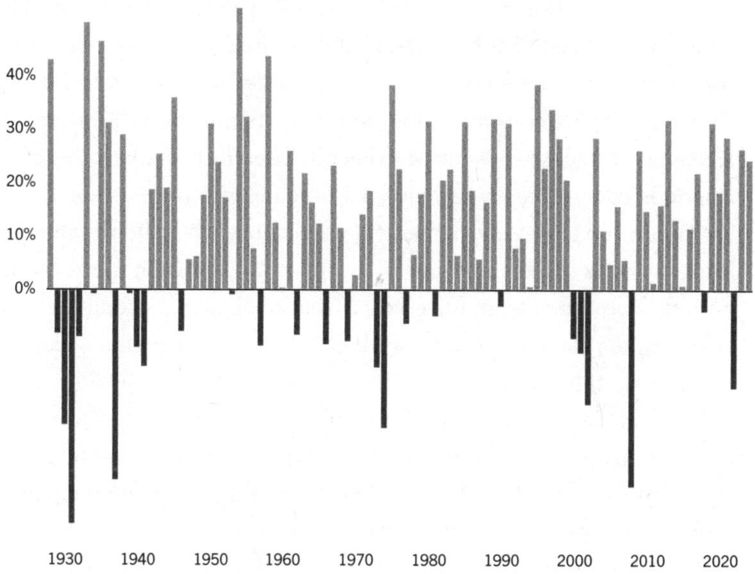

The Wall Street bull, a quasi-religious symbol of American capitalism and prosperous markets, is notably represented by its bronze statue on Wall Street, where tourists from distant places flock to engage with its symbolism—and its anatomical elements. (Fine, I'll just say it. People go to Wall Street to cup his balls. *I'm so tired.*) Bear markets represent investment periods in decline, which I remember because they leave you feeling "bare."

Looking back at history, the best year in the US stock market was 1954, when shares surged 52.5% as they finally recovered from the massive losses of the Great Depression. The worst calendar year was 1931, with a -43.8% return, but the stock market has lost *more* than 50%, when measuring from peak to trough, on several occasions. All that falls in between represents the full range of possibilities in the stock market.

And there is something else I want you to see here, too. Yes, bull markets are long and strong (Sir Mix-a-Lot voice: *and down to get the friction on*), and bear markets are painful but shorter-lived, but neither can be nailed down into entirely predictable patterns. While I tend to generalize and say that full market cycles, including both a bear and bull market, last about a decade, some cycles last longer and some shorter. We mostly exist during bull markets, but bears can happen anytime—often when we least expect it. Therefore, the best thing we can do is accept that it's coming on a timeline we cannot predict.

When you look at stock market performance, two patterns emerge. First, the stock market is up and down and up and down in shorter-term periods like one year and five years. That's volatility. Second, despite volatility, the stock market moves higher over longer periods, like ten or, more reliably, twenty years. Thirty years is even better. Forty years is better than that. What do you think this means for your investments?

Reliable, predictable, and average results in the stock market take time. That's the essence of passive investing: The stock market tends to reward patience over the long term.

Annualized Returns Over Rolling Periods + Volatility

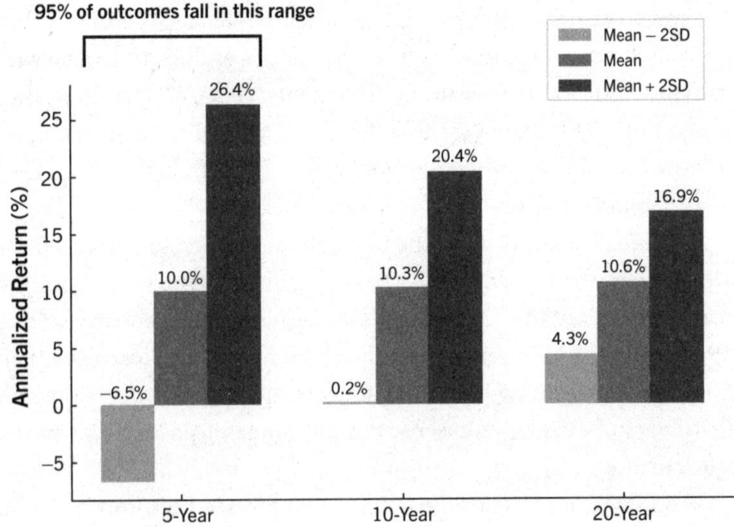

The graph above shows rolling returns based on month-by-month US stock market data, looking at *every possible* five-, ten-, and twenty-year period from 1926 to 2024. On average, the annualized return was about 10% across all time horizons. But averages alone don't tell the whole story! The volatility of those returns was far greater for five-year periods than for ten- or twenty-year periods. We can measure this with a calculation called *standard deviation,* which captures how widely outcomes tend to spread around the average. A common way to frame this is to look at two standard deviations above and below the mean—an interval that contains 95% of all historical results.

For five-year periods, that range stretches from -6.5% to +26.4%. Said another way, history tells us it has been entirely possible to endure five years of compounding losses at around -7% per year, and just as possible to enjoy five years of 26% returns per year. For ten-year periods, the range narrows, with outcomes clustering between roughly 0% and 20%. For twenty-year periods, the results are even tighter, falling between about 4% and 17%. And that's not because the market stops being wild. No, no, the ups and downs are still there! But over time, those swings get absorbed, balanced out by more chances for recovery and growth.

This can feel abstract until you see it play out in real life. Take two recent back-to-back decades. The US stock market lost about 9% in total across the 2000s, weighed down by the Dot-Com Bubble and the 2008 financial crisis on either end. That worked out to an annualized return of roughly -1% per year, about as bad as it gets for a ten-year stretch. But in the 2010s, the following decade, the market roared back with an incredible 256% gain, compounding at 13.5% per year. This is typical: Long, sluggish decades are often followed by more prosperous ones.

Using this information, my personal conclusion is that it's ideal to keep your money in the stock market long enough to catch at least two upswings (bull market cycles). I know that reading this can feel frustrating, especially for those who don't envision themselves as having twenty-plus investing years. (Although, I bet most of you do have twenty years. You'll be investing money you need to use long beyond the day you retire.) It's also totally fair if you think this sucks. But I firmly believe it's better to be honest, because cheerily lying to you about how this works would suck way more.

One last thing. I spent the chapter focusing on the US stock market because it will likely make up the majority of our investing strategies—and it's the focus of so much cultural attention. But for most of us, it won't be the only market that we invest in. International stocks are on a similar wave as US stocks but will have periods where they do better than US stocks and worse than US stocks. We cannot know, in advance, when these times will be. (This, again, is a case for diversification.) Bonds will sometimes perform in tandem with stocks, and other times they won't. For both stocks and bonds, many of the same lessons apply. Not all years are positive (but most are), the markets produce patterns of behavior we can track over time, and **the big decision we make as investors is whether we want to participate in these patterns.**

Investing the Squishy Middle

I'm often asked, sometimes sheepishly, whether investing for shorter-term goals is *allowed*.

And the answer is, of course you're allowed! And logistically, it's simple. Open a (non-retirement) brokerage account and you can invest however you want and for whatever reason you want. No one is going to investing jail for investing on shorter timelines! It just requires that you accept the extra risk and keep your expectations completely realistic.

By now I hope you can see why stocks are most appropriate for long-term goals, because you can ride out any choppy weather and take advantage of compounding. Placing cash in a HYSA (or CD) is usually best for short-term goals, which I'd classify as anything with a hard deadline in the next five years.

But what about everything in between? This is what I call Investing the Squishy Middle. Imagine a woman who is twenty-two years old and fresh out of college. She has started contributing to her 401(k), but she is thinking about saving for a future home and maybe a wedding, though she has no immediate plans to jump into either. Knowing she is already saving, should she also invest that money?

It all depends on your risk tolerance. When looking at the historical returns of the S&P 500 index, about 27% of calendar-year periods have been negative, meaning the other 73% have been positive.

Certainly better odds than you'd get playing roulette, but still odds that demand some careful consideration. Twelve percent of five-year periods are negative, and even 6% of ten-year periods are negative. (Remember the 2000's Lost Decade?) You have to ask yourself: For this particular goal and considering your best approximate timeline, are you okay with those odds?

If you're willing to be on the market's schedule—that is, able to wait to tap into the money only once you're ahead, even if that takes longer than you'd expected—then maybe that's your answer. If, on the other hand, you know you'll need the money in the next few years and don't want to risk losing any of it, well, maybe that's your answer, too.

This doesn't have to be an all-or-nothing decision, either. An easy thing to do is split the money evenly between cash, stocks, and bonds. (Using index funds of course.) If this makes you skittish and you want more help deciding on an asset allocation for short-term goals, consider using ROBO-ADVISORS, which I cover in chapter 29. (And don't forget: Because you aren't investing in the tax shelter of a retirement account, you'll owe taxes on any investment gains!)

20

MARKET CRASHES

How do I protect myself from crashes?

You may think I'm done talking about volatility, but I'm not! I'll never shut up about it because I have seen firsthand how market crashes can make a person demolish their own investment plan. There's no point in getting people invested if they're going to self-sabotage as soon as we have a market crash—as did so many of the investors I worked with during the financial crisis of 2008.

The timing was impeccable. I was in my first year of work after college, starting my career in investment management. The US stock market had just begun its now-historic nosedive, ultimately losing 57% of its value between October 2007 and March 2009. Somehow, it gets worse. Part of the firm's sales pitch to prospective clients was that our research team would "catch" the next crash, moving our clients to a "defensive strategy," aka cash.

Spoiler alert: We didn't! And because of it, our clients terminated us swiftly, and in numbers. Way back then, terminations required a signed fax, and I was a lowly associate, tasked with processing them. On one especially brutal day, the firings came so relentlessly that, in a spectacular allegory for the market itself, our fax machine burst into flames.

In the chaos, I witnessed, firsthand, otherwise intelligent people—doctors, engineers, business executives—destroy their nest eggs by selling out at exactly the wrong time: the market's absolute lowest point. Imagine working your entire career to build a $10 million portfolio, only to panic and cash out when it temporarily drops to five.

Watching people actively undermine their own well-being, in a workplace thick with fear and anger, was harrowing for me, too. 2008 is permanently etched into my nervous system; it is also the reason you're holding this book. I wish I could say I got into this work to help my friends get filthy rich. But that's not totally true. I got into it because I've seen how quickly things can go wrong, and it made me scared for us.

In 2010, I moved into the role of investment counselor, where part of my work was persuading our clients to stay the course; begging them to hold on. The market was recovering but still at a massive loss, and trust in the system (and our firm) had been shaken. Many of our clients continued to believe that their money was safer out of the market. They broke and sold, locking in their losses, many of them never returning to the market. If they *had* held on, that $10 million portfolio that had shrunk to $5 million would have boomed back, worth over $40 million today.

Understandably, many people could not see past their pain. 2008 was the worst market crash since the Great Depression. And it wasn't just the markets but the entire economy in free fall. Major banks imploded. Millions of people lost their jobs. In the face of such economic horror, the instinct to protect whatever money you have left—the hard-earned, numerical embodiment of your entire life's work—gets primal.

To safely handle market crashes, which is essential to your success as an investor, I firmly believe that you have to know *why* they happen. To show you, I want to introduce another of history's most stunning bear markets: the Dot-Com Bubble. Grab a hot cup of tea and crawl into your favorite couch groove because Grandma is going to tell you about a time, not so long ago, when you couldn't send someone a photo of your butthole that would self-destruct in twenty-four hours. That's right, this is a story about the invention of the internet.

It was the late 1990s when the internet began to infiltrate our lives in earnest, and the user growth of the new technology was unlike anything we've ever seen in history. (So far.) A vast new frontier of unlimited information and unsolicited dick pics was upon us, with economic excitement rapidly reaching a fever pitch. Everyone wanted their share of these hot, new internet stocks, even though many of these companies did not have a clear path to profit or even a viable product. To investors, that didn't matter. That these companies would someday do business on the World Wide Web was more than enough. The Nasdaq index, a benchmark for tech stocks, climbed 86% in 1999, capturing the market's fervor for new technology companies.

And then the bubble burst. To understand why, we have to know how it formed in the first place.

Remember our ol' pals from Econ 101, supply and demand? In a *free market*, supply (how much of a thing is available) and demand (how much people want a thing) set the price for that thing.

A stock, a parcel of company ownership, is also a thing for sale in a free market, subject to the forces of supply and demand. On any given day, there are only so many shares of stock available; a fixed supply, more or less. Demand, though, is in constant flux. On a day where mass amounts of people buy into a stock, this buying is the mechanism that pushes the price higher. When demand rises, sellers can charge more.

It works in the other direction, too. If no one wants a stock, sellers may have to drop the price to entice buyers. That's the heart of it: **The price of a stock is a reflection of how much we want it; or how much we don't.**

Supply matters too, but shifts in the supply of stock tend to be slow. It's a big deal for company stock to be destroyed or for a company to create new stock to be sold in the stock market, called an *initial public offering (IPO)*. Demand, then, can be blamed for a lot of the visceral ups and downs we experience day to day.

In the investment forecasting industry, *investor sentiment*, the technical term for vibes/mood/feelings, is considered one of the most powerful influences on stock prices on any given day or year. It feels very high school, doesn't it? Really, the stock market is just a big, fickle, continuous, never-ending popularity contest.

During the Dot-Com Bubble, prices increased *because* people kept buying into extremely popular but vapid stocks. Economist Robert Shiller, author of *Irrational Exuberance*, explains such investment manias as a series of *positive feedback loops*: Stock prices experience a price boost, which gets them more media coverage, which further stokes prices. The guys who were lucky enough to be the first investors make loads of dough, and then brag to all their friends about how rich and smart they are. This in turn influences even more people to invest, who, despite reservations about what seems like unusually high prices, are irrational with envy and simply cannot help themselves. The increased buying is what spurs even more buying. (The crypto markets are a more recent example of this buy-*because*-it's-expensive behavior.)

But this can't last forever! There comes a time when demand for stocks can no longer run off euphoria alone. Just as I might pull an Irish goodbye on day three of a music festival, my serotonin stores running bone-dry, investors will inevitably sober up, question the clarity of their initial calculus, and quietly start to sell their trendy stocks to secure whatever profit they can. Demand is in decline. More people sell because they see prices creeping lower, which then causes even more people to sell—a *negative feedback loop* in action.

By March 2000, the market began to boil over, and before the end of the year, investors were in a full flight response. Prices collapsed as people panic-sold all stocks. Internet stocks fared the worst; the tech Nasdaq index lost 77% from its peak, and only about half of all tech companies made it through the crash.

Both statements are true: (1) This "cleaning out" of the market was necessary because the market can't run on vibes/mood/feelings alone. These companies had no profit, which is generally required for investors to stay interested long-term. And (2) sensationalism—a bias to which humans are especially susceptible—amplified extremes on both high and low ends. (Hence Schiller's use of the term *irrational.*)

Therefore, the stock market isn't just a reflection of how companies are doing; it's a reflection of how we *feel* about how they're doing. Over time, company profits tend to rise in a relatively steady, grounded way. But stock prices? Hoo boy, they're much more dramatic, because they're powered by the full spectrum of human emotion. Sometimes, we get high on rising prices. Sometimes, we crash out. Eventually, emotion settles, and the market gravitates back toward the actual performance of the businesses beneath.

And because the global system of buying and selling is the ultimate voting machine, the stock market does a spooky good job of reflecting the real-world profitability of the companies we own, even despite the interim theatrics. This is what people mean when they say that *the market prices in all known information.*

It's hard to fault anyone in that situation for instinctively wanting to sell their stocks. Especially if you are holding individual stocks for sinking ships like Boo.com or Flooz.com—to name two notable flops of the era—cutting your losses is a logical move. But if you were investing across the entire market, like through an index fund, it calls for a completely different strategy. Selling in a panic during a downturn would be a mistake. Negative years are undeniably frightening *and* a part of the investing journey. You don't buy investments just to sell them when they are at their absolute, temporary worst.

Instead, a most wretched 2002—and an utterly terrifying 2008—were incredibly *good* times to invest. Counterintuitive as it may seem, the best chance for good returns in the future is when we are in a "bad market." With time, investors will slowly buy back into stocks, unable to resist the market's incredible deals. This buying in will push the prices back up—and the cycle repeats itself. This is true in the other direction, too. The highest likelihood for bad returns in the future is when we are presently in a "good market." Good markets, usually after years of positive returns, mean buying in at higher, possibly overblown prices, when the market may be due for a price *correction.*

That's why I try to avoid using the words "good" and "bad" to

describe markets at all, because "good" and "bad" are subjective. They have everything to do with your vantage point. Yeah, a "bad" market, like 2002 or 2008, is really freaking bad if you are trying to live off your investments. But a "bad" market is *great* if you are trying to buy investments. Think about it: Would you rather buy a house for cheaper or more expensive? Cheaper, of course. Would you rather buy shares of companies for cheaper or more expensive?! The answer is cheaper. And here's what's really trippy. The *worse* the market is—in terms of both price decline and duration—the *better* it is for young investors who are collecting shares. The more shares you're able to collect during down times, the better your positioning when it swings back around.

Now, no one needs to go wishing for a bear market. That's gross and dark because real people get hurt. But because our current retirement system requires we be investors, we must accept investing's basic mathematical premise: It is a better time to buy when prices are low. Of course, this is difficult to see with clarity when your 401(k) is bleeding out. But as the old investing adage goes, "Be fearful when others are greedy, and greedy when others are fearful."

That's also not to say I think you should be trying to time the markets. Not at all. As I hope you can see, they are very difficult to predict, because major economic events and the human behavior around them are very difficult to predict. Instead, here is my very best advice for handling a market crash:

Stay cute. Stay unbothered. Stick to the plan. Keep investing.

Remember what it is that you own when you own a stock: It is a proportional share of ownership in a company. During a bad year, you don't own any less of that company; the market is simply valuing it at less. The only thing a stock's current price tells you is what you could get if you sold it right now.

Last, I ask that you learn the ways that your brain may be working against you. When the next crash hits, the people around you will be in a panic. That is a promise. At that time, it will take real clarity and nerve to paddle against the emotional current. We are herd creatures, and learning from our peers helped us survive in conditions far harsher than a crypto winter.

That instinct hasn't gone away. Our primal groupthink tendencies still show up all the time in modern economic life. Just look at fashion trends. Sure, 2016's cold-shoulder sweater wasn't exactly on any cavewoman's practical survival checklist—because *brr*!—but the desire to belong absolutely was. Being part of the group meant safety, protection, and a better shot at not being eaten. Don't be surprised if you feel wracked with self-doubt if you find yourself going against the crowd during the next big crash.

That's not all! We are hardwired and chemically programmed to take action when we sense danger—even when that danger shows up in the form of a falling stock portfolio. Our brains read losses as threats and it may send us hurtling into survival mode. It's your internal caveperson yelling, *Somebody, quick, kill it!* and grabbing a club to go bash the danger before it gets any closer.

These big, beautiful brains of ours have done a great job keeping us alive through millennia of real-world threats. However, they are relatively mismatched for navigating capital markets, which have only existed for about a hundred years. When it comes to investing, those ancient instincts don't always serve us well. In fact, they can have us catwalking right into the mouth of the saber-toothed tiger. When markets drop, your instinct will be to act. But in most cases, the best action is inaction; doing nothing at all. That may feel completely wrong, which is exactly why we need to talk about it now—*before* things get primal.

As Morgan Housel writes in *The Psychology of Money*, "Your success as an investor will be determined by how you respond to punctuated moments of terror, not the years spent on cruise control."

Stay cute. Stay unbothered.

The Stock Market Versus the Economy

I want to pause, for a moment, and place investment markets in the context of something bigger: the economy.

The economy includes the investment markets, but it stretches far beyond to include all forms of production and spending. It's the big stuff like trade policy but also the small, everyday stuff: your rent payment, Dad's disability check, the tamales you buy from the vendor down the street. Said another way, the economy is people. The stock market, on the other hand, is exactly what it says on the tin—a marketplace for stocks. Some of us own them. Many of us don't. The stock market and the economy are deeply connected, and what happens in one can affect the other, but even then, the economy is more important than the stock market.

When the economy shrinks, we call it a *recession*. When stocks lose significant value, that's a bear market. They don't always move in lockstep but often they do. And both tend to move in cycles, which many economists and educators, myself included, often refer to as inevitable. In the last two chapters, I spoke about these patterns as if they are as natural as the seasons or the tides. But are they?

Under our current system, yes, probably. But for what it's worth, I don't think they have to be. Some recessions, like the 2008 Great Recession, are caused by big businesses and banks chasing profit in risky ways, as they're encouraged to do under a profit-seeking economic model. And when it doesn't work, the little guy pays the price. Governments use our taxpayer dollars to stabilize and stimulate the system, bail out institutions, and keep things from spinning out of control. It is by this mechanism that the losses of these corporate behemoths are socialized, paid for by us, but their gains are privatized, benefiting only the shareholders.

Meanwhile, a retiree can be wiped of everything they ever worked for—and for what? So a multi-billion-dollar bank can make a shady bet? This isn't the economy I want to live in. Changing entrenched systems would be hard, and it may not happen in our lifetime. I certainly don't have all the answers. But why not dream big? Why not question the systems we've inherited? Every rule, every operating principle in our political and economic structures was made by humans, and that means we can remake them.

To initiate a Great Remaking, I believe we must begin from an honest place. I'd like us to start by loudly admitting that we don't live in a "free market" economy. Companies like Boeing, Tesla, RTX, and many others exist largely thanks to massive infusions of US taxpayer dollars in the form of contracts, subsidies, and bailouts. And once we accept government planning as a feature of our current capitalist system, *not* an anomaly, we can ask the brave question: What would it look like to plan an economy that's more thoughtful, more stable, and more democratic?

For now, this is the system we've got. We can and should expect cycles, including the negative bits.

Please understand that recessions and bear markets require different handling, even if they are happening simultaneously. Recession prep is an act of conservatism: You reduce spending, build savings, and prepare for a potential job loss. But a bear market doesn't call for conservatism. Instead, boldness is the best bear market strategy. Of course, it is tough to hold the two ideas, one in each hand. If you're scared, economically, you may not be able to be bold in your investment choices. And that's okay: You must always take care of Present You first. But we're also investors now, so it's crucial that we clarify the difference between the two.

21

UNDERPERFORMANCE (STOCK PICKING)

Should I pick my own stocks?

We know we can invest and capture returns close to the stock and bond markets' averages by using index funds. Still, many investors choose a different route: picking individual stocks or hiring someone who does.

This is active management and introduces the risk of *underperforming* the average. In the previous chapter, we discussed one of the most dramatic ways we can underperform the average—selling in and out of the market based on emotion. But sometimes it's the quiet stuff that does the most damage, like active management and all the fees tucked inside it.

Active Management aka Stock Picking

Contrary to popular belief, picking stocks will not necessarily make you a better investor. Often, the exact opposite is true.

In January 2024, I was speaking with an acquaintance—I'll call her Ruby—at a Sunday soup party. (A gathering I highly recommend for affordable, cozy wintertime hangs.) She mentioned her stock market success in the previous year and was willing to talk numbers. I love talking numbers. On about $100,000 invested, Ruby's selection of individual stocks had gained a collective $13,000. Can't be mad about $13,000, right? And 13% is better than the historical 10% annual returns for the stock market! *Right?!*

The US stock market, as measured by the S&P 500 index, was up 26% that year. Relatively speaking, she performed a helluva lot worse than the market she invested in. This is a big deal, because it factors into her personal average. Over the course of an investing lifetime, **one cannot return the average if they underperform the average!** If you routinely do half as well as the market, like Ruby did, then your average will be half the market's average. If we assume historical returns, that's 5% to the stock market's 10%. You'd be taking all the risk of being invested in the stock market—yet receiving only half of the market's returns.

Now of course, it could go the other way. You could certainly pick all the right stocks and do much better than average. For example, if you had owned only Amazon stock over the last two decades, you would have smashed the index average. This is the allure of stock picking. But alas, nailing one drunk karaoke song does not make you Lady Gaga, and the elusive *outperformance* investors are seeking rarely materializes. And there's a funny reason why: Most stocks perform worse than average.

Uhm, that's not how averages work, you'd be reasonable to think. The job of an index is to provide the average performance of the market it measures. So, it must mean that about half of stocks do better than the average, and half do worse. That would make sense if stock returns were evenly distributed. But they're not!

Here's the technical explanation; hang with me. The stock market has a *positive skew,* meaning a small number of extreme outliers, like Apple or Exxon, deliver such exceptional returns that they pull the average higher. Meanwhile, the majority of stocks lag behind. Put another way, the average return is higher than the median or "typical" return because a few extreme outperformers buoy the average. It's like in school, when one person—probably you—did the entire group project while the slackers coasted their way to the same good grade.

A study of all US stocks between 1926 and 2015 found that only 4% accounted for all the net wealth generated in the stock market. Allow that to sink in: Just one in twenty-five companies is responsible for *all* sustained stock market gains. The other 96% of stocks either underperformed or are outright failures. Of the 23,500 US stocks studied, more than half delivered negative lifetime returns. And the most common outcome for an individual stock over its lifetime? A total loss of 100%. Most businesses do not last forever.

This is not to imply that stock picking is wrong or can't be successful. Indeed, picking the right stock can result in lottery-like returns. The problem is that it's hard to win the lottery.

There is no universal formula for identifying the superstar stocks *before* they become superstar stocks. If there were, every single one of us could feasibly follow said formula and, with the use of leverage, become infinitely rich!! But no formula can account for the future's many unknowns. Predicting the financial future is a largely futile pursuit and yet people (men) try and try and try, fancying themselves something of a fortune-telling Miss Cleo in a Patagonia fleece vest.

Additionally, managing a strategy of individual stocks requires an extraordinary amount of energy. This is fine if (1) this is energy you'd like to expend, and (2) you understand the very serious risk of getting it wrong and underperforming. That said, it doesn't have to be all or nothing, either. I think it's fine for young people to take a few big swings. I personally wouldn't do it with more than 5% or 10% of my total invested strategy.

If you aren't interested in stock picking, great! There is no need to spend your days studying earnings reports and SEC filings, because there is little chance it will make you any richer than doing the boring, easy thing.

Actively Managed Mutual Funds

Even if you aren't picking stocks for yourself, you may still be engaged in active management. If you have a broker or financial advisor who is picking stocks or other investments for you, that is active management.

More commonly, you might own actively managed funds. For example, if you have a hodgepodge of mutual funds in your 401(k), I'd bet at least a few of them are run by active managers who charge fees. As we discussed in chapter 16 on INDEX FUNDS, this means that there is a guy with a research team who is attempting to pick the "best investments" for the fund.

So then, the question du jour: Can professionals pick the best investments? The short answer is *no, not with any consistency*. Professional managers may have finance degrees and every forecasting tool at their disposal, and still they regularly perform worse than the index average. In fact, 97% of actively managed mutual funds invested in the US stock market underperformed the S&P 500 index over the last twenty years. You would do better than the vast majority of professionals by buying an S&P 500 (or similar) index fund. And yet, when they inevitably do not keep their promise of outperformance, it is only you, the investor, who suffers. It is not as if they'll return their fees when they underperform.

The underperformance of active funds stems not only from the challenge of picking winning stocks but also from the added hurdle of covering their own fees. For example, if the market returns 10% and a fund charges a 1% fee, the manager must achieve an 11% return just to earn you 10%. As the data shows, managers are largely unable to do this.

Next, we'll delve into the performance erosion caused by the hidden fees involved in investing—a topic so epic it deserves its own chapter. This discussion builds on our exploration of underperformance and uncovers yet another critical factor at play.

But first, take a quick break! Splash your face with ice-cold water, come back, and let's talk fees.

What Are the Risks of Indexing?

In these pages, I'm doing my best to share what I believe are the best practices in investing. And the truth is, any expert who understands the risks of underperformance will recommend index funds for anyone who doesn't have the space to take on additional risk. But I also accept that indexing is not above criticism nor do I operate without any bias.

As indexing has grown in popularity, some economists and market observers have raised concerns about what happens when too much of the market becomes passive. Not because it's bad for you personally, but because it could change how markets operate on a larger scale.

Index funds buy stocks automatically, based on what's in the index—not based on whether a stock is a good investment. That kind of blind diversification has worked well for individual investors: It spreads out risk, lowers costs, and requires very little guesswork.

But what's good for individual investors isn't always great for the overall health of the market. Because indexing doesn't evaluate companies on their merits, it can start to disrupt a key function of financial markets: *price discovery*, the process by which investors assess a company's value and collectively decide what it's worth. Basically, active investors keep these companies, and their stocks, honest.

Take this example: When a company is added to the S&P 500 index, its stock price often jumps. Not because the company did something extraordinary, but because all the index funds that track the S&P 500 are required to buy it. That demand bump isn't earned; it's automatic. And it reveals the deeper issue: If too much of the market becomes passive, prices can become distorted, rising higher than they should, or falling harder than they deserve, especially during mass sell-offs.

That said, active investors still own about half the US stock market—which amounts to trillions of dollars still actively voting on stock prices. And anyone who's spent time on Robinhood knows that for every stock going "to the moon," another is on the fast track to the grave. This isn't to downplay the risk. If passive investing ever became truly dominant, market efficiency could suffer. And to be totally honest, no one knows the breaking point, if there is one.

For individual investors, I still personally believe that index funds remain the best choice for long-term wealth building. The risks of passive investing are real and market-wide, but active investing carries its own big bag of risks. Further, active management won't necessarily shield you from the risks of a prospective passive indexing bubble and crash; in a major sell-off, all stock prices will fall, no matter how you hold them.

That said, I'm telling you this as an invitation to disagree with me.

22

FEES

How much should I be paying to invest?

Investment fees are sneaky little bastards.

First, you don't get a heads-up about the fees that you are being charged. This is especially true if you are investing with actively managed funds. Instead, the fund managers simply help themselves to your money. If you were sent a bill, I bet you'd lose your goddamn mind. They make Airbnb and Ticketmaster fees look like child's play.

Second, investing fees appear deceptively small. Consider the standard 1% management fee, whether paid directly to a financial advisor or embedded in a fund. (When in a fund, that management fee is called an *expense ratio*.) Now, you might see 1% and think, *Whatever, that's nothing!* And I get that. In the "real world," 1% does seem like nothing. Imagine a store advertising a sale with a 1% discount on all sweaters. *Wow, the generosity!* Or how about a happy hour with 1% off all drinks? *Hmm, okay! I'll just pay full price, thank you very much!*

Naturally, we think of 1% as one piece of a hundred-piece pie. And with a hundred-piece pie, you'd think there was plenty of pie for everyone! Unfortunately, that's not how it works. Here's how to think about it instead. One percent is assessed on the total amount invested; not just profit. To fully grasp the impact, subtract the 1% fee from your projected returns.

So, if you are making a cautious projection of 7% returns into the future, and your fund's expense ratio is 1%, well, 7% minus 1% leaves 6%. You're not giving up one piece of a hundred-piece pie. You are giving up one piece of a seven-piece pie—that's 14.2% of your pie, right out of the gates!

And it gets worse! Just as your investing returns compound over time, so do fees. Have a look at the graph below. Over forty years, an investor who's doing just about everything right—consistently investing $1,000 per month and earning a 7% return—would lose $568,553 to a 1% fee. That's 28% of their total gains after decades of compounding!

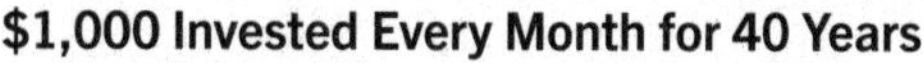

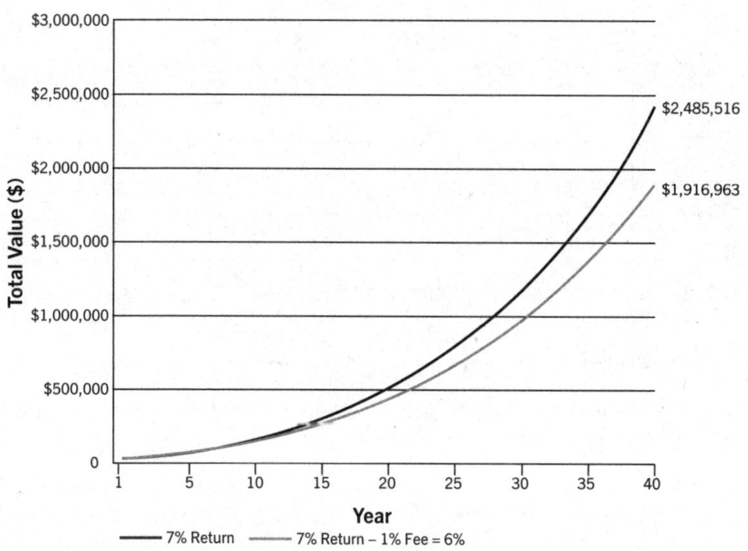

Even fees less than 1%, like .75% and .5%, can take a serious bite out of your cookie over time.

It'd be one thing if you could pay for outperformance, but as we've discussed, you can't. And so, just as you must subtract fees, you must subtract underperformance. Consider a year where the market returns -20% and your actively managed fund returns -22% due to underperformance. Despite the negative year, and despite their underperformance, managers still take their 1% fee, leaving you with a -23% return.

Now, extrapolate this forward. Say your active fund manager performs, on average, 2% worse than the markets. Back to our easy math!

Seven percent (cautious return expectation) minus 1% (fee) minus 2% (underperformance) equals 4%. *Four freaking percent!* How unnecessarily dangerous. You put up with the drama of the markets only to get the same returns as if you'd kept the money in your high-yield savings account. (Not to mention, the real returns after inflation are actually closer to 1%.)

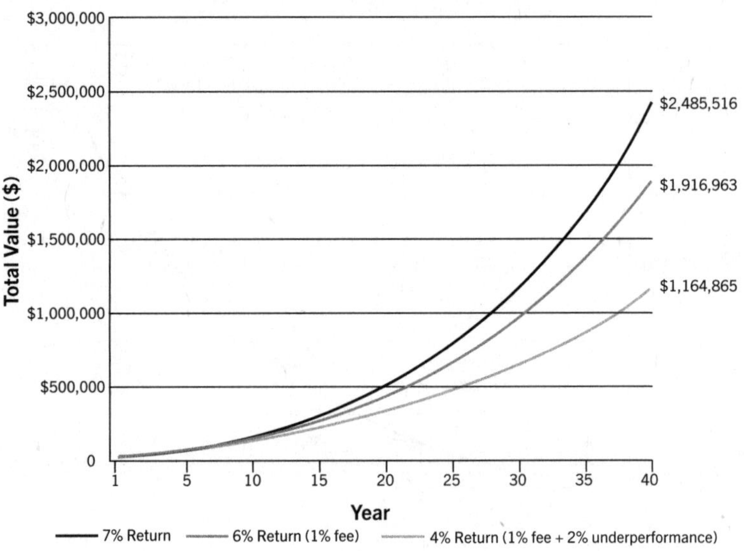

The stated purpose of active management is to give you, the investor, the chance to "outperform." But the real purpose? The *real* purpose of active management is to extract fees from you. In fact, the entire industry—from actively managed mutual funds to hedge funds to annuities—exists for the purpose of fee extraction. That's the BIG, HIDDEN SECRET that the consumer finance industry doesn't want you to know. Whether they deliver outperformance or not, and whether the market is up or down, none of it matters. No matter what, they get theirs.

I've talked a lot about expense ratios in funds, but these may not be the only investing-related fees you encounter. Below, I've split the fees into two categories: first, those assessed on the account level, and second, the fees you might find lurking inside your funds. So, for example, if you have a brokerage account at Morgan Stanley, the bank charges you a yearly account fee. Inside of that account, you own actively managed funds, each of which has its own set of fees.

Investing Fees

Fees you might encounter on a bank or account level:

Account fee, maintenance fee: charged on a monthly, quarterly, or annual basis

Transaction fee: a trading fee, usually a dollar amount, when you buy or sell an investment

Management fee: paid to an advisor or broker, usually expressed as an annual percentage rate

Fees built into funds:

Expense ratio: management fees within funds, expressed as an annual percentage rate

12b-1 fees: usually included within an expense ratio, a 12b-1 fee is an annual marketing charge paid from fund assets to cover promotional costs and to compensate brokers or advisors for selling the fund to investors. (If you see one of these, I would run in the other direction.)

Front-end load fees: a fee to buy into the fund (like a cover charge at a party)

Back-end load fees: a fee to sell out of a fund (like a charge for cancelling your gym membership)

A student of mine, Honey (not her real name), had her first investment account via her dad's financial advisor. Even though she didn't meet his usual minimum account size, he took her on as a "favor." The advisor was charging a management fee *and* buying her actively managed funds, which *also* had management fees. Looking through her account statements, we also discovered an annual account maintenance fee of $275. And if this was not enough, as she moved her money away after having taken my course, they stuck it to her one last time: A few of her funds had 5% back-end load fees, costing her over $800! All of it—the account fee, the double dip of management fees, the load fees—erased all the gains Honey made in her first five years investing. Who exactly was the recipient of the favor here?

Don't worry, many finance professionals can and will help you. I'll tell you more in chapter 40 on HIRING HELP. But a lot of the investment services industry does not exist to help you. No, they're laughing all the way to the bank, knowing that busy, regular people will never know about the hidden fees they charge. At the same time, people believe that their retirement accounts exist as nothing but a goodwill gesture from their workplace, when in fact they are administered by yet another private, for-profit industry looking out for itself first.

Worst of all, high-fee products like actively managed mutual funds, annuities, and whole life insurance are often marketed as "safer" options to economically marginalized (and therefore potentially more risk-averse) communities, including low-income people, people of color, and women. This is a prime example of how we are vulnerable to an industry that preys on financial insecurity and illiteracy.

The easiest way to avoid all this madness is to, yep, use index funds. Index funds have minuscule expense ratios, ranging from free (Fidelity now has zero-fee index funds) to .3%. (That's three-tenths of 1%.) It is common to see index funds with expense ratios like .01% or .04%. The fees are tiny because index funds have no research analysts, no marketing teams, and no one trying to pick the best investments. Straightforwardness is the point and by design.

And as we now know, indexing is consistently the more successful way to invest, ensuring that you take home your fair share of the markets' returns. Knowing that the markets are going to give us only so much pie, the question is: Do you really want to give a piece to the finance industry? Or would you rather share the spoils with your loved ones—or have it to yourself?

23

COMPOUND RETURNS

Are compound returns really the magic they say they are?

Especially if you are a Young, at some point during your short life, an Old has lectured you about compound returns. Or, you've read the thunderous screeds about the magic of compounding interest at the beginning of every personal finance book, as if abstract math that takes decades to materialize is supposed to spark something in the average twenty-two-year-old.

But alas, the Olds are right. Your youth is a gift. Not just because you can function on three hours of sleep or produce collagen on demand, but because you have something us old heads can't fake: time. With a long runway, you can build wealth in a way that an older person could not match, even with significantly more money and more effort. Put another way, starting earlier lets you be much lazier overall. Compound returns are what allow for such aspirational laziness.

So yes, the nagging is well-intentioned. But I also agree that it is hard to feel the magic of compounding without the full context, which we have now built together. That's why I've put this chapter at the end of our big section on investing basics. Only now are we ready to truly see compound returns, along with the steps necessary to achieve them.

With compound returns, also known as *compound interest,* you earn profit not only on the moola you invest—the principal—but on all profits. Your money makes you money, and then that money makes you MORE money, which makes you EVEN MORE MONEY. And the more time you give it, the more scrumptiously out of hand the results.

To better understand this, let's take a moment to compare compound returns to its more understated counterpart, *simple interest.* With simple interest (or returns), you receive the promised payout and that's the end of the investing story. For example, say you own a bond. And when you receive interest payments, you take the money and spend it at the sandwich shop. Well, we cannot compound growth on money you spent on a meatball sub. Looking at numbers will help illustrate what's happening here.

5% Rate of Simple Interest Paid on $1,000 Over Ten Years			
Year	**Principal**	**Rate of Return (RoR)**	**Profit**
1	$1,000	× 0.05	$50
2	$1,000	× 0.05	$50
3	$1,000	× 0.05	$50
4	$1,000	× 0.05	$50
5	$1,000	× 0.05	$50
6	$1,000	× 0.05	$50
7	$1,000	× 0.05	$50
8	$1,000	× 0.05	$50
9	$1,000	× 0.05	$50
10	$1,000	× 0.05	$50
Total			**$500**

But what if all of those profits were reinvested? Or what if it were an investment that, instead, was growing bigger each year? To envision compound returns, picture a stock that grows at a rate of 5%. With each year of growth, we are calculating 5% returns on top of a bigger base.

This profit carries over to the next year, creating a bigger base

5% Rate of Compound Returns Earned on $1,000 Over Ten Years			
Year	**Base (Principal Plus Prior Profit)**	**RoR**	**Profit**
1	$1,000	× 0.05	$50
2	$1,050	× 0.05	$52.52
3	$1,105.50	× 0.05	$55.12
4	$1,157.62	× 0.05	$57.88
5	$1,215.51	× 0.05	$60.78
6	$1,276.28	× 0.05	$63.81
7	$1,340.10	× 0.05	$67.00
8	$1,407.10	× 0.05	$70.36
9	$1,477.46	× 0.05	$73.87
10	$1,551.33	× 0.05	$77.57
Total			**$628.86**

Compounding your returns resulted in an additional $129. To achieve this fun "bonus," you did not save more of your own money. You did not earn a higher rate of return. You simply asked your profits to get to work as well.

I know, I know, $129 might not seem like much! That's, like, five and a half hours of enjoyment out of a Diptyque candle. It is true that in the first decade, compound returns can feel subdued. But look at what happens over longer periods, like forty years. Let's revisit my example in chapter 4, DEBT VERSUS INVEST. Say you invest $10,000 and earn a 7% rate of return. To be clear, you invest $10,000 only one time. (Of course, *you* will be adding more as you go! Here, I want you to focus on the power of compounding alone.)

Look at the growth line between thirty and forty years. See how it curves up? That's when the lights flash on and the mechanical bull turns damn near vertical. (Ride it, cowgirl.) What you're seeing is a form of

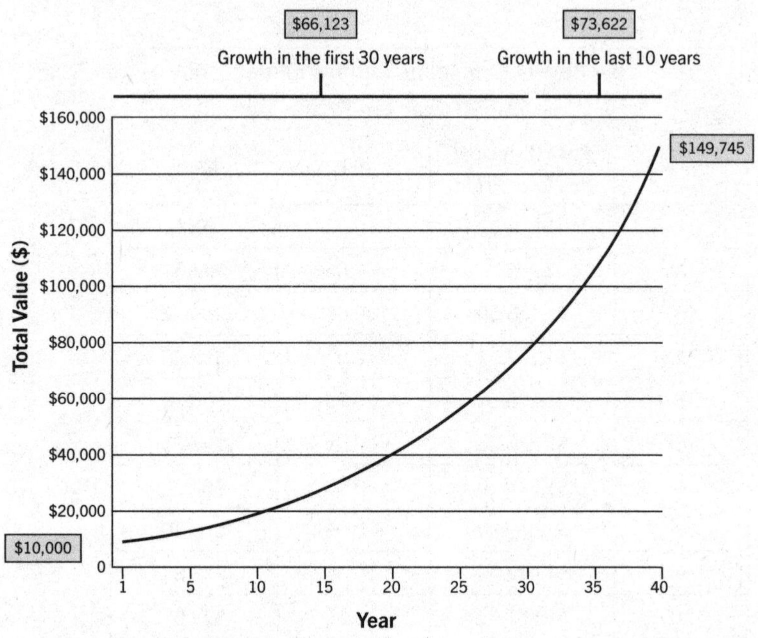

exponential growth, where the growth itself *increases at an increasing rate*. Despite making no additional contributions, you make more and more and more money. Between years one and thirty, investing earned a total of $66,123. Between years thirty and forty, investing earned $73,622. The last quarter of time produced more than 50% of the returns!

Let's say your financial independence goal is $2 million. To reach this target over a forty-year period with a 7% return, you must invest $840 per month. During these forty years, you would have chucked in $336,000 of your own money. **The remaining $1,664,000 would come from investment growth.** Now, compare this to a twenty-year investment period. To reach the same $2 million goal, you must invest $4,050 per month, contributing nearly one million of your own dollars to the cause. When you begin early, compound returns do the majority of the heavy lifting—so you don't have to.

Monthly Contribution to Reach $2 Million			
Years	Monthly Contribution	Total Contributions	Investment Returns (7%)
40	$840	$336,000	$1,664,000
30	$1,760	$528,000	$1,472,000
20	$4,050	$972,000	$1,028,000
10	$12,050	$1,446,000	$554,000

The math is compelling, but let's reground in reality. Starting a career at twenty-two often means student debt, lower salaries, and life expenses that can make investing large monthly sums feel totally out of reach. The point of this exercise isn't to discourage you; just the opposite. This is merely a number nerd's rallying cry to start as soon as you're able. If you're "young," excellent. Use your youth to your ultimate advantage. If you're not, who cares? You still have plenty of investing ahead of you, and you'll be so glad you started now instead of ten years from now.

Best of all, now you know what you're doing. You understand that it's not enough to invest for a long time; *how* you invest also matters. Things like your asset allocation, relative underperformance, and the fees you pay will have a tremendous influence on your long-term results. In the land of compounding interest, your rate of return really fucking counts.

By now, I hope you feel totally ready to go out and achieve compound returns. Get invested, stay invested, and reinvest dividends and interest. The good news is that most of this can be set up to run quietly in the background, so you can go on living your life while your money does its thing.

To me, compound returns have a kind of feminine magic: It is the practice of digging a hole, dropping a seed, and planting a tree. One day, when your youth is gone and you're a Rich Old Lady, you'll look back and marvel at how much it's grown. The tree, you note, has deep roots and wide branches. A tree provides shade, food, and a place for wildlife. Its growth allows it to be more generous and connected with others as it ages. Screw the collagen—you're a tree. I'm always very touched to think of a person who planted a tree decades ago so that I could enjoy it today. You can do this for yourself and your beloveds, too.

Creating Passive Income with Your Investments

With any investment that grows or provides a stream of income, it is well within your right to spend those profits, should you choose. For example, you could use dividends paid out by funds and stocks as spending money. This is the crux of the popular *passive income* movement.

But you should also be aware that when you spend all or some of your investment profits, you are robbing your future self of not only those profits but also all the compounding growth that happens on the profits and the profit's profits, and so on. It's not just the $100 or $1,000 in dividends, it's the thousands or tens of thousands you could have made by keeping that money invested.

I want everyone to be able to use investing to add ease into their lives, and I am not discouraging passive income streams. But when it comes to investing in markets—and funding our financial futures—most people simply can't afford to rob their Rich Old Lady of this growth. Saving and investing enough to reach financial independence is an insanely difficult job, and compounding returns is the single best tool we have to make it happen.

PART III HOMEWORK: Design Your Strategy

Here, use everything you've learned to design your desired strategy.

1. In the circle below, draw out your desired asset allocation; the mix of US stocks, international stocks, and bonds:

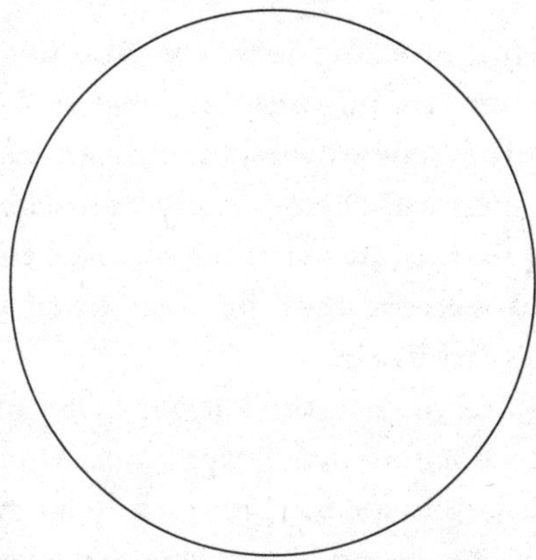

2. Briefly describe the strategy you will utilize to "build" that asset allocation (ex: "I will use three index funds" or "I will use one target-date index fund"):

____

____

3. Describe three ways that you can ensure that you perform as well as the markets you invest in:

____

____

4. Write out a plan for how you will remain calm and resolved during the next market crash:

____

____

RICH OLD LADY REFLECTION

Isn't it incredible that investing doesn't require all of your time or mental energy? I can certainly imagine some yucky alternate reality where the only people who get to retire are obsessive stock-pickers and day traders with their sixteen screens, freebasing alpha delusion and Red Bulls while searching the markets for arbitrage opportunities and ignoring their precious loved ones. But no! That's not the reality we live in.

Turns out, the less you overthink it, the better off you are. For example, no one tries harder than hedge funds. And yet, time after time, hedge funds lose to a basket of stocks your grandma could own. (No, seriously, hedge funds consistently perform worse than the S&P 500.)

I'm grateful for this fact: You do not have to be obsessed with investing to be good at it. You do not need to make money your whole personality to become financially independent. A big part of why I took on this mission is because I wanted to show *my* people—the weirdos, lovers, artists, and mothers—that smart investing strategies are well within their capacity, even if they're busy or have better things to think about. I hope this knowledge settles into you in a real way, clearing the path for pure, uninterrupted whimsy.

All that's left is to get your automated systems set up and get your ass outside, honey, because life is for living. Watch a bird, not a stock. Unless, of course, you *want* to watch a stock—then by all means.

PART IV

BUILDING AND MAINTAINING YOUR STRATEGY

Turning theory into action. This is where we go from "thinking about it" to "doing it"

24

BANKS

Where do I invest?

We have come to the point in our investment journeys when we can begin to build a strategy—not just hypothetically but literally. Yeehaw! The first step is to decide where.

If you're currently using a workplace retirement account, like a 401(k), your bank is chosen for you. You can skip to the next chapter, if you'd like. But if you are planning on opening your own investment account, you're going to have to choose a bank.

Or, you might decide that you don't want to build your own strategy at all. If you're thinking, *Keep your yeehaws to yourself, lady. I do not consent to your yeehaw. I would simply like this handled, please.* I hear you. It sounds like you might prefer an automated investing service that builds a portfolio of index funds for you. If that's the case, skip ahead to chapter 29, ROBO-ADVISORS—and do so with my full blessing.

That said, learning this is completely doable. And I'm going to show you how. First step: opening a brokerage account at a brokerage bank.

Because you know I'm a sucker for placing jargon in its historical context, let's talk about the word "brokerage." In the days before computers, if you wanted to buy a stock, you had to pick up the phone (gross!) and call your guy on Wall Street. Your guy would then take your order to the New York Stock Exchange (or similar marketplace), where he would broker the deal, finding a seller to your buyer. He is a stockbroker, facilitating an exchange known as a *trade*.

These days, trading is done online, and while you no longer need to talk to a broker, you still need to use a bank with the ability to trade investments—that's a brokerage bank.

Now that we've discussed the harm of fees, you won't be surprised to learn that I'm mostly just looking for a brokerage bank that allows me to invest for as close to free as possible. Because, ladies, we are not here to make the banks rich! The banks are doing just fine. We are here to make *you* rich. Tell your girls! Tell everyone! *SKANKS BEFORE BANKS!*

What I am looking for in a brokerage bank:

Free accounts
Free trades
Good, low-cost investing options
SIPC bank insurance, which insures $500,000 per brokerage account per bank

Luckily, lots of *discount brokerage banks* meet these qualifications. I like Charles Schwab, Fidelity, and Vanguard (let's call them the Big 3), but there are others. Compare this to *full-service brokerage banks* like Merrill Lynch or Goldman Sachs, which prefer to work with rich people and generally charge you for accounts and investing services.

If one item on my list were to trip you up, I bet it might be "good, low-cost investing options." I have to include this because there's a chance you could end up at a small mutual fund shop that limits you to their actively managed fund products. Luckily this isn't a problem at the big brokerage banks, where you can access almost any investment in existence.

All the major discount brokerages offer pretty much the same stuff. For example, each bank has created its own "line" of index mutual funds. Vanguard famously made the very first S&P 500 index mutual fund, but Charles Schwab and Fidelity make their own, too. And because each is built against the same index, they are materially the same investment. If this is confusing, remember that funds are financial products and there are lots of banks that want in on the action. Both Vanguard and Fidelity offering their own versions of a total bond market index fund is the same concept as Wells Fargo and Bank of America each offering a checking account.

Part of what makes these brokerage banks so great is that there are ways to get started investing with just $1. This is the minimum for some index mutual funds and ETFs at Fidelity, some index mutual funds at Charles Schwab, and index ETFs at Vanguard. (Vanguard has higher minimums to get started with index mutual funds—$1,000 for your first purchase of a target-date fund, and $3,000 for mutual funds.)

Last, no conversation about brokerage banks would be complete without dragging them for their user design. Navigating these platforms can feel like using a remote control from 1998. It works, I swear, but you have to know which buttons to press and in what order. No matter which brokerage bank you choose, a part of the process is learning its quirks and clicking through its clunky little menu.

Before I send you along, let me float another idea, a kind of "third way": M1 Finance. Think of this investing platform as halfway between DIY investing at a brokerage bank and using a fully automated robo-advisor. You choose your allocations and funds with their "pie" system, while the platform handles the grunt work, like automatic investing and rebalancing. I personally use the old school brokerage banks but for some of you, this could be the Goldilocks option: not too self-directed, not too hands-off, but just right. That said, it probably makes the most sense for investors with more than $10,000, because otherwise there's a $3 per month fee. Pin it in your mind for later, and I will revisit again in chapter 28, UPKEEP.

When you are ready to pick a bank, do so and don't look back. More important than the bank you pick is—you know what's coming!!—opening an account and putting it to use.

Should You Use Robinhood?

I prefer the Big 3 over stock- and crypto-trading apps like Robinhood, which are designed to encourage harmful behaviors like compulsive trading and risky options bets. While the user experience is undeniably better than what you'll find at a traditional brokerage, trading apps have taken a page straight from Mark Zuckerberg's handbook on creating an addicted user base. To do this, Robinhood uses a process called *gamification.*

Robinhood led the charge in making stock and ETF trading free and accessible, which is great in theory. But of course, they must get paid somehow. Instead of charging you up-front, Robinhood makes its money by selling your trade orders to large financial institutions—a practice that becomes profitable only if they're selling lots of trades. Therefore, Robinhood nudges you into trades with confetti emojis, animations, and dopamine loops—that's gamification. And it works. One report in early 2020 revealed that Robinhood users traded nine times as many shares as E*Trade customers, and forty times as many shares and eighty-eight times more options contracts than Charles Schwab customers. Engaging with an investing app in this way is not investing. This is gambling.

Selling our trades—and, effectively, our behavioral data—to Wall Street firms that can (and do) bet against us is real narc behavior. And although it's not only Robinhood that does this, it's definitely most hilarious for an app called Robinhood to do this. A name that claims to be robbing from the rich, all while tipping off the Sheriffs of Nottingham.

But hey, maybe it's not that serious. You can trade stocks on Robinhood with some splash-around fun money, if that's how you like to spend your splash-around fun money. You can also totally choose to use a trading app to build a buy-and-hold strategy. But you have to do so while resisting design that is engineered to chip away at your willpower. Considering I can't keep myself from checking Instagram any less than six times before lunch, I figure I probably shouldn't put my retirement savings into the TikTok equivalent of a casino. Maybe we don't want the influence of our Orwellian App Daddies anywhere near something as important as our long-term financial well-being.

25

RESEARCH

How do I find and research investments?

For me, the panic of having too many options sets in when I'm shopping at the big Bloomingdale's on Manhattan's Fifty-Ninth Street, ordering from the biblical menu at the Cheesecake Factory, or sifting through investment options on a brokerage bank's website. And when I venture in without knowing exactly what I want—whether the perfect jeans, a carb-based entrée, or a sensible index fund—I might just abandon the mission altogether.

Because I know how paralyzing it can be to have too many options, I'll show you exactly how to find the investments you need to build your diversified strategy. Next chapter, TRADE, I'll show you how to buy them.

This process will look a bit different depending on whether you are using a workplace retirement account or opening an account at a brokerage bank.

Workplace retirement accounts usually limit you to a short list of investment options—typically around thirty mutual funds. This is done to reduce overwhelmedness by narrowing your number of choices. Your job, then, is to research those limited options and pick the best ones available. When you're investing independently, though, you're faced with the entire universe of investment options. In theory, more choice is better. But in practice, it can make decision-making harder—this is what I call the Cheesecake Factory Paradox.

So, the exact process may look a little different depending on whether you're choosing from a curated menu or an open buffet. I'll detail each in a moment, but let's start with the skill you're going to need either way: researching an investment fund.

How to Research Funds

Allow me to show you, in worksheet format, the information you need to know about any investment fund you are considering.

Fund Name ________________________________

Ticker (the two-to-five-letter "identifier") ________________________________

What market does this fund invest in? (What are the holdings?)

____

Is it an index fund or actively managed? If index, what is the underlying index/benchmark?

____

What is the expense ratio of the fund? ________________________________

Any other fees associated with buying the fund (transaction fees, load fees, 12b-1 fees)?

____

Is it a mutual fund or an exchange-traded fund? (Hint: Mutual funds always have a five-letter ticker that ends in an X, like ABCDX) ________________________________

The information you need to fill out the worksheet can be found through your bank, retirement account provider, or Yahoo Finance.

Yahoo, I know, so vintage, but weirdly, it is a very solid and easy-to-use resource for fund research. Go to finance.yahoo.com.

To show you how this works, let's look up a fund on Yahoo Finance together. In the search bar, type "FZROX." This is Fidelity's version of a total US stock market index mutual fund. On the summary page, you'll find just about everything you need to know about this fund.

Find more information about Fees & Expenses under the Profile tab:

Summary
News
Chart
Community
Historical Data
Profile
Holdings
Performance
Risk
Purchase Info
Sustainability

Fees & Expenses

Expense	FZROX	Category Average
Annual Report Expense Ratio (net)	0.00%	0.84%
Prospectus Net Expense Ratio	0.00%	--
Prospectus Gross Expense Ratio	0.00%	--
Max 12b1 Fee	--	--
Max Front End Sales Load	--	5.18%
Max Deferred Sales Load	--	1.28%
3 Yr Expense Projection	0	--
5 Yr Expense Projection	0	--
10 Yr Expense Projection	0	--

Using the information from Yahoo Finance, fill out the worksheet:

Fund Name *Fidelity ZERO Total Market Index Fund*

Ticker (the two-to-five-letter "identifier") *FZROX*

What market does this fund invest in? (What are the holdings?)

The total US stock market

Is it an index fund or actively managed? If index, what is the underlying index/benchmark?

Index fund, the index is the "Fidelity US total investable market index"

What is the expense ratio of the fund? *0.0%*

Any other fees associated with buying the fund (transaction fees, load fees, 12b-1 fees)?

No load or 12b-1 fees, no transaction fees when purchased at Fidelity

Is it a mutual fund or an exchange-traded fund? (Hint: Mutual funds always have a five-letter ticker that ends in an X, like ABCDX) *Mutual fund*

Now, that's all fine and good if you have some funds in mind to research, but what if you don't? How do you find the funds to research in the first place?

Workplace Retirement Account

Your workplace retirement plan is probably already invested. Most likely in a mix of mutual funds or a target-date fund (TDF). This default strategy is what you signed up for on that sweaty first day at work, whether you remember it or not.

Default investing isn't bad, especially considering 401(k)s used to dump your money into cash and leave it there until you did something about it. Still, you should never, ever accept your default strategy without question. If your provider is defaulting you into financial products, there's a decent chance they're steering you toward the ones that quietly make them more money: actively managed mutual funds or, worse, high-fee annuities dressed up as "retirement solutions." You cannot trust that the default was designed with you in mind.

You should begin by having a look at your current investments. Fingers crossed they're already great! Then have a look at the other options available.

Step 1: Log into your account.
Step 2: Find your list of *all* the investing options available in your plan—not just the ones you are currently invested in.
Step 3: Narrow down by index funds and index TDFs.
Step 4: Using the fund research worksheet, research those funds' holdings and fees.
Step 5: Build a strategy with the best available options.

Selecting investments within a workplace plan is an exercise in working with what you've got! Given your limited options, make the best possible selections.

I'd estimate that about 15% of my students have workplace retirement accounts with zero good investing options. If you find yourself in this situation, I'm so sorry. Here are a few options to explore:

1. Try contacting your plan provider and asking if the account can be "opened up" to allow for the purchase of investments outside of those on the designated list. To be clear, you are *not* moving money out of the account. You are asking for access to other investing options within the account.

2. Consider investing outside of your workplace account, where you have total control. For example, you might contribute up to your match in your workplace plan—yes, it's still worth it—and then you

make any additional contributions to a Roth IRA at a bank of your choosing.

3. Stage a company-wide uprising. I'm being dead serious. Demand better for yourself and your comrades. Pass along a copy of this book to your HR. When you think about it, it is pretty wild that the retirements of an entire workforce hinge on decisions made by a person who's probably never been trained in investing.

Investment Options Inside of 403(b) Accounts and Thrift Savings Plans

Although a 403(b) and Thrift Savings Plan are technically equivalent to a 401(k), they are unequal in practice.

403(b) Accounts

403(b) accounts are notorious for their terrible investment options and sky-high fees. These are 401(k)-like accounts offered to public school teachers, employees of some hospitals, and nonprofit workers. In other words, these plans serve a workforce that is disproportionately female. Financial firms targeted school districts and nonprofits as easy pickings: under-resourced, without benefits departments, and exploitable. The worst investing options I've ever seen live inside teacher 403(b)s. It makes me want to flip a table. ("Ma'am, this is a Cheesecake Factory.")

Although every workplace account needs to be researched, my sweeties with 403(b)s must be on high alert.

Thrift Savings Plans

It's worth noting that when institutions have both the capacity and the knowledge, they tend to choose what's best for people: low-cost index funds. You can see this in the Thrift Savings Plan (TSP) for federal government employees—a well-resourced, intentionally low-fee system that stands in stark contrast to the quagmire of many 403(b)s.

Instead of picking index funds by name, TSP participants choose from letter-coded funds that correspond to different market indices—see below. It's simple, streamlined, and exactly what you'd expect from a system built with the participant in mind. Because all your options are low-cost and index, you only need to pick your mix—your asset allocation.

G = Government bonds
F = Fixed income aggregate (mix)
C = US stock market
I = International stock market
S = Small-cap stocks
L = Lifecycle funds

Investing Independently

When you are investing independently, the easiest way to find what you're looking for is to have someone point you in the right direction. That someone is me! If you want to do this the easy way, start with the index funds that I have provided throughout this book.

Index Funds: Page 116
Index Target-Date Funds: Page 125
Ethical Index Funds: Page 206
Market Category Index Funds: Pages 212 and 215
REIT Index Funds: Page 219

That said, this is a teach-a-bitch-to-fish operation. Here's how to find low-cost index fund options at whatever brokerage bank you're using.

Step 1: Start at your brokerage bank's general website. They will have a tab for both "mutual funds" and "ETFs." Take your pick.

Step 2: Look for the bank's branded funds. (Don't worry, they'll be front and center.)

Most banks let you buy their own self-branded mutual funds for free. So, if you're opening an account at Charles

Schwab, start by looking at Schwab's list of mutual funds; they will have "Schwab" in the name. If you try to buy, say, a Vanguard mutual fund at Schwab, you'll likely get hit with a trading fee. And there's no reason to pay that fee when Schwab offers its own version of the same fund.

With ETFs, the good news is that most brokerage banks let you trade all of them for free. Even so, your bank or brokerage should have a list of "no-transaction-fee ETFs" or something like this—use that as your starting point for research.

Step 3: Sort by "index."

Step 4: Find options for the markets you'd like to invest in.

Step 5: Using the worksheet, research any finds that look interesting to you.

Step 6: Build your strategy using funds that suit your needs.

10-MINUTE MISSION

Research the funds you are currently invested in and the funds you are considering. You can use finance.yahoo.com or google.com/finance, or search for the fund's fact sheet.

You can download and print copies of the fund worksheet at richoldlady.com.

26

TRADE

How do I buy an investment?

I saw a tweet* the other day about "Forcing Parties," where friends get together and force each other to do the stuff they've been putting off forever: applying for a passport, getting to inbox zero, that kind of thing. Someone in the replies called it a "Party of Done." Another referred to it as "an Executive Function."

I actually clapped. This is exactly what I do with my friends and students, but with Roth IRAs and index funds!

I recently sent an invite to some friends that read: "Bring your laptop and a bottle of somethin'. We're clicking buttons and buying investments." They'd been lamenting that they knew *what* to invest in but were struggling to actually make it happen. So, as the resident finance friend, I offered myself up as emotional and technical support. I also host several "Clicking the Buttons" parties throughout the year for my investing course students.

Even though I can't be with you physically—dang, wouldn't that be fun?—it's time for our very own Forcing Party/Executive Function/Party of Done/Clicking the Buttons Party. I'm with you here on the page and I'm with you in spirit. Please grab a comfort beverage, put on the musical stylings of your favorite pop princess, and walk us over to your computer. We are going to do this together.

Like we discussed in the last chapter, this process will be different depending on whether you're using a workplace account or investing independently. If you're using a workplace account, updating your investments won't feel like placing trades, but that's what you're doing.

---

* Tweet by @TylerAlterman

Once logged into your portal, you will look for wording along the lines of "make changes to investments." As you make changes, be sure to adjust both your current and future investments.

For the rest of the chapter, I'm going to talk about purchasing investments when you invest independently.

The first step is to open an account, and then to fund it with cash. Most people will link their checking account up to their new investment account. If you are transferring over an old workplace retirement plan like a 401(k), call the 401(k) company to conduct a rollover into your new account. When doing a rollover, remember to place Traditional/tax-deferred with Traditional/tax-deferred, and Roth with Roth. (See chapter 10, RULES, for a refresh.)

Depending on the type of transfer, it could take a day or two. A rollover can take a few weeks. Once the money has arrived in your investment account, it's time to party! On page 178, I've written out exact, can't-mess-this-up, step-by-step instructions for buying an investment at each of the major brokerage banks. However, these processes change from time to time as the banks update their customer portals. So, here's a big-picture summary of the process:

Find a tab or button that says trade, transact, or buy
Enter the investment's ticker symbol
Indicate how much you want to buy, using either dollars or shares
If it's an ETF, indicate the *order type*—likely a *market order*
Review for any sneaky transaction charges or fees
Click "buy"

Exchanges and Order Types

When you buy an ETF or a stock, your order goes through a brokerage, which connects you to an exchange like the New York Stock Exchange or the Nasdaq. These exchanges are digital marketplaces that match buyers and sellers.

Exchanges are open during weekday business hours (9:30 a.m.–4:00 p.m. ET). It's usually best to place an order while the market is open, but it's also okay to trade after hours; it will be executed during the next trading session. Keep in mind that prices can fluctuate significantly at the market's open due to overnight news or events. All good, you're a long-term investor and not worried about what you can't control.

When you place an order on an exchange, it will ask for an *order type.*

A *market order* is executed right now (or as soon as the market is open). I remember this by saying, "Let's go to the market!" with urgency or "This little piggy went to the market." (I am the little piggy here.) When your goal is to get invested as soon as possible, a market order is the way to go. As long as the market is open, your trade will typically be filled within seconds. Not immediately, though. When purchasing in shares rather than dollars, be sure to leave a small cash buffer in case the share price jumps.

A *limit order* places conditions on a trade. For example, you could indicate that you want to buy an ETF only if a share drops below a certain price. Or, you want to sell only if it exceeds a certain price. Limit orders are triggered only when that condition is met. Limit orders are popular with traders, who place a lot of value on the short-term swings of the market.

Money Market Funds

Cash in a brokerage account is held in a *money market fund*. Seeing the word "fund" can be tricky, because we tend to think of funds as holding stocks or bonds, but money market funds very much hold cash and *cash equivalents,* like super short-term bonds. Many, many an investor has come to me, curious why her investment accounts aren't growing, only to discover that her investment fund holds cash. You might want to go check your accounts now.

As if this were not confusing enough, money market funds are also sometimes called *settlement funds* because it is where cash in the account settles after a trade, and *sweep funds* because that's where idle cash is automatically swept. No matter what it's called, it's basically just a holding tank for your cash.

Reinvesting Dividends

At some point in the purchasing process, you will be asked whether you want to "reinvest dividends." Say yes! Let's keep all that money growing and compounding. If you already own funds, make sure your funds are also set to dividend reinvestment. You can usually do this by clicking on the investment itself, which should generate a menu of options. (Almost all workplace retirement accounts automatically reinvest dividends.)

If cash accumulates in your account's money market fund, it's a sign that one or all of your funds are not set to automatically reinvest and the cash is being paid out to you directly.

How to Place a Trade at the Big 3

Banks change their processes all the time. Don't get hung up if these instructions don't perfectly reflect what you're seeing.

Charles Schwab Mutual Fund

Go to the "Trade" tab
Choose "Mutual Funds"
Type in the symbol (ticker) of the investment you want to buy
Select an action (buy, sell, or sell and buy another)
Type in dollar amount
Click "Reinvest dividends and capital gains"
Click "Review Order" (don't worry, this won't place the order!)
Review the order and double-check for transaction fees
Click "Place Order"

Charles Schwab ETF and Stock

Go to the "Trade" tab
Choose "Stocks & ETFs"
Type in the symbol (ticker) of the investment you want to buy
Select an action (buy or sell)
Enter number of shares—you must buy full shares of ETFs
Click "Reinvest Dividends"

Select "Market" order
Review the order and double-check for processing fees and commissions
Click "Place Order"

Fidelity Mutual Fund

Go to "Accounts & Trade" tab
Click "Trade"
Choose "Mutual Funds"
Choose the correct account
Type in the symbol (ticker) of the investment you want to buy
Under "Action," select "Buy"
Type in dollar amount
Click "Preview Order"
Review the order and double-check for transaction fees
Click "Place Trade"

Fidelity ETF and Stock

Go to "Accounts & Trade" tab
Click "Trade"
Choose "Stocks/ETFs"
Choose the correct account
Type in the symbol (ticker) of the investment you want to buy
Under "Action," select "Buy"
Select share or dollar amount; type in share or dollar amount
Select "Market" order
Check for a trading commission (fee)
Click "Preview Order"
Click "Place Trade"

Vanguard Mutual Fund

Go to the "Transact" tab
Choose "Buy & Sell"
Enter the ticker symbol for your investment and click "Get Quote"
Select "Buy"
Choose an account

Enter in dollar amount

Click "Continue Order"

Choose your funding source ("settlement fund" is your cash!)

Click "Preview Order"

Click "Submit Order"

Vanguard ETF and Stock

Go to the "Transact" tab

Choose "Buy & Sell"

"Enter ticker symbol" for your investment and click "Get Quote"

Choose an account

Click "Buy"

Enter in share or dollar amount

Under "Order Type," select "Market"

Check for commissions (fees)

Click "Preview Order"

Click "Submit Order"

27

AUTOMATION

What is the trick to being a good investor?

Any good Rich Old Lady will tell you that collecting interesting pieces of driftwood or sea glass at the seashore is not a onetime act. It is a ritual, a practice. You have to think about investing the same way; collecting shares like they're shells at the shore. The best way to invest is through a consistent practice, and here is where automation can help. Each time you get more money in your life, automatically invest a part of it.

Dollar-cost averaging is the way-too-complicated term we use to describe what I call *regular investing* or *paycheck investing*. Investing consistently, like with each payday, allows us to build wealth through small, steady actions that compound over time into something significant.

We all know that investing $100 each month is better than investing $100 whenever we remember to do it. But this is about more than bypassing forgetfullness; automation is a powerful way to embrace the essential strategy of staying invested, even when the world feels uncertain or the market is down. A lack of a consistent, automated strategy—one instead fueled by fear or hubris, expressed through what we call *market timing*—can destroy your shot at investing success.

Success in investing isn't about timing the market; it's about spending time in the market. Statistically, we know that the market moves up more than it moves down. Every day you wait on the sidelines, it's more likely that you are going to miss out on upside than downside. We cannot know when the good days, months, and years will be, but they will come. Therefore, it's a good investing strategy to get your money invested as soon as you have it. For most people, that's as it rolls in with each paycheck.

If you're investing through a workplace account, the automation is done for you—removing money from your paycheck, depositing it into your account, and purchasing investments. Same with a robo-advisor if you set up a monthly deposit. But if you're investing independently, you can (and should) fully re-create this automation experience for yourself. Ideally, you are automating both the contribution of cash into your investment account and the purchase of investments with that cash.

Automation is what allows a strategy to be fully passive. You can eat Cheetos off your tummy table while you lie on the couch watching Olympic ice-skating and still somehow be a gold-medal investor. To automate is to build wealth while doing literally nothing at all.

How to Set Up Automated Investments

As always, these instructions may change as the banks update their websites.

Charles Schwab

Charles Schwab offers an Automatic Investment Plan (AIP) that allows you to schedule recurring investments into eligible mutual funds. You will need to already own the fund; make a one-time initial purchase and then set up automatic investments into that fund.

Log into your Schwab account. From the main menu, go to Trade > Mutual Funds > Automatic Investing.

Select an account. You'll see a list of mutual funds you currently hold that are eligible for automatic investments. Click "Enroll" next to the fund you wish to set up for automatic investing.

Specify the investment amount, frequency (weekly, monthly), and start date.

Review the details and confirm.

Fidelity

Fidelity allows you to automate investments into mutual funds, ETFs, and stocks through their recurring investments feature.

Log into your Fidelity account. From the main menu go to Trade > Reoccurring Investing.
Select an account.
Select the security type (mutual fund, ETF, stock) and enter the ticker symbol.
Specify the investment amount, frequency (weekly, monthly), and start date.
Choose the funding source: probably a linked bank account.
Review the details and confirm.

Vanguard

Vanguard allows you to automate investments into mutual funds and ETFs. You will need to already own the fund; make an initial one-time purchase and then set up automatic investments into that fund.

Log into your Vanguard account. From the main menu, go to Transact > Automatic Investments.
Under "Create Reoccurring Transactions," choose "Vanguard ETFs" or "Vanguard Mutual Funds."
Select an account.
Specify the investment fund, the investment amount, frequency (weekly, monthly), and start date.
Review the details and confirm.

28

UPKEEP

In terms of upkeeping my strategy, what is required of me?

Once you've carefully mapped out your landscaping and planted your garden, all that's left is a bit of ongoing nurturing and upkeep.

Here's what you'll need to do:

Annual rebalancing
Annual relative performance check
Shift into a more conservative (bond-heavy) strategy over time

1. Annual Rebalancing

Your big annual responsibility is called *rebalancing*. It is the equivalent of planting and pruning for the New Year. What didn't make it through the winter? What do we need more of? What can we trim back?

One of your plants has grown much larger and faster than everything else, choking out the garden's diverse flora. From what little I know about invasive plant species, it's probably English ivy. It used to take up a thoughtful percentage of your space, and next thing you know it's wildly overgrown and everyone is talking about it behind your back at the co-op meeting. Stocks are the English ivy of a garden. Growth is good, but left to grow unchecked, a balanced portfolio may become dominated by stocks over time.

Rebalancing is the process of restoring a portfolio to balance, snapping it back to the asset allocation you determined was best for you based on your goals and risk tolerance.

Say you'd determined that an allocation of 80% stocks and 20% bonds was best for you. After twenty years without rebalancing, and knowing that the different markets grow unevenly, perhaps the stock allocation makes up 95% of your portfolio. Stocks do tend to outpace bonds, and so this shift is to be expected over long periods. But that's not really what we wanted, now was it? Presumably, you had bonds there for a reason. If anything, we may want your proportion of bonds to (slightly) increase over time.

This may seem like the type of trading in reaction to the markets I've been cautioning against. But it's not in the reactionary way one might expect. If US stocks have a bad year, rebalancing teaches us to do the opposite of what our panic might tell us to do. (Remember: *cute and unbothered.*) Instead of bailing, we fill out our position: We buy more. This is an act of consciously sticking to the strategy we had determined was best for us given our goals, risk tolerance, and timeline, and knowing that temporary market conditions are just that—temporary.

To rebalance, you sell the funds performing relatively better and buy into funds that are lagging. This is not a comfy exercise! You'll likely find yourself with a preference for the year's winners, not the losers! But you are training yourself to *sell high* and *buy low*. You know that what performed best in the past might not perform best in the future. You accept that big sea changes come but take decades. It's true, thinking in terms of decades is hard for humans. But if you wrongfully assume that one category will always dominate, you run the risk of letting it take over your strategy right as some other category picks up speed.

Rebalancing can be done in one of two ways. First, as mentioned, by selling what has gotten too big and using the proceeds to buy into what is now relatively too small. Or, and this is so much easier, just redirect all new contributions to whatever category needs the boost. This strategy might take more time, but then you can avoid having to sell anything, which is nice.

Though it's best to be in the practice of rebalancing once per year, truthfully, you may not need to rebalance each year. Unless something dramatic happens, it's fine to rebalance every few years. And when you do, make your life easy and use a simple online rebalancing calculator to guide you. Look, I made one for us! You can find it at richoldlady.com.

Rebalancing in Action

Janelle has a portfolio of $100,000 invested in a 50/30/20 strategy. Left to grow on its own, it does so unevenly. This is the outcome of diversification, and to be expected. After five years, her investments are worth $160,000 with (let's say) an asset allocation of 46/40/14.

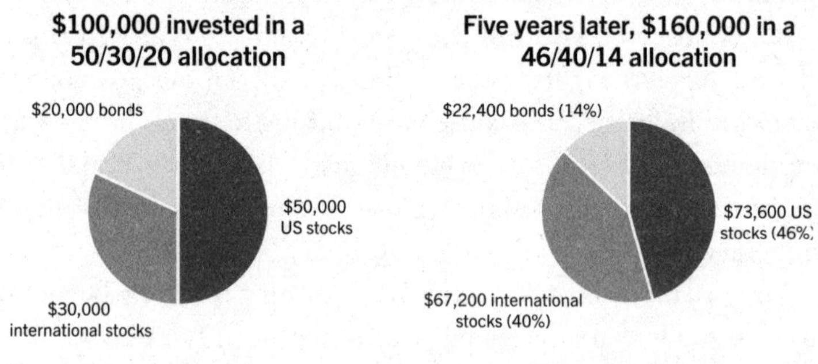

Janelle would like to rebalance to a 50/30/20 asset allocation, because that is the allocation that she had decided best suits her goals, timeline, and risk tolerance. She can do this in one of two ways.

Rebalance by Selling and Then Buying

Step 1: Find Your Target Dollar Amounts

Multiply $160,000 by your target percentages:
50% of $160,000 = $80,000 (US stocks)
30% of $160,000 = $48,000 (International stocks)
20% of $160,000 = $32,000 (Bonds)

Step 2: Find Your Current Dollar Amounts

$73,600 (US stocks now)

$64,000 (International stocks now)

$22,400 (Bonds now)

Step 3: Calculate the Moves Needed

Compare current and target amounts:

US stocks: $73,600 → needs to **increase to $80,000 → buy $6,400**

International stocks: $64,000 → needs to **decrease to $48,000 → sell $16,000**

Bonds: $22,400 → needs to **increase to $32,000 → buy $9,600**

Step 4: What You Actually Do

Sell $16,000 of international stocks

Use the $16,000 you just sold to:

- Buy $6,400 of US stocks
- Buy $9,600 of bonds

This brings all three categories to your desired 50/30/20 target allocation.

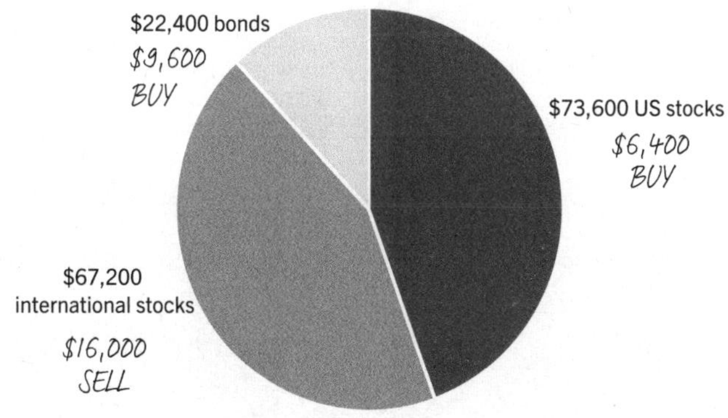

Note: If this is a taxable account (like a regular brokerage account), selling could trigger capital gains taxes.

Rebalance by Contributing New Money

If you don't want to sell anything right away (to avoid taxes or trading costs), you can rebalance gradually using new contributions.

Step 1: Identify the Underweight Assets

Compare your current allocation to your target:

- US stocks are slightly underweight (currently at 46%, needs to be 50%).
- Bonds are heavily underweight (currently at 14%, needs to be 20%).
- International stocks are overweight (currently at 40%, needs to be 30%).

Step 2: Redirect New Contributions

Direct 100% of your new contributions to US stocks and bonds. Shut off investments in international stocks.

Step 3: Adjust Over Time

Every three months, check your allocation. As US stocks and bonds get closer to their targets, you can resume contributing proportionally to all three according to your intended 50/30/20 split.

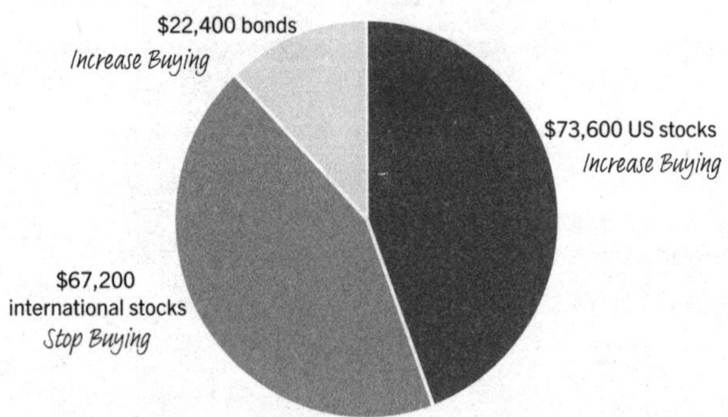

Want help crunching your numbers? You don't have to do this on your own. Head to richoldlady.com.

If you are feeling intimidated by rebalancing, you're not alone. Fortunately, I predict this service will soon be offered for free, even at DIY brokerage banks. If you'd prefer a robot to handle your rebalancing (along with every other part of building a strategy), consider a robo-advisor, discussed in the next chapter. Another option is M1 Finance, the "third way" option I introduced in the BANKS chapter. With M1 Finance, you choose the allocations and investments, but the platform is able to automatically rebalance your strategy with the click of a button.

2. Annual Relative Performance Check

At the end of the year, do a quick relative performance check because, remember, we are trying to perform as the markets do. If you are significantly underperforming the markets, we may need to troubleshoot. Revisit chapter 21 on UNDERPERFORMANCE for ideas on why this might be.

Find your portfolio's annual performance, which should be provided by your brokerage bank, and compare it to the performance of the markets you're invested in. I use the S&P 500 index for US stocks, the MSCI World ex USA for developed international, and "the AGG" for bonds. (It's easiest to find these performance numbers plastered all over financial news media on December 31.)

Let's go through an example. Suppose my asset allocation is 50% US stocks, 40% international stocks, and 10% bonds. If, at the end of the year, the US stock market is up 12%, the international stock market is up 18%, and the bond market is up 4%, the overall performance would be 13.6%, a *weighted average* of these returns based on my asset allocation.

$$\text{Weighted Average} = (0.12 \times 0.50) + (0.18 \times 0.40) + (0.04 \times 0.10) = .136 = 13.6\%$$

If my money had been fully invested for the entire year, the performance should be around 13.6%. It won't be exact, but it should be close! However, if I were investing gradually throughout the year—as I typically do—my performance might come in a bit lower, since not all of my funds would have benefited from the entire year's returns.

3. Shift into a More Conservative (Bond-Heavy) Strategy Over Time

Annual rebalancing is the act of returning a portfolio back to its intended asset allocation. But over time, you will also want to revisit the asset allocation as *your* needs change.

On an episode of his show called "Money," John Oliver gave some funny but shrewd advice: You should shift into more bonds every time they choose a new actor to play James Bond. According to a quick review of the James Bond Wikipedia page, it looks like we get a new Bond actor about once a decade. This is pretty spot-on. And though you might not actually make a shift into more James Bonds each decade, especially if you are in the first half of your career, it's good practice to reevaluate on your five-year birthday intervals: thirty-five, forty, forty-five, and so on.

To enact a strategy shift, use a process similar to rebalancing. Use a rebalancing calculator for help. Adjust the current investments as needed, and make sure that any new money also reflects your desired changes.

All right, Rich Old Lady! These are your responsibilities for upkeeping your investment garden. After you get the hang of it, the process shouldn't take more than a few hours per year. Per year! How great is that? Otherwise, all you gotta do is sit back and smell those roses.

29

ROBO-ADVISORS

Should I use an automated investing service?

Growing up, I loved going over to Teddi's. Once, I walked into her house, and her mom, Tracy, was blasting Metallica over the home stereo while blasting glitter onto the ceiling using a spray gun. *You can do that?* I wondered. From pantsing each other at sixth-grade basketball practice, to a spirited (but very last-place) performance of MC Hammer's "U Can't Touch This" at the eighth-grade talent show, to getting suspended for drinking raspberry Smirnoff at the senior homecoming dance, Teddi and I found trouble as easily as we found each other. Today, she owns a successful salon, cutting hair for the cool girls of New York City.

One day, we were reconnecting—a couple of Oregon girls makin' it in the big city—and we started talking about investing. I taught her how to build her own strategy, as I have for you in these pages. But I could sense a hesitation. "There is another option," I offered. "If you don't want to do this on your own, you can use a *robo-advisor.* Everything I just explained will be done of for you." Teddi, whose business success is built on her ability to move quickly and outsource, said yes immediately. Right then and there, we set her up with an investment account using one of the major robo-advisor services, including an automated monthly contribution. Several years later, she has a sizeable investment portfolio that *she would never have otherwise.*

Can you invest on your own? Yes, absolutely. But perhaps the better question is, *will* you invest on your own? Although you can totally do what a robo-advisor does, better and cheaper, it doesn't matter *if you don't do it at all.* How *much* we invest is going to be the single most important variable to our success. Instead of waiting until you know more, waiting for the right time, waiting, waiting, waiting until the weeks turn into months turn into years, get your thumbs out of your butt and over to your phone and download a robo app. You can be up and running in the next ten minutes.

Robo-advisors are mostly the same and they're mostly all fine. Betterment, Wealthfront, and the robo services you can now access at the brokerage banks generally buy portfolios of index ETFs that invest in the stock and bond markets. (I'd steer clear of any robo *not* using index funds.) Your mix of stocks and bonds is determined by, you guessed it, how you answer their questions about your goals and risk tolerance. In addition to choosing your allocation and index funds, the service takes care of any upkeep. Most allow you to invest within a regular brokerage account or a number of retirement accounts, like a Roth IRA or a SEP IRA.

Typical Robo-Advisor Portfolio

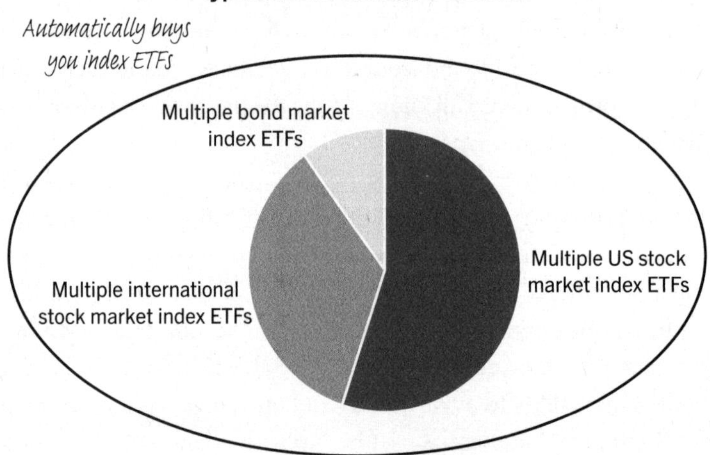

Knowing this, here is another way to frame the to-robo-or-not-to-robo debate: *Should you pay a robo-advisor to buy your index funds, or should you just buy the index funds yourself?*

Though robo-advisors are widely regarded as providing a solid service, it does not come without a cost. Usually, you pay a fee to the robo-advisor *and* there are fees embedded in the funds themselves, creating two layers of fees. It is a parfait of fees.

Example Robo-Advisor Holdings	Fund Expense Ratio
US Large Cap - VV	.02%
US Mid Cap - SCHM	.03%
US Small Cap - VB	.03%
International Developed - VEA	.03%
International Emerging - VWO	.07%
US Bonds - AGG	.03%
International Bonds - BNDX	.07%
Emerging Markets Bonds - EMB	.39%

+.25% robo-advisor fee

A typical robo management fee is one-quarter of 1% (.25%). Much more affordable than the typical 1% you might pay a traditional wealth manager, but can still amount to tens of thousands of dollars over time. Someday, you will have $1 million invested. (I believe!) A .25% robo fee on $1 million is $2,500 per year. That's $2,500 annually for a service that buys and maintains index funds. Investing $300 a month for forty years and assuming 7% returns per year, a .25% fee will cost $53,173 over those forty years. And this doesn't consider the fees embedded in the funds themselves. Still, the fees are worth it if the alternative is not investing at all, or if using an automated service would inspire you to invest more. **Choose more!**

Opinions are mixed on whether robo services help people become better and more consistent investors, but I think they do. That said, it's also true that users with less financial literacy may lean on robo services, and they would be well served by more proactive education about what they're investing in. A common misconception of robo portfolios is that they "only go up." Nope! You're in bear country, just like the rest of us.

A few summers ago, I did a six-day hike across the northern region of Glacier National Park in Montana with my friend Alexis. Before they hand over the permits, the park requires backcountry campers to watch a twenty-minute grizzly bear safety video on VHS. Bears, I learned, should never be surprised by your presence. You need to let them know you are coming. They recommended yelling "Bear!" every thirty seconds, which we did for six days straight, which, just take me now, bears. It worked, I guess—we didn't end up seeing any bears! Apparently, an interaction with a bear remains unlikely, even in remote regions of northern Montana.

But we *are* all but guaranteed another bear market or five during our lifetimes. So, then, where is my scratchy educational video hosted by a 1980s lady in long cargo shorts and Reno bangs teaching me how to handle a bear market? I genuinely believe that this type of education should be mandated for any automated investing service—robo-advisors, 401(k) accounts, all of them.

Still, for anyone second guessing themselves, it is a great option.

Is Tax-Loss Harvesting as Great as the Robo-Advisors Claim It to Be?

You'll often hear robo-advisors selling a service called *tax-loss harvesting*. They will claim that the tax savings from tax-loss harvesting will pay for the robo's fees. Is this true? Maybe. I believe the value of this service, when done in an automated or algorithmic fashion, is both real and probably overstated.

First, know that you don't need this service for retirement accounts, where you don't pay capital gains tax.

When done in a taxable brokerage account, tax law allows you to sell investments at a loss proactively (this is the proverbial "harvest") to cancel out gains that you'd otherwise have to pay a tax on. There are some situations in which tax-loss harvesting can be valuable, like if you're going to have a large capital gains tax bill and also have the losses to offset the gain.

However, it will not benefit everyone. For example, the strategy may be harmful to investors who are already paying a low (or zero) capital gains tax because they are a low earner. If they were to sell investments at a loss, only to repurchase a comparable fund at the same price level, not only would there be no tax savings but it also stamps them into a lower purchase price (called *cost basis*). This could cause a bigger tax burden in the future because the distance between your purchase price and what you sell it for will determine your capital gain, and you will be taxed on that larger spread. In this case, automated tax-loss harvesting prioritized a short-term tax strategy that (1) a person didn't need, and (2) will actually cost them over the long term.

Tax-loss harvesting can get quite nuanced and generally requires an understanding of a person's total financial picture, including where they sit on taxes. A robo-advisor very likely will not collect such detailed information. So, it may or may not work for you. It's fine but it's not *why* I'd use a robo-advisor. Use a robo-advisor if it will get you to invest more.

10-MINUTE MISSION

If you have decided you would like to use a robo-advisor, you are ready to invest. Go do it! The best thing about a robo-advisor is that getting invested is truly a 10-minute mission.

Be prepared by knowing:

- *Which account type you will open. (Revisit part II if necessary.)*
- *That there will be questions about your goals and risk tolerance, which will directly impact your ratio of stocks to bonds.*
- *How much to set as a monthly contribution, which will be automatically invested.*

PART IV HOMEWORK: Make Shit Happen

This is a HUGE moment—the moment you've been waiting for!

It's time to put together everything you've learned in part II (accounts), part III (investing theory), and part IV (building a strategy). This is where we turn theory into action. Use the checklist below to stay on track as you take the steps to get invested. On the other end, a celebration awaits.

Independent Investing

- ❑ Choose a bank
- ❑ Open an account
- ❑ Make an initial transfer of cash from a checking account, or transfer in another investment account
- ❑ Purchase investments according to the strategy you determined on page 159 and using investments you researched on page 174
- ❑ Set up automated contributions and investing
- ❑ Check in next month to make sure automations are running smoothly
- ❑ Set an annual calendar reminder to rebalance and check for relative performance around the New Year
- ❑ Celebrate this fabulous achievement

Workplace Retirement Account

- ❑ Set up an account through your workplace portal, if necessary
- ❑ Set your contribution as a dollar amount or as a percentage of your income
- ❑ Set your investments according to the strategy you determined on page 159 and using investments you researched on page 174
- ❑ Although most workplace plans automatically rebalance, set a calendar reminder to check for rebalancing and relative performance around the New Year
- ❑ Celebrate this fabulous achievement

Annual Investing Checklist

Rebalance

Did your portfolio experience a year of uneven growth? __________

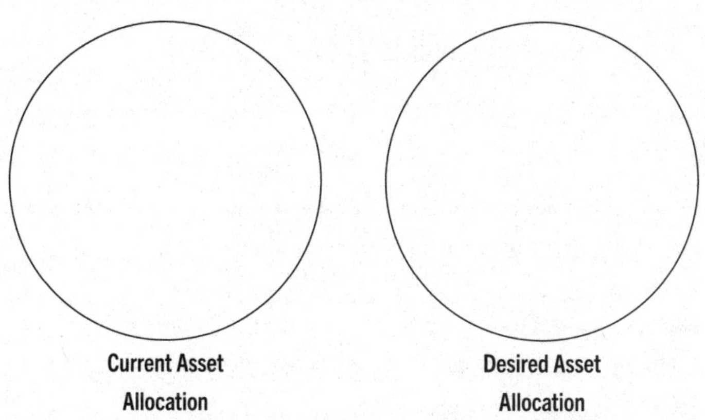

Use a rebalancing calculator to determine how you will bring your strategy back into balance.

Relative Performance Check

My annual performance: ______________________________

Compare this to the weighted performance of the:

S&P 500: ______________________________

MSCI World ex USA: ______________________________

Bloomberg US Aggregate Bond Index: ____________________

Take a weighted average performance of the market's performance using your asset allocation:

(RETURNS × WEIGHT) + (RETURNS × WEIGHT) + (RETURNS × WEIGHT) =

Example:

(0.12 RETURNS × 0.50 WEIGHT) + (0.18 × 0.40) + (0.04 × 0.10)
= .136 = 13.6%

(___ RETURNS × ___ WEIGHT) + (___ × ___) + (___ × ___)
=______ =______%

How did your performance stack up? If you underperformed the market, what is a possible source of underperformance? ______________

Every five years: Does your asset allocation feel appropriate given your goals, investing timeline, and risk tolerance? If not, what changes will you make?

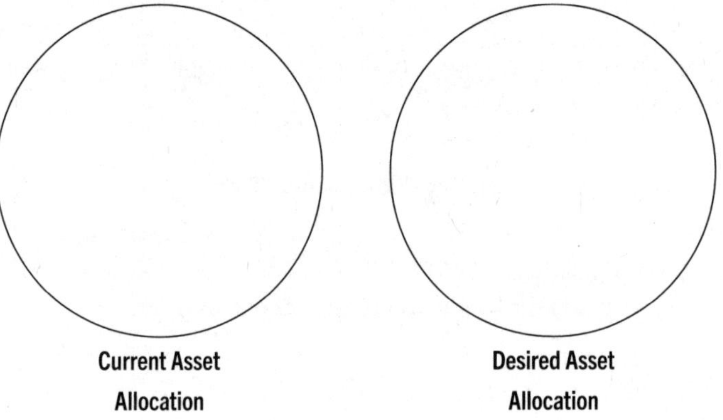

Current Asset Allocation

Desired Asset Allocation

Bonus

- Make a bonus end-of-year (or beginning) contribution to investment accounts, or increase your contribution percentage.
- Manually invest any lingering cash and double-check all automations, including automated dividend reinvestment.

RICH OLD LADY REFLECTION

Roth or Traditional? Mutual fund or ETF? Vanguard or Schwab? Robo or DIY? 90/10 or 80/20?

I know—it can feel like one wrong move will have you crying into your spreadsheets, haunted by every bad, stupid, terrible decision each time you log into Fidelity's living nightmare of a website.

But guess what? That's not how this works. At all. Your financial success doesn't hinge on being a flawless investor. It hinges on investing consistently and staying the course. That's it. No one's asking you to nail a perfect switch leap on your first try. You just need to get your ass on the dance floor.

If you're investing, you're already doing it right. Yes, you'll make mistakes. Yes, some might cost you money. That's part of the deal. But investing rewards persistence, not perfection.

Here's a Rich Old Lady rule of investing: If the choice is between taking an easy route you're not 100% sure about or doing nothing, take the easy route. Got a retirement account at work? Start there. Using a robo-advisor? Amazing. You can tweak your routine later.

Forget perfect. Boogie on.

PART V

FINE-TUNING THINGS

Optional ways to tweak your investment strategy

30

ETHICAL INVESTING

How do I invest in a more ethical way?

Short answer: Instead of regular index funds, use index funds that screen out weapons and oil.

Long answer: Investing in the stock market can never be truly ethical. But just as we can make *more* ethical choices with our jobs and what we consume, we can make *more* ethical choices with how we invest.

Any honest conversation about investing begins with understanding what the system was designed to do and for whom it was built. Modern wealth, especially in the West, has largely been amassed through horrific acts of violence: colonialism, environmental destruction, and exploitation. Wall Street itself, the symbolic heart of American finance, was first a slave market. And while we can choose "less bad" companies to invest in, the underlying structure is still extractive. By "extractive," I mean a system that generates profit by pulling value *out* of people, communities, and the earth, often without consent or reciprocity. Extraction treats labor like it's a line item and global resources as inputs to be acquired by any means necessary.

Therefore, investing indeed carries moral weight. But opting out doesn't erase that weight—it just shifts who carries it. In the US, personal investing has quietly become our system of elder care. Yes, there's Social Security, but that alone likely won't be enough, especially if politicians take a hatchet to the (widely popular, successful) program before we get a chance to collect our checks. And most people cannot afford to ignore how inflation eats away at their savings over time. Compounding investment returns is one of the only tools regular people have to build enough resources to live with dignity, especially in old age.

And I hate to state the obvious, but having money does not somehow become less necessary just because you're old. You are at your most vulnerable (and unemployable) as an older person. If you decide not to invest at all out of resistance to capitalism, you don't escape the system, because that's not actually possible. You either continue to provide your labor to that same exact system, or you transfer the cost. And given what we know about who absorbs the burden of unpaid elder care, that cost will likely fall on your daughter.

Under a more just system, workers would own a meaningful stake in the value they help create. That idea—worker ownership—is central to many cooperative visions of a fairer economy. Ironically, one of the only ways to approximate that kind of shared ownership right now is through investing in the stock market. Further, companies rely on public infrastructure, subsidies, government contracts, and a publicly educated workforce. In addition to our tax dollars, companies become profitable through our labor and our consumption. Knowing this, I think it's fair to ask whether we're entitled to a share of what this system produces. Yes, the mechanism is clumsy, exploitative, and only available to those who can afford to buy in. But maybe that's still better than letting a handful of billionaire buttheads own absolutely everything.

There are no right answers. Personally, I've decided that my best path forward is to work for a better system for all while also taking care of myself in the system we've got.

To invest more ethically, look for keywords like *social, responsible, sustainable,* and *ESG* when shopping for funds (or robo-advisor services). ESG stands for environmental, social, and governance, and is a framework investors use to evaluate how companies handle concerns around climate impact, labor practices, and executive pay. Ethical or ESG funds typically include companies that score well on these factors, although definitions and scoring methods can vary. Still, they represent our starting place.

I view this decision like a Venn diagram. In one circle, I have "make good financial decisions" using the principles of investing we've discussed so far. In the other, it's "make more ethical choices." For me, ESG index funds that specifically omit oil and weapons companies are where the two circles light a responsibly sourced soy candle and scissor tenderly. Let me explain.

In my "make good financial decisions" bubble: Just because a fund is labeled ESG doesn't mean that it is a good financial decision—and not for the reasons you might think. It's not because more ethical stocks will perform worse moving forward—we can't know that. However, what we do know is that high fees and active management destroy returns for investors, and this fact doesn't change because the fund is ethical. And while I am sure that lots of active ESG fund managers really care about worker protections and endangered sea turtles, there is no denying that the demand for more ethical options creates a big opportunity for the finance industry, whose fees sure have found an epic hiding place behind the ethical-investing label.

In my "make more ethical choices" bubble: At least with index funds that cut out weapons and oil, I'm not profiting off Lockheed Martin every time America gets a war boner. But even then, they often still include Big Tech giants like Google, Amazon, and Palantir—companies now actively profiting from genocide, war, and surveillance. You'll also find Big Banks, health insurance providers, and mining companies. Once you start peeling back the layers, you see with your own eyes how hard it is to invest truly ethically.

Because this is about your ethics and your money, you're welcome to put whatever you'd like at the center of your Venn diagram. Maybe you conclude that ethical investing in your 401(k) really isn't possible, so you scrap the idea for now. Or, maybe you're okay taking on fees to have more control. Here's a newer offering gaining some momentum: *direct indexing*. You build your own index fund using the stocks in an established index, like the S&P 500, and then hand-screen certain companies or industries. That said, this is a costly option that probably only makes sense with bigger sums of money.

If you'd like to pursue a strategy of using slightly-more-ethical index funds, it's simple. Use all the methods you've learned so far but swap out your regular index funds for the ethical funds I've provided on page 206, which screen out *both* weapons and oil. (Alas, not all of them do.)

You may be limited by what you have access to. Not all workplace retirement accounts will have an ethical option, and even fewer will have an ethical index option. All you can do is the best you can with the tools you have available to you right now.

Whereas my friend Jules, who is self-employed, was able to buy ethical index funds in their Roth IRA and a brokerage account at Fidelity, their sister, Casey, found herself in a bit of a conundrum. She is investing in her 401(k), which includes only one ethical option—an actively managed ESG fund with a 1.2% expense ratio, which she knows is quite high. She has decided to opt for the regular index funds available to her and show up for the world in other ways.

For those in a similar situation but who are committed to financing a sustainable future, I recommend focusing on your bank. Whereas you'd risk elder poverty by totally opting out of retirement investing, you lose nothing when you don't use a big bank. Commercial banks like Chase, Citi, Wells Fargo, and Bank of America use bank deposits (your money!) to invest in fossil fuel projects, private prisons, weapons manufacturers, and governments committing known human rights abuses. Meanwhile, credit unions use deposits to reinvest in their community members.

Whatever choice you make, thank you for caring, just like a Rich Old Lady should.

Ethical Index Funds That Screen Out Oil Companies and Weapons Makers

	Type	Market	Provider
ESGV	Index ETF	US Stock Market (broad)	Made by Vanguard, available to purchase at most brokerages
VFTAX	Index Mutual Fund	US Stock Market (large-cap)	Made by Vanguard, will likely have a fee to purchase elsewhere
VSGX	Index ETF	International Stock Market	Made by Vanguard, available to purchase at most brokerages
EAGG	Index ETF	US Bond Market (mix)	Made by iShares, available to purchase at most brokerages

Sample Portfolio Using Ethical Index Funds

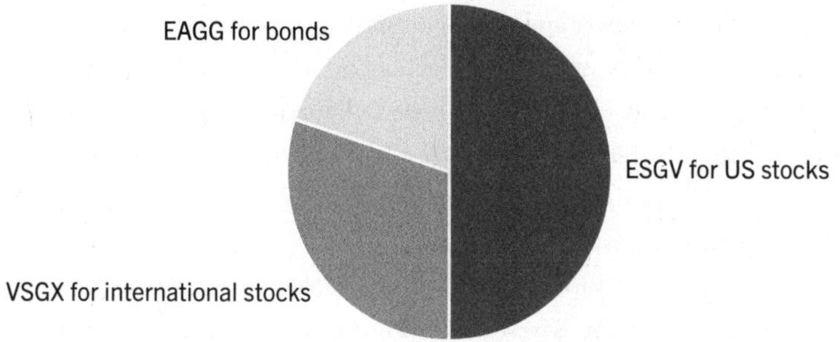

Does Ethical Investing Drive Meaningful Change?

Ethical investing is frequently accused of being a *greenwashed* solution to our world's most pressing issues. As in, it is the personal finance equivalent of putting a C☪☮E✡I☯✝ bumper sticker on your mid-sized SUV. This is fair.

Critics on the left argue that ESG investing is hardly enough to halt the US's continued acceleration toward a corporate oligarchy that threatens social welfare and the environment.

Critics from the finance end of things will point out that refusing to invest in certain types of stocks may do little to affect those companies' share prices. To alter the stock price in a meaningful and sustained way, it would likely be necessary to alter a company's profit in a meaningful and sustained way.

It is true that mass movements to sell certain stocks could drop prices—that's supply and demand for you. But in financial markets, a temporary drop is not the end of the story. Lower prices create an opportunity for other market participants to buy the stock at this lower price and there will always be investors willing to overlook murky ethics for a good deal. This includes the companies themselves, which frequently buy back their own stock (*stock buybacks*) when they believe it's selling for cheap.

Knocking off the bud won't stop the growth; if you want to kill a weed, you have to dig it up from the roots. The best way to thwart corporate power on an individual level is to (1) vote for politicians who are serious about regulating it, (2) unionize your workplace to reclaim collective power and when necessary, withhold your labor, and (3) *stop giving them your money!* Remember, stock prices are a downstream effect and will ultimately reflect the underlying profitability (or belief in the future profitability) of a company. While big-money investors will gladly swoop up the Amazon stock you sell, no one will buy the Prime membership you cancel.

Then again, the *divestment* movement knows today's stock prices aren't really the point. Divestment movements aim to pressure major institutions, like foundations and universities, to sell off investments in industries seen as harmful, like tobacco or weapons manufacturing. Bill McKibben, a leader in the fossil fuels divestment movement, explains that divestment aims not to drop share prices but to revoke the *social license* of certain companies—eroding their social and political power and moral standing within a culture. Divestment is seen as one tool in a broader toolbox to effect change. Ethical investing, then, aligns with the divestment movement's goal of reshaping the social and ethical landscape in which these companies operate.

In conclusion, yes, be aware of the limitations of ethical investing. But I firmly believe that the best investing strategy is one that you understand, feel good about, and therefore, will stick with over the long term. If you've vetted your ethical fund options for fees and can sleep better at night, you have my cosign.

31

MARKET CATEGORIES

How can I perfect my investment strategy?

Esther sits back in her chair and cackles. "I am decoding the Rosetta stone right now. How is anyone supposed to know what any of this means?" She was looking through the list of mutual fund options available within her 457(b). "Mid-caps, value stocks, and dividend funds. What about these? Do I need to invest in them, too?"

I told Esther, "you may already be invested in them!" and explained that by utilizing a broad three-fund index fund strategy, you already own practically everything—including mid-caps, value stocks, and dividend-paying stocks. These funds simply represent narrower categories of investments, for folks who want to focus on specific corners of the market.

It is a common misconception that buying into more funds inherently adds diversification. Students often come to me with a Jackson Pollock approach to investment management: chaotic smatterings of everything. But because they may lack the touch of a skilled craftsmen, the outcome is brown and muddled and doesn't represent much of anything at all. If you are going to add more funds, it behooves you to understand what you're adding and why. You can't just start throwing paint.

For example, people often ask me if they should buy an index fund that only invests in tech stocks. (Like QQQ or anything that says *Nasdaq*.) But if you already own a total US stock market index fund or an S&P 500 index fund, you already own tech stocks! And *a lot* of them!

Currently, tech stocks compose nearly 40% of your typical US stock market index fund. Therefore, purchasing a tech sector fund would *not* increase diversification; it would concentrate your position relative to the market itself. It would be a kind of doubling down on tech stocks.

Esther certainly could build a strategy of the narrow funds provided by her 457(b), but this would be to dabble in active management as she makes personal decisions for and against categories relative to the broader market. That, by the way, is what professional managers do. They *overweight* and *underweight* categories of investments and individual investments that they think will perform better or worse than the market. Here's an example. Healthcare stocks currently make up about 11.2% of the US stock market. If an active manager were to believe that the healthcare industry was going to outperform relative to expectations, they may choose to bump their strategy's healthcare stock exposure to 18%. My guess is that most people won't be interested in this level of involvement, especially considering it introduces a lot of room to get things wrong. Instead, we are generally best served by keeping our strategies simple and passive.

Still, it's good to understand the terminology. It will make our brains bigger and our convictions stronger. And who knows, maybe you will want to fine-tune your portfolio. So, here are some of the most common stock market categories, along with how each would change the shape of your strategy.

As you consider the category, ask yourself these questions: (1) Will this category increase my diversification, because it is something that I am not yet invested in, or does it make my strategy more concentrated in a certain category, reducing diversification? And (2) how does this category change the overall risk and potential return profile of my strategy?

Market Capitalization ("Market Cap")

When you add up the value of a company's stock, you get its *market capitalization*—the stock market's way of measuring a company's size. Large-cap companies are economic Andre the Giants, such as Nvidia and Coca-Cola. Small-caps, on the other hand, aren't household names.

In general, the smaller the company, the riskier it is; many small companies fail. But small- and mid-cap companies also have more room to run and have historically performed better than large stocks. If you caught Nvidia stock on its way up from nothing, you'd be reading this from your chalet in the Swiss Alps or from the thousand-acre miniature horse sanctuary you've self-funded.

	Historical Annualized Returns
US Large-Cap	10%
US Small-Cap	12%

The big boys, especially the tech giants, have become so large they dominate our market-weighted indices (and therefore, funds). The Russell 3000 Index, which covers most of the US stock market, is weighted at approximately 80% large-cap stocks, 15% mid-caps, and under 5% small-caps. The S&P 500 index is even more concentrated, with about 85% in large-caps, 15% in mid-caps, and essentially no exposure to small-cap stocks.

Given this, you could consider increasing your exposure to small- or mid-cap stocks, especially if you are using an S&P 500 index fund. You can do this by adding a small- or mid-cap index fund to your strategy. While this approach may ultimately overweight you to smaller stocks relative to the market's current composition, I agree with the concerns about the dominance of mega-monster companies. It is valid to explore diversification strategies that were once viewed as beyond the scope of traditional passive investing in order to limit the risk of putting too much of your strategy in any one stock or handful of stocks.

Let's ask our questions: (1) Will this category increase diversification? Answer: Adding or overweighting small-cap and mid-cap stocks may or may not add diversification depending on whether you already own them. (2) Does this category increase or decrease my portfolio's overall riskiness? Answer: Popular theory tells us that small- and mid-cap stocks will increase your strategy's risk profile and therefore return potential. But in the age of ballooning Big Tech exposure in US stock indices, it could *also* be true that it decreases single stock risk.

If I were to overweight a category beyond a passive, three-fund strategy, small- and mid-caps would be my top choice. For example, you can do this by paring back your S&P 500 index fund and replacing with a small-cap, mid-cap, or small-cap value index fund (more on small value next). I'm personally aiming for 20% of my overall strategy allocated toward small- and mid-cap stocks, but remember, that's a reflection of my risk tolerance. You do you.

Small-Cap and Mid-Cap Index Funds				
	Charles Schwab	Fidelity	Vanguard	iShares
Small-Cap Index Mutual Fund	SWSSX	FSSNX	VSMAX	
Small-Cap Index ETF	SCHA		VB	IWM, IJR
Mid-Cap Index Mutual Fund	SWMCX	FSMAX	VIMAX	
Mid-Cap Index ETF	SCHM		VO	IJH

How Is Market Capitalization Measured?

Market cap is calculated by multiplying the current share price of the company's stock by the total number of outstanding shares.

Market Capitalization = Share Price × Number of Outstanding Shares

If a company has ten million shares outstanding and each share is priced at $70: 10,000,000 shares × $70/share = $700,000,000 market capitalization.

Category	Market Cap Range	Description
Mega-Cap	$200 billion and up	Global giants (Apple, Microsoft)
Large-Cap	$10 billion–$200 billion	Established leaders of industry
Mid-Cap	$2 billion–$10 billion	Mature companies with growth potential
Small-Cap	$300 million–$2 billion	Emerging players, more risk and reward
Micro-Cap	$50 million–$300 million	Very small firms, often less liquid
Nano-Cap	Under $50 million	Tiny, speculative companies

Growth and Value Stocks

In investing, *growth* feels like a fairly straightforward term, but alas, it has multiple meanings. "I'm investing for growth" is totally something you might say to describe investing in stocks generally. But growth also refers to a specific *style* of stock. So does the term *value.* If you see the word *growth* or *value* in the name of your stock fund, it almost certainly refers to this particular style of stock, *not* your desire for growth or value more generally. Therefore, the terms *growth* and *value* should be an immediate indication that the fund represents a narrower category of the market.

A value stock is undervalued by the market relative to comparable companies. A growth stock is relatively overvalued. Think of it like this: A value stock is unpopular, and a growth stock is popular. Investors are tripping over themselves to invest in growth stocks, like Apple. Value stocks? Not so much. Value stocks are often bedraggled companies, maybe because they are going through a difficult time as a business or there's not a lot of excitement on the horizon.

Now, why would someone want to invest in a bedraggled stock? Well, you might be able to get it for a great deal, and if this tough period is only temporary, there could be a big payoff in the comeback. Warren Buffett is famously a value investor, buying what he believes are essential American companies when they go on sale. It is counterintuitive, but it can be a good investing strategy to buy into Debbie Downer stocks, because they are the ones trading at low prices compared to the value of the business.

Currently, the stocks that dominate our market are growth stocks in the tech industry. They're like buying into Beyoncé stock when she is already at the top of her game. You might have to pay a higher relative price for this stock, but perhaps you expect continued domination. Value stocks, on the other hand, would be like investing in a big star after an album flop or during the kind of cancellation campaign we often reserve for famous women. Which is to say, when her stock is down. Value stocks are a bigger risk, especially on an individual-stock basis, but there's also a bigger possible spread between where they are and where they can go.

	Historical Annualized Returns
US Growth	10%
US Value	13%*

According to the famous Fama-French dataset, value stocks have outperformed growth stocks by about 3% per year when measured over long stretches of history. When you focus on stocks that are both small and value, the spread is even larger, more than 4%! Still, not everyone is convinced. Legendary investor Jack Bogle, for example, doubted that everyday investors could capture much of this advantage at all. (Hence the asterisk.) Of all the return figures in this book, these may be the toughest to replicate with index funds. (For example, the index funds below don't track the exact Fama-French factors used to calculate these return figures.) Even so, I hold to the core investing belief that higher risk, as in the case of value stocks, *could* lead to higher returns over time. Just know that with all riskier, narrower categories, you will likely face long periods of underperformance, just as we saw during the Big Tech boom. For this kind of investing, you need to have tiger blood.

In summary, having a combination of value and growth stocks is considered ideal for diversification. The stock market is a mix of both, and you own both within your broad index fund. That said, growth stocks are much larger and tend to dominate the indices. Because investors generally already have ample exposure to growth, some choose to tilt toward value (or small value) in hopes of better long-term performance. Overweighting value stocks (1) may or may not increase diversification in your investment strategy because you already own them, and (2) would increase both risk and the potential for higher return in your strategy. But, it is also true that being too concentrated in large growth stocks is a newer risk that overweighting value stocks relative to the market may help temper.

	Fidelity	Vanguard	iShares
Small-Cap Value Index Mutual Fund	FISVX, FIMVX (mid-cap)	VSIAX, VMVAX (mid-cap)	
Small-Cap Value Index ETF		VBR, VIOV, VOE (mid-cap)	IJS, IWN, IJJ (mid-cap)

Sectors

There are eleven stock market *sectors,* the stock market's way of saying "industry." Investing in an index fund invests you across every sector in its relative market weight. Sectors are categorized as either *cyclical* or *noncyclical.*

Cyclical sectors are more sensitive to booms and busts, and are considered riskier.

Information Technology (tech)
Consumer Discretionary (unnecessary goods)
Industrials (machines)
Materials (mining)

Energy
Financials
Real Estate

Noncyclical sectors are less sensitive to booms and busts, but have less growth potential.

Healthcare
Utilities
Consumer Staples (necessary goods)
Telecommunication Services (phone service providers)

Overweighting a specific sector in your portfolio (1) does not necessarily increase diversification since you probably already own it, and (2) will alter the risk and potential return profile depending on the sector.

Dividend Stocks

Just as the name says, these stocks focus on paying dividends. Dividends, those quarterly payments from the company to the shareholders, are a smaller but still essential element of the stock market's total return. Companies are not required to pay dividends, but most do. You own dividend-paying stocks in your stock market index funds.

It is true that dividend payments can come at the cost of higher share growth. Think about it like this: The cash is either being paid out to you or reinvested in the company's quote-unquote own damn self. Generally, companies can only get away with not paying a dividend if they promise otherwise booming growth. Tesla and Amazon do not pay dividends. But they can also fail on their promise of growth, and then you're left without growth *and* without dividends. It's a risk! Compare that to utilities companies, which can make no promise of banger returns and therefore tend to pay higher dividends.

Adding dividend-paying funds is a common strategy for investors who are shifting away from maximum growth and toward producing income, especially around retirement. Grandpas *love* dividends.

If you overweight dividend stocks, you are (1) not necessarily increasing diversification because you already own them, and (2) decreasing risk and potential returns to instead focus on producing income.

In closing, I'm serving up a hearty dose of real talk: The long-term return averages I've presented throughout this book may not come to fruition. Past performance never guarantees future results. Further, it is helpful to understand that these averages are academic in nature—numbers calculated in a lab, far removed from the messy realities of actual investing. In practice, your mileage may vary. What is certain is that all future averages, whatever they may be, require you play a wicked long game.

To diversify is to accept that some parts of your portfolio will outshine others on a schedule you can't predict. Be careful here: Investors tend to chase recent winners—categories that have already run hot—and end up moving in and out at exactly the wrong time. (Ironically, the better bet is often the category that's been sucking for years.) Timing mistakes are easy to make, and they'll cost you. That's why many pros recommend adopting a passive strategy and committing to it wholeheartedly.

32

REAL ESTATE (REITS)

How can I own real estate without owning a home?

For a long time, everything I knew about real estate investing came from TV. First, there were the early-aughts DIY shows, like TLC's *Flip That House*, where camera crews followed passive-aggressive, plaid-shirted couples teaching themselves how to caulk a wall in the hopes of flipping their house for a profit. Then A&E came out with their own version of the show, called *Flip This House*. Genius. Fast-forward a few years, and I'm watching the deeply tanned cast of *Selling Sunset* sip on martinis while throwing professional jabs at each other at Nobu and only very occasionally selling $20 million homes. Luckily, what I've also learned through the years is that you don't actually have to wear red bottoms or get filmed 24/7 while sweatily excavating a basement to invest in real estate.

Of the major asset categories, we've now spent a lot of time talking about cash, stocks, and bonds—the core building blocks of any strategy. But real estate is another big category that I bet you're considering, especially as you do the thoughtful work of diversifying. And there is a way to invest in real estate even if you can't afford a home (yet) or have no interest in becoming a landlord, and that is through *real estate investment trusts* (REITs). Sure, you could start a reality show, stage a fake argument over backsplash tile, and hire a drone to film your open house. Or you could just buy REITs.

Here's how they work: Each REIT is a company that owns and manages income-generating real estate, like office buildings, hotels, warehouses, storage facilities, or cell phone towers. (Investing in a shopping mall REIT? It's like the mall is finally paying *you* back for all those dollars you blew at Spencer's and Limited Too.) By law, REITs are required to return at least 90% of their taxable income to shareholders as dividends, so as an investor, most of your profits will come from those payouts.

Investing in a REIT is as simple as buying shares of a real estate company, just like purchasing stock. There are three main types of REITs: equity, mortgage, and hybrid. Equity REITs are the most popular. They own and operate income-producing properties, earning revenue primarily from rent. For example, your employer might rent office space in a building owned by a REIT, and the rent payments contribute to the REIT's revenue. After accounting for expenses, the REIT passes a significant portion of that revenue to investors in the form of dividends. Mortgage REITs earn income from the interest on mortgage loans, which are then passed to investors as dividends. Then there are hybrid REITs, which combine the two.

So, should you invest in REITs? Currently, there isn't a real industry consensus on whether REITs should be part of an investment strategy. Proponents for REITs point to the added diversification. Why not have something besides stocks and bonds? REITs have outperformed bonds and, in many cases, owning real estate outright. This is particularly true when compared to a primary residence, which does not generate income like a REIT. In fact, REITs appear to have performed even better than large US stocks. But it's a bit of an apples-to-oranges comparison; REITs are a newer offering, and we don't have the same century of data that we do for stocks and bonds. The annualized return figure I cite here only dates back to the 1970s. (Notably, this excludes the Great Depression, a period reflected in the stock and bond data.)

	Historical Annualized Returns
REITs	10–11%

Critics of REITs argue that they can add unnecessary complexity to an investment strategy. More moving pieces can lead to higher costs and timing mistakes. Additionally, the performance of stocks and

REITs appear to be correlated; both stocks and REITs got pummeled in 2008 and 2022. REITs may not diversify your portfolio as much as you'd expect.

Investing in a real estate company's REIT is similar to buying a company's stock: Some will thrive, while others may suck. That's just the nature of business. Buying individual REITs gives you the most control over your investments, but it also requires more effort and carries greater risk because you're less diversified. For most investors, a REIT index fund is likely the better starting place. These funds invest in a whole bunch of REITs, helping to spread out risk while keeping things simpler to manage.

So, how much of your portfolio should be invested in REITs? Again, there's no rule. Although real estate is considered its own asset class due to its unique characteristics, I think of real estate as just one economic sector, like technology or healthcare. Personally, I wouldn't allocate more than 15% to REITs. Also, consider this in the context of your existing real estate holdings—many Americans who own a home are already heavily exposed to real estate.

REIT Index Funds

	Charles Schwab	Fidelity	Vanguard	iShares
US REIT Index Mutual Fund		FSRNX	VGSLX	
US REIT Index ETF	SCHH	FREL	VNQ	IYR

What about the Ethics of Owning REITs?

Although REIT index funds provide diversified exposure across the real estate sector, it is absolutely reasonable to have ethical concerns, particularly around corporate ownership of residential properties. While the majority of REIT holdings are concentrated in sectors like industrial warehouses, data centers, and infrastructure such as cell towers, single-family rental homes do account for a small portion of most REIT indices. Typically, around 3% to 4%. Apartment buildings represent another 9% to 10%.

Financialization is the process of turning things we rely on to live into assets for financial markets to trade and profit from. Personally, I believe the financialization of housing should be illegal. It puts everyday people in the untenable financial position of having to bid against Blackstone and foreign hedge funds for the only available home on the block. And it's not just financial, this severs public trust in the political systems that claim to protect us.

That said, we are all just trying to survive within the same system that, for example, has made it nearly impossible for Black families to build intergenerational wealth through homeownership. It would be pretty wacky for me, a white person whose grandparents were able to buy homes in a city with a notoriously racist history of redlining (Portland, Oregon), to deny anyone the opportunity to use these tools. I want you to take care of yourself, and I trust you to make that judgment call.

One alternative is to buy individual REITs, focusing on property sectors that better align with your values. You would be taking on some active management risk—think of it like picking a stock—but if that trade-off lets you invest with a clear conscience, it might be worth it. I wouldn't allocate more than a small proportion of my portfolio to any one individual REIT.

33

CRYPTOCURRENCY

Should I invest in cryptocurrency?

Treat cryptocurrency like that sparkly clutch you take out on a Friday night. You have to be okay with accidentally leaving it in a taxi.

Which is to say, don't invest more than you can afford to lose. This is not a commentary on whether crypto is good or bad (although that's coming). It's simply a statement on that risk-and-return trade-off I keep yammering on about. In terms of investing risk, crypto has large, unpredictable swings to both the upside and downside—more pronounced than even the worst volatility in the stock market. Also, the future of cryptocurrency is unknown, no matter what anyone says.

That said, crypto does not appear to be going anywhere. It's likely to be shoehorned into our shared, global future regardless of how many acres of Amazon rainforest it burns down in the process, or how much it fails to improve everyday life. Though designed as an alternate way to transact, crypto remains too expensive, clunky, and volatile for most people to actually use. Instead, its primary purpose seems to be providing the ultrawealthy with another place to park their money, and private equity firms a shiny new frontier for which to invest.

But before we go any further, let's back it up. What is cryptocurrency?

Your worst cousin will corner you at Thanksgiving and tell you that *it's simple*! It's money, but money that you can't really use to buy things. You wake up in the morning, and you don't know whether you can afford a sandwich or a house. It's created by computers solving Rubik's Cubes really, really fast. Tom Brady got on a Super Bowl ad to tell you to get it at a fake bank that *oops!* collapsed like a Jenga tower within the year.

What's not to get?!

Okay, okay, it is a digital currency. Cryptocurrency is *decentralized,* meaning it isn't controlled by any government, and you don't need a bank account to use it. Cryptocurrency can be created in several different processes, like *mining* or *staking*. One such mining process is called *proof of work,* and it's basically just computers completing calculations. You can think of it like a competitive video game. The first computer to beat a level (a block) gets a coin. Then, you move on to the next level. Each new level (block) requires more complex calculations, which means the computer needs even more processing power and energy to solve them. Every completed level also adds a permanent record to a shared game board (called the blockchain) so everyone knows the score.

Now, at this point, you might be like, *so what?* What about this process gives it value? And frankly, these are very good questions. Make no mistake, these otherwise throwaway calculations have value only because a bunch of people decided that they have value. Yep! Value is a social construct, baby! And it's not just crypto. Society is propped up by numerous made-up systems that require our collective belief. The US dollar, the Supreme Court, and diamonds all require that we collectively believe in their value. If everyone at once decided diamonds were a scam, and there was no demand for diamonds, the market would collapse.

The success of any and every cryptocurrency ultimately boils down to the same thing: our collective belief in that cryptocurrency (and its value). Remember our chat about supply and demand? If people bail and sell a coin, the price goes down. The more people buy in, the higher the price goes. And people buy into a coin because they believe in it. Therefore, predicting which cryptocurrencies will still be in use ten, twenty, or thirty years from now requires knowing which cryptocurrencies people (and institutions) will *want* to use decades into the future.

As of this writing, the front-runners are Bitcoin and Ethereum. Bitcoin has the first-mover advantage, institutional backing, and a reputation as "digital gold." (There is a fixed supply of Bitcoin, which appeals to the investors who see the government as inflating away our savings so they can print ever more money for wars. Which—yeah?!) Ethereum, on the other hand, is liked for its flexible and usable technology.

Then, there are memecoins; joke currencies that aren't designed to do anything except go viral and make early buyers rich. Memecoins appear to be fueling crypto-based gambling addictions, especially among young men chasing quick wins in apps designed for dopamine, not financial planning. There's Elon's beloved Dogecoin, the president's blindly corrupt $TRUMP project, and yes, there's CumRocket. Yeah, I am not personally out here buying CUMMIES, but if it becomes the global dystopia's default currency in thirty years, I guess . . . I can't . . . be mad?!

Therefore, it is not so simple as researching your way into knowing which cryptocurrency will be the best cryptocurrency twenty years from now. That's like looking at a bunch of babies and guessing which will grow up to be prom king—or whether we're even still doing the whole prom court thing. That's not to say you shouldn't do your homework if you're planning to invest in crypto—you should—but don't break your back trying to know the unknowable. The truth is any cryptocurrency's future depends on collective belief systems, cultural trends, technological advances, regulatory decisions, institutional adoption, whims of the wealthy, unforeseen events, attention spans, and *luck*.

Compare this to a productive asset like a stock. Not only does a stock often predictably share a portion of its profits through dividends but there's also an entire business behind it—real people working together to create value and generate profit. Most cryptocurrencies, on the other hand, lack any underlying cash flow or dividends, making their value wholly speculative. Crypto adheres to the *greater fool theory* of investing: Your only hope is that, somewhere down the line, a fool greater than you will be willing to buy it from you for more than you paid.

We've seen this speculative dynamic play out in crypto, where early adopters and the wealthy—those who got in before the hype—have reaped the most benefits, often at the expense of smaller investors chasing gains. Crypto *whales* are large holders who can manipulate markets by triggering massive price swings with their trades, frequently leaving small investors butt naked holding the bag. Everyday investors "with narrow margins for losing money [are] taking on risky financial products that extract profit for elite asset holders at the top," writes Tressie McMillan Cottom. "One might say, the risk and reward structure is shaped like a *pyramid*."

If you've ever wondered why the crypto bros speak about their favorite coin with what feels like a religious fervor, this is why. Their personal success requires ever-increasing buy-in. That's it. That's why. They might tee up a fine financial, political, or technological argument, but it's probably about the money. Knowing this, please don't ever feel bullied into an investment that you are not comfortable with. Especially considering the serious ethical concerns—like the attendant strain on power grids, its frequent use in shady or outright corrupt schemes (see again: $TRUMP), and the near-total lack of basic financial protections that leave everyday people vulnerable to scams and wipeouts.

Perhaps paradoxically, it's precisely because I'm a bit skeptical of our current institutions that I still invest a tiny sliver of my investments in crypto. It's less an enthusiastic endorsement and more a hedge against the outside chance that traditional systems fail. If you decide to invest in cryptocurrencies, follow these three simple rules:

1. **Set a clear limit:** After doing a personal risk assessment, decide what percentage of your investing strategy you're comfortable allocating to crypto—and stick with it!
2. **Invest regularly, not reactively:** Stick to a steady, monthly investing routine. If you feel tempted to buy crypto only after a massive price surge—when everyone's buzzing about it—you're doing it wrong. That's not investing; that's chasing hype. Buying crypto only when it's at its most expensive is a sign you're not ready for crypto.
3. **Learn about crypto security:** You can start on a trading platform to get familiar with the process, but if you're putting significant sums into crypto, it's crucial to learn how to use a *hard* (as in hardware) *wallet* like Trezor or Ledger. It's your best protection against hacks and loss.

I will end with a prayer for crypto: May it live up to its promises, make up for its massive ecological destruction, and leave no one behind. If its only purpose was to help a handful of guys get rich at the expense of the many more who lost, it will have been for nothing.

PART V HOMEWORK: Tweaks and Fine-Tunes

1. Will you add or overweight additional investment categories? Describe how this will change the risk-and-return profile of your investment strategy:

Category: ______________________________
Underweight or overweight: ________________________
Why? ____________________________________
Will this increase or decrease risk? __________________
Will this increase or decrease potential returns? ___________

Category: ______________________________
Underweight or overweight: ________________________
Why? ____________________________________
Will this increase or decrease risk? __________________
Will this increase or decrease potential returns? ___________

Category: ______________________________
Underweight or overweight: ________________________
Why? ____________________________________
Will this increase or decrease risk? __________________
Will this increase or decrease potential returns? ___________

2. Draw out an updated asset allocation breakdown:

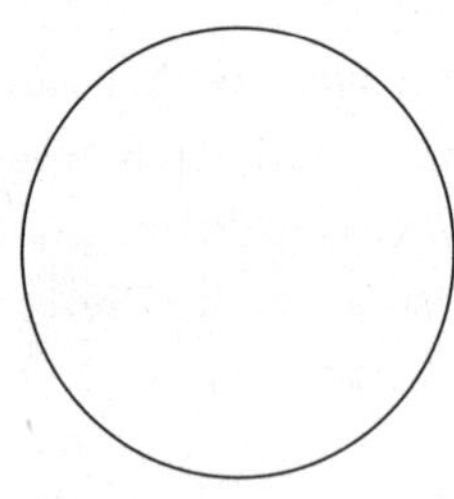

3. Make changes in your strategy! Make swaps and/or add funds, and set up any additional automations, if necessary.

RICH OLD LADY REFLECTION

For a long time, my dream was to be the Rich Old Lady who leaves 2,000% tips on her Miller High Lifes at the local watering hole. Well, bad news for bartenders and good news for anyone concerned for me after the opening Reno sequence: I'm sober now! But this hasn't stopped me from making spontaneous, joyful, regret-free giving a core part of my Rich Old Lady lifestyle. These days, it just looks more like leaving a twenty-dollar bill on the counter for a cup of diner coffee.

Because while it's great to make someone's day, I also do it because it makes *mine.*

I believe that when I feel bad, whether it's my low-grade depression, despair over our brutal, violent world, or compulsive behavior tendencies, the only way out is by helping others. And the sicker I feel, the *more* urgent it is to help someone else. Not because I need some sign that I'm a good person, but because it pulls me out of the suction of my own butthole for long enough to feel the fresh air. Don't get me wrong, therapy and self-reflection are important, but sometimes you just need to help a friend move a couch.

Recently, my friend went through a hard breakup, and I was able to send an eighty-dollar Uber to extract her from her ex's apartment, no questions asked. I have paid for the abortions of women I will never meet. With the help of my students and social media followers, I've sent over $50,000 in mutual aid to feed people in Gaza. This is community care, yes, which for me is also a form of radical *self-care.*

Luckily, this practice doesn't have to cost money! These can be acts of your time and energy. Still, feeling financially stable helps, even with energetic giving. Whether I'm investing in abortion pills or writing a sweet note to a friend, I believe radiating generosity in this life is the ultimate luxury. And, my desire to be recklessly thoughtful serves as a great motivation to understand my money.

PART VI

PEARLS OF WISDOM

Big-picture and advanced topics from the perspective of a Rich Old Lady

RETIREMENT CALCULATIONS

How much do I need to save for retirement?

"Invest 10% of your income for retirement" is advice you've probably heard before.

I have to say, generalized budgeting rules always make me nervous. I can appreciate the intent. They give us something tangible to work toward, and that makes people feel like they are in control. Perhaps a false sense. Because while a 10% investing rate might work for some, and is certainly an achievement, it will not work for everyone. Think about it. To reach the same goal, a fifty-two-year-old with no retirement savings will need to save and invest *significantly* more as a percentage of her income than a twenty-two-year-old who can spread the same work across many more years—and take maximum advantage of compounding.

To determine how much *you* need to invest, we need to look at *your* numbers. To begin, a quick reminder that in the introduction, we defined financial independence as having an annual investment income greater than your spending rate.

The first puzzle piece is your annual spending rate. More specifically, the annual spending rate when you are retired. Now, you don't need to predict your spending forty years from now down to the last dollar. That level of precision is neither realistic nor necessary. Start with a rough estimate; you can refine it as your circumstances become clearer. Oh, and make this budget in "today's dollars." We'll account for inflation later, in our calculation.

This exercise is deeply personal. Everyone is going to have or want a different retirement spending rate. Everyone should think through factors like homeownership versus rental costs and increased medical expenses, but this is also the time to consider your Rich Old Lady. Will she want spa treatments? To travel more? A yarn budget? As a reminder, you are still going to be yourself when you're older, so if you're a coffee snob now, well, you better book that into the plan. Whatever your spending rate, round it up by 10% to cover income taxes, 20% if you're in a high-tax state or will have lots of income in retirement. (If you're prioritizing Roth accounts, you can round down a little, because you won't owe taxes on those withdrawals.)

Next, multiply your spending rate by 25. That's what I am going to call your "Big Number." Your Big Number is the asset base you need to create investment income greater than your spending rate. Why 25? That assumes that your big investment number produces profit at a conservative rate of 4%. So, if you want to spend $60,000 per year in retirement, you multiply it by 25 to get $1.5 million. (In reverse, 4% of $1.5 million is $60,000.) Once you've grown your investments to $1.5 million, you have reached financial independence.

Now you've got your Big Number target! (At least, for the time being. We will bump this number up as stuff gets more expensive. That's inflation for you.)

The final step is determining how much we currently need to invest, monthly or annually, to reach the Big Number. To do this, I recommend trial and error using an online compound interest calculator, like the one on investor.gov. I admit it's not the most elegant approach, but I think it's better than asking you to dust off the ol' TI-89 or fire up an Excel spreadsheet.

Enter into the online calculator your current investments and years until retirement. For your estimated interest rate (or rate of return), I recommend using 4% or 5%. While we hope (and expect) you will earn much more than this, a 4% or 5% rate assumes a diversified strategy *and* takes inflation into account. Because we are only accounting for real growth beyond inflation, this gives us a sense of our future Big Number in today's dollars, not some big wacko inflated future dollars that would feel impossible to plan around. Then keep tweaking your monthly contribution until the calculator shows you hitting your Big Number by your desired financial independence date.

Let's practice using our example from above. Sly has a Big Number goal of $1.5 million for a spending rate of $60,000 in retirement. They would like to reach financial independence in thirty years and currently have $50,000 invested. They are making $80,000 a year after taxes.

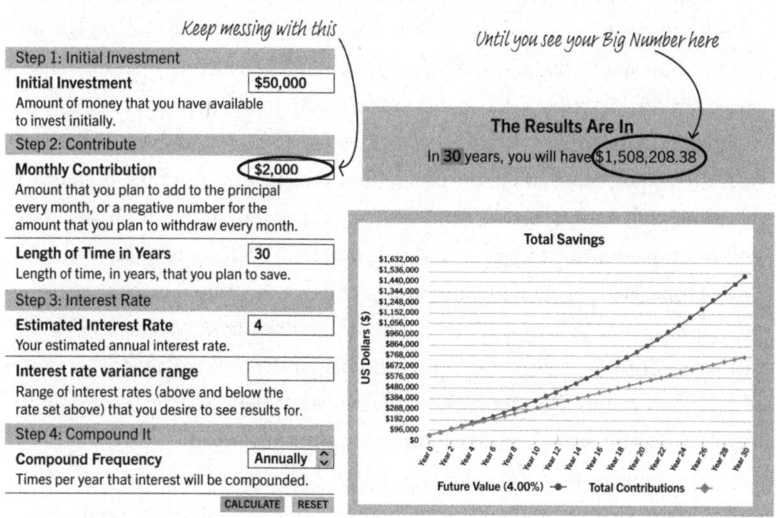

A 4% rate of return would require Sly to invest approximately $2,000 per month to reach their Big Number goal of $1.5 million. This amounts to 30% of their take-home pay. With a 5% rate of return, they would need to invest about $1,600 per month, which amounts to 24% of their take-home pay. (Or about 20% of their before-tax pay.)

Related, this is why you really cannot be sleeping on company matches. If Sly had a 10% company match, this would help lighten their load tremendously, reducing what they need to contribute by half or a third.

It's a crude calculation, I admit. For one, it doesn't account for life's vicissitudes or your future raises, or how making these contributions may not be possible now, but may be possible later. Still, I would like you to take a turn. But before you do, let's stop for a coffee refill. There we go, top you up. You're going to want it. As you putz around on the calculator, you may feel confronted by what you see. If you're like the vast majority of

Americans, you need to invest more for retirement. Potentially *a lot* more. The honest truth is that for most people on an average American salary, it is freaking hard to plan to live for thirty-plus years with no income. Think about it. For many of us, this will be nearly half of our adult life! And although investing is essential to growing our wealth beyond inflation, it can't spin thirty years of living expenses out of nothing. Investing for financial independence requires a serious outlay of consistent effort and time.

I know this can be disheartening. That's why I've waited until so late in the book to share this information with you. I feel a strong urge to shield you from this; to tell you to "just do your best!" and then "look over there, a squirrel!" And while I do believe that all you can do is your best, I also believe it's my responsibility to be honest about the challenge we're up against.

Here's what I can assure you: Even if you do not hit your target, you will be so glad you tried. It is so much better to rock up to your Golden Girls Gone Wild years with something and not nothing. You will not regret doing what you can. Like, maybe it's not bottle service at the club, but isn't your bestie showing up with a bar of dark chocolate and a case of Raspberry Rose Poppi for the *Vanderhouse Is Blind* season 74 reunion watch party still great, and way better than nothing?

Also, I admit that the calculation above is a bit of a worst-case scenario. Many people will have other sources of income in retirement, like passive business income or a pension—and if you do, fantastic. That's less work for your investments. This is also true of Social Security, the federal government's pension system for retirees. In 2025, the average Social Security payment was nearly $2,000 per month or $24,000 per year. For a future spending rate of $60,000, that leaves just $36,000 for you to cover. In our example from above, Social Security steps in and cuts Sly's personal burden *nearly in half.* But at the current political moment, Social Security is in serious jeopardy. May this retirement calculation exercise be the political motivation we need to do everything we can to save it.

How to Live Off Your Investments

The 4% withdraw rule was born from the Trinity study, which examined how long invested money lasts considering different withdrawal rates and asset allocations. They found that withdrawing 4% annually was sustainable, meaning the money lasted the thirty-year period, particularly with portfolios allocated 50% to 75% in stocks and the rest in bonds.

Here's the general idea. Even if you expect your portfolio to return an average of 7% in a portfolio of stocks and bonds, we still need to account for 3% inflation. To do this, we subtract inflation from our expected returns to get our inflation-adjusted returns. Seven percent minus 3% is 4%. These are our *real returns.* (It's like with guys on Hinge; automatically subtract three inches to get his *real* height.) The idea is that you are only skimming genuine profit off the top of your portfolio, never eating into the principal.

Not everyone believes that 4% is a *safe withdrawal rate.* This is especially true if you plan on living off your investments for very long periods. The study only looked at thirty-year periods, not perpetuity. If you have even one year where you need 10% or 20% of your portfolio because life does not always fit into a 4%-sized box, you will significantly reduce your portfolio's chances of survival. Then again, some market optimists think 4% is way too conservative or that it asks too much of the average investor. I think aiming for 4% is just fine.

As you contemplate retirement spending, keep this in mind: You are now on the market's timeline. We have to learn to work with the new reality that our retirements will be invested in the stock and bond markets. We know that market returns can be highly variable, and that won't change just because we are approaching or in retirement. Averages are just that, averages.

Therefore, the 4% rule should be treated as an average, too. In addition to your multiple stock and bond pots of money to draw from, enter into retirement with a strong cash reserve. In a strong stock market year, you can pull from your profits. In a down stock market year, avoid touching your stock investments and rely on cash or bonds instead. In great stock market years, take a little more and replenish your cash reserves to be ready for the next stock downturn. Do not fight the waves. Instead, allow them to carry you.

10-MINUTE MISSION

Let's walk through a retirement calculation together. Pull up both a regular calculator and the compound interest calculator provided by investor.gov.

How much money do you want to spend each year in retirement (in today's dollars)? Round up by 10% to 20% for taxes if you are primarily pulling from a Traditional/tax-deferred account.

*$*________________

Subtract any other sources of retirement income.

\- *$*________________
\- *$*________________
= *$*________________

Multiply your spending rate by 25 to get your Big Number.

*$*________________

Using a 4% rate of return, where does your current rate of investing land you at your ideal retirement age? What about 5%?

____

____

How much would you need to increase your monthly contributions to reach your Big Number?

____

____

35

SOCIAL SECURITY

Will I get Social Security?

Social Security is the federal government's retirement safety net, providing retirement income to elders. If you pay income taxes in the US, you are paying into the program right now. Social Security and Medicare are a separate tax, called FICA taxes, that we pay in addition to our federal and state income taxes.

Despite what you've heard about Social Security "running out," the program will disappear only if politicians kill it. A lie frequently parroted by those who want to eliminate social programs is that our Social Security is being squandered away by immoral politicians. While one could certainly mount this argument regarding our general income taxes, it is not true of the Social Security trust, whose assets are, by law, only used to pay Social Security benefits.

Now, it is true that Social Security has a *funding shortfall*. But here's what's really going on. Social Security was designed as what we call a "pay as you go" pension system. The trust is funded by taxpayers and the money is then passed through to elders (called *old-age recipients*) and folks with disabilities. Yes, young people pay for old people's benefits, but the program keeps track of what you pay in, and eventually someday when you're old, young people will pay the taxes that fund your Social Security.

Sound like a pyramid scheme? I mean, yeah, it kinda is. (But then again, *so is the stock market*!) But the funding shortfall isn't caused by deceit; it is caused by (drumroll, please) a slowdown in population growth. The stats nerds did their best when the program was created, but they predicted a future where we were going to be having *way* more babies. *Sweet, sweet little taxpayers!* Between a shortage of wages to fund the program and a flood of boomers aging into Social Security and collecting checks, there's not enough active funding. This does not seem to be improving anytime soon, with the birthrate declining in recent years.

But the situation is not as dire as people think. From now until the year 2033, the Social Security trust is fully funded, and old-age recipients will receive 100% of their benefits. After that point, the incoming taxes will fund a majority but not all of the benefits. Beginning in 2033 and projected through 2097, there will be a gradual decline in benefits from 79% to 69%. So, even young people are expected to receive about three-quarters of their benefits. This is not ideal, but it is also not *nothing.* And this is if no changes are made!

The program is not carved in stone; policy adjustments can and should be made to address the funding gap. For example, this problem could be solved by allowing for more legal immigration or removing the Social Security tax cap. And HELLO, just because the population growth is shrinking *does not* mean the taxable wealth base is! That wealth is now just concentrated at the top. Tax math is reworked ALL THE TIME, especially to benefit the rich. If I were queen, I would supplement current funding with an additional tax on the ultrawealthy. Because it is only possible to become ultrawealthy via the exploitation of low-wage workers, who deserve and would benefit most from a fully funded Social Security program, I believe it should be the responsibility of the ultrawealthy to make up for the shortfall.

To ensure our access to Social Security, vote, yes, but also stop spreading misinformation. The latter plays right into the hands of the politicians who want to crush it. I admit that the program is far from perfect. It was perhaps naive to think that population growth would never slow. (Maybe, if they want us to have more babies in this country, they should make it a little bit easier to have babies. Just spitballin' here!) And yet, the program remains a vital lifeline keeping millions of our elders out of abject poverty; particularly elder women who spent a lifetime locked out of financial opportunity. I'm open to exploring alternatives, but that becomes impossible if we let politicians convince people the real problem is corrupt leftists squandering the trust fund on transgender operas in Colombia or whatever. That's not happening.

To all the libertarians and tax hackers who hate paying FICA taxes because *they can invest that money better themselves,* I mean, maybe? But what if that doesn't work? The S&P 500 is not guaranteed to repeat its past performance. Returns are not in our control. And when the market tanks, as it inevitably does from time to time, you know what diva doesn't bat an eyelash extension? Social Security. In ninety years, in good times and bad, Social Security has never missed a check. To me, having a source of retirement income that is completely detached from corporate share prices is not just comforting; it is essential diversification.

For your very unsexy afternoon activity, create an account at SSA.gov. Then go to "My Social Security." It will display the amount you are expected to receive in payments, determined by what you've paid in and the age you begin to withdraw. For those born in 1960 or after, sixty-seven is the age at which you can receive your *full benefit*. You'll get less if you choose an *early benefit* at age sixty-two and more if you take a *delayed benefit* at age seventy.

How do we integrate this number into our planning? I'll admit, it's hard to say. On the one hand, your expected payout figure will be bigger than the number you see currently, as it will be adjusted upward for inflation. On the other, benefits could be further reduced, or if certain politicians have their way, Social Security will be eliminated. For this reason, I agree with the financial planners who recommend that you don't rely on Social Security for planning purposes. I am trying to hit my target without the help of Social Security—*and* I remain hopeful about and will fight for the program's future.

10-MINUTE MISSION

Create an account at SSA.gov and go to My Social Security. Provide your best estimate for your average annual future salary. Fill in the following:

Early monthly benefit: $______________________

Full monthly benefit: $______________________

Delayed monthly benefit: $______________________

To determine your expected annual benefit, multiply by 12: $______________

36

WHAT NEXT

I've maxed out my retirement account. What do I do next?

Wow! Congratulations. Maxing out your retirement account is impressive, hard work. Keep up this level of skill and your Rich Old Lady will be wiring her Life Alert button to the piña colada machine and at the front of the conga line twice daily.

Your first order of business is to celebrate. Then, once you've treated yourself nicely, take stock. Are you feeling stretched thin? Then rest! You've done what is needed for now. If you have more financial fight left in you, then read on.

There are a few reasons *why* you may want to keep going, if you're able:

The more money you invest, the closer in you yank that retirement date. Or you keep the retirement date where it is and increase your retirement spending rate, leading to the nicer apartment at Blue Hair Oaks, or an extra trip every year, or shopping at the fancy grocery store instead of the discount outlet, or more Chappell Roan concerts, which by then will probably be at those casinos on the coast. Having more investments, like having more money in the bank, only creates more freedom and options.

As you know by now, the contribution limit you've bumped up against has nothing to do with how much money you will actually need in retirement. Instead, we want to follow the lead of our personal RETIREMENT CALCULATIONS from chapter 34.

To invest more, you need to find the next spot to invest. (To collect more treasure, you need another Caboodles that you can pack full of treasures.) That could be another tax-advantaged account you qualify for, or it might be a regular degular brokerage account.

Tax-Advantaged Accounts Beyond Your Workplace Retirement Account

1. Roth IRA or Backdoor Roth IRA

If you haven't opened one already, a Roth IRA is an easy choice, so long as you are under the income requirement. If you earn too much to contribute to a Roth IRA, a Backdoor Roth IRA *might* be the answer. It's a sneaky, mostly legal way for high earners to get money into a Roth. But of course, there are rules. To nail the financial triple axel that is a Backdoor Roth IRA, see the instructions on page 244.

2. Health Savings Account

Check with your health insurance provider to see if you qualify for an HSA. Some folks choose to use their HSA as a bonus, tax-advantaged retirement account.

More on HSAs in the next chapter.

3. Mega Backdoor Roth via your workplace retirement account

Not every workplace retirement account allows it, but if it does, you could contribute up to an additional $46,500 to a Roth account via your 401(k). And that's *beyond* your $23,500 traditional contribution! Mega, indeed. Like a Backdoor Roth IRA, this won't be for everyone, and there are rules. See the instructions on page 244.

4. SEP IRA for self-employed income

If you also have self-employed or contract income (that you will report on your taxes), you could contribute approximately 20% of those earnings to a SEP IRA. For a refresher on self-employed retirement accounts, head back to chapter 10, RULES.

Investing in a Regular Degular Brokerage Account

An easy option available to anyone is investing in a regular brokerage account, which you can do with any amount and for any reason, including retirement. Do not be scared of a brokerage account! They're great! What a brokerage account lacks in tax breaks, they make up for in flexibility, including easy access to your money sooner than retirement age. Every year, I try to max out my retirement accounts first and then scootch right on over to my brokerage account without hesitation.

Amy and her wife are both high-earning, overworked lawyers together earning nearly $1 million per year. They each invest the maximum $23,500 in their respective 401(k) accounts, but they want to make the most of their good fortune and know they can't work like this until retirement age. They reached out to me because they don't want the IRS's rando retirement account limits to stop them from doing as much as they can right now. After exploring their limited options, they decided to add $200,000 to their regular brokerage accounts. And this is how it goes. Wealthy people tend to end up with more money in brokerage accounts than they do in retirement accounts.

Whether you're in Amy's position or not, never let a lack of retirement account options prevent you from doing the real work of investing. It is way better to start today with a brokerage account than to wait around for another year or heaven forbid five years because you can't figure out which retirement account you qualify for.

As for your investment strategy, you can simply replicate whatever you decided was best in your 401(k)—unless this money has a different goal. My brokerage and retirement accounts look the same because they share the same goal of moving me toward my financial independence. Remember, our hopes, dreams, and flair for risk are expressed through the investments themselves, *not* the account. The account just tells us how the money is taxed.

We may want to make a few adjustments around taxation, though. Because of how they're built, ETFs tend to be slightly more tax-efficient, so consider using index ETFs instead of index mutual funds in a brokerage account. Dividends on REITs are often taxed at your highest income rate, so keep those inside the tax shelter of a retirement account.

With a brokerage account, you will need to report your investment earnings each year, so earnings that come from dividends, interest, or *realized* capital gains. You "make real" a gain (or loss) by selling out of an investment. You do not pay taxes on *unrealized gains.* Don't worry, you won't have to bust out the abacus to painstakingly tally up investment earnings yourself. Your brokerage bank does that. At the beginning of each year (usually in February), the bank will provide you with a *consolidated 1099* (or separate 1099s for dividends, interest, and realized capital gains). Use this document to make a paper airplane. Just kidding! Slap it on your pile of tax documents to deal with come tax time.

Taking the Back Door

Backdoor Roth IRA

If you don't qualify for a Roth IRA, you can weasel your way in by putting money into a Traditional IRA first and then transferring the money to a Roth IRA. That's the "back door."

1. Open a Traditional IRA
2. Contribute to the Traditional IRA
3. Convert to a Roth IRA ASAP (or transfer the money, if you've already got one!)

Never hesitate to call your brokerage bank customer service for assistance. They are paid to help you.

Mega Backdoor Roth

Some 401(k) programs will allow a mega backdoor maneuver, which potentially allows you to contribute up to $46,500 in Roth money to your 401(k). Here's how this works:

1. Ask HR or your 401(k) bank whether your 401(k) supports a mega backdoor Roth

2. Max out your 401(k) normally
3. Make an "after-tax contribution" to your 401(k) and immediately convert to a Roth IRA or Roth 401(k)

If you choose the Mega Backdoor Roth method, you are not subject to the usual income or contribution limits. In 2025, you may be able to contribute up to $46,500 via a Mega Backdoor Roth, though your employer may have limits due to funding rules. Ask to be sure!

The Pro Rata Rule

Here's where it gets convoluted. Both Backdoor Roth and Mega Backdoor Roth maneuvers get complicated if you already have money in a Traditional IRA or SEP IRA. Think about it like this: With the Backdoor, you're moving money from Traditional (pre-tax) to Roth (post-tax). For it to become post-tax, *you have to pay taxes.* When dealing only with new money, it's all good: You *are* going to pay income taxes on this money because you aren't deducting these contributions.

But if you've *already* got Traditional money, who's to say that the older, existing Traditional money shouldn't get moved to the Roth first? This would be a Roth conversion, a movement from pre- to post-tax, and you would owe income taxes. So, when you already have existing Traditional money, the *pro rata rule* requires that you move proportional amounts of old and new Traditional money. (By *new,* I mean the money passing through a Traditional IRA as a backdoor to your Roth.) Honestly, the calculation gets a tad gnarly. Personally, I'd pursue a Backdoor only if (1) I did not have Traditional IRA or SEP IRA dollars, or (2) I had only a small amount of Traditional IRA dollars and was comfortable converting them all to Roth, paying all the necessary taxes.

Please consult a tax professional.

What Is FIRE?

Those in the *FIRE (Financial Independence, Retire Early)* movement aim to invest as much money as possible, with the goal of retiring as young as possible. Achieving FIRE usually requires both a serious commitment to living frugally and a high income. Within the FIRE movement, it is common to see people investing up to 70% of their income.

While I, too, am aiming for financial independence, I don't quite fit in with the subculture of FIRE bloggers and Redditors. I find it admirable to minimize unnecessary consumption where you can, but just like anything, it can be taken too far. Some of the tactics you read about in the online FIRE forums can border on the psychotic. Guys, it is extreme loser behavior to measure out your wife's shampoo usage or refuse to tip service workers when you're already very rich.

Reducing spending to such an absolute bare minimum clashes with both my personal values and financial philosophy. I hold generosity and supporting community structures as core principles—not only as a moral stance but as a vital investment in the future I aspire to live in. This is a position that is at odds with the hoarding encouraged by some in the FIRE movement.

So, I will be working to become financially independent sooner rather than later, but you won't catch me cosplaying pioneer times just to retire alone by forty-three. For me, financial independence is about freedom of choice. I want the option to not have to work, or to choose work because it feels meaningful. This is more along the lines of what I envision for myself: having ever more flexibility to choose my work as I get closer to financial independence.

If you're looking for a thoughtful take on financial independence that prioritizes values-driven approaches to rethinking work and wealth, I highly recommend *Work Optional* by Tanja Hester, as well as *Cashing Out* by Kiersten and Julien Saunders.

37

HEALTH SAVINGS ACCOUNTS

Should I use my HSA to invest for retirement?

I think, by now, we know better than to believe anything is a "secret hack to wealth." Health Savings Accounts (HSAs), a darling of the personal finance internet, are no exception.

An HSA is an account where you can save money for healthcare expenses. It's available only for folks with high-deductible health insurance plans; like a motorcycle sidecar for your HDHP. You can contribute to an HSA (so can your employer, if they do that sort of thing), and the money is yours to keep forever, rolled over from year to year. For this reason, most HSAs allow you to invest the money held inside.

Here's where it gets spicy. The money you put into an HSA may *never* be taxed if it's used for *qualified medical expenses*. An HSA is *triple tax-advantaged*; there are no income taxes on the way in, no income taxes on the way out, and no taxes on investment gains. From a taxation standpoint, this gives it a leg up on a retirement account, which always has one point of taxation.

HSA Taxation When Used for Qualified Medical Expenses

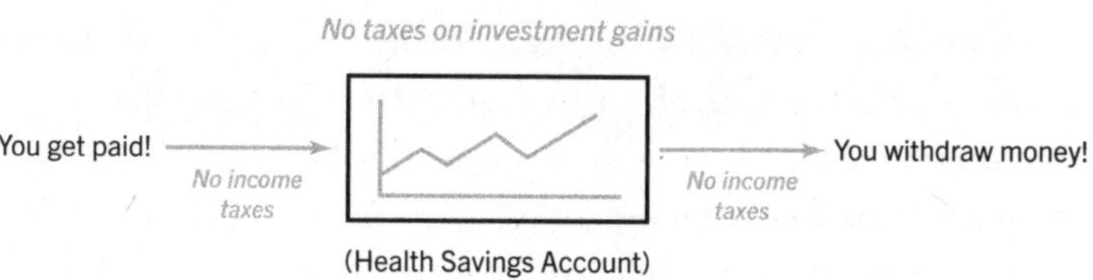

Qualified medical expenses include just about everything you'd consider healthcare except your monthly insurance payments. Surgery, crutches, IVF, even your fancy GOOP sunscreen counts. You can expect to have plenty of healthcare costs in retirement, using HSA funds to reimburse yourself. If you're worried that you won't have enough healthcare costs, you can save receipts from earlier years. The withdrawal does not have to happen in the same year you spent money on healthcare.

And if you are indeed a miraculous exception to the inevitabilities of aging and have no medical expenses in retirement to justify tax-free withdrawals from an HSA, not to worry. After the IRS's retirement age of fifty-nine and a half, any withdrawals that can't be justified with a healthcare expense will be treated as income, same as a Traditional/tax-deferred retirement account. So, if you wanted to pull $10,000 from your HSA to throw yourself a ninetieth birthday rager, you would not be penalized, but you would need to pay income taxes on that amount. (If you pull the money to, say, throw yourself a bachelor party next month, both taxes *and* penalties will apply. Take it from my friend who accidentally used his HSA debit card at an ATM in a strip club during one such soiree. He was on the hook for taxes and penalties, despite his claim that—*sigh!!!*—lap dances have health benefits.)

HSA Taxation When Used for Non-Medical Expenses in Retirement (Traditional/Tax-deferred Taxation)

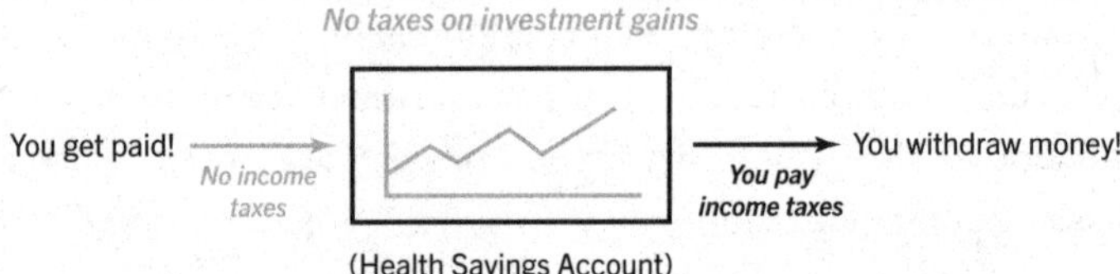

Because it is the only completely tax-free way to invest when the money is used for qualified medical expenses, money nerds see the account space as too valuable to use on the Robitussin you may need next month. With an HSA, your money can grow for decades while making the most of tax-free compounding.

Sounds pretty great, huh? And it is true that an HSA *can* be a great way to save for healthcare expenses in retirement for a person who is young, healthy, and has extra money to save. But there's always a catch. An HSA is not great for everyone (or society, for that matter). If you are choosing a healthcare plan with an HSA, you are likely picking the plan with less coverage. And when people have less health insurance coverage, they frequently put off the care they need. My apologies to the HSA evangelists but having adequate healthcare coverage trumps the tax benefits of an HSA every day.

That said, I have one. It's not exactly by choice. As a self-employed person, my options for healthcare are limited. I buy the cheapest plan on the New York state marketplace, which is still $700 per month for very little coverage. I choose it because I'm relatively healthy and paying more feels criminal. It also happens to be compatible with an HSA. So, it's the first place I max out each year because I can't resist the tax savings. But I have made the promise to myself that having a high-deductible plan with an HSA *cannot* come at the expense of my health now. Those tax-free healthcare dollars sure won't do me a lot of good if I'm not around to use them.

As with any money that can be invested, the first step is to devise a strategy as per your goals for that money. If you want to use an HSA the way it was intended, reimbursing yourself for healthcare costs throughout the year, you'll likely want to keep the money in cash. It's too risky to invest money you might need in the near term. If you are committed to paying for healthcare costs out of pocket and want to use the HSA as a turbocharged retirement account, then you can invest the money. I invest my HSA exactly like I invest my retirement accounts. You can also split the difference. Keep some cash available to use and invest the rest.

2025 Health Savings Account Contribution Limits				
Coverage Type	Contribution Limit	Catch-Up Contribution (Age 55+)	Minimum Deductible	Maximum Out-of-Pocket
Self-Only	$4,300	$1,000	$1,650	$8,300
Family	$8,550	$1,000 per eligible individual	$3,300	$16,600

We Are Getting Scammed

People love their HSAs, but it's imperative that we recognize them as a product of conservative efforts to erode healthcare benefits during Obamacare (Affordable Care Act) negotiations. The argument was simple: Make people "healthcare consumers" by forcing them to bear more of the up-front costs of medical care while offering a tax-advantaged way to save for those expenses. In theory, this would encourage price shopping and curb rising healthcare costs.

In reality? Healthcare costs exploded, and price shopping became impossible in a system designed to be opaque and confusing. You can't compare costs when providers straight-up won't tell you the price of a procedure and when different insurers negotiate different rates.

So instead of becoming savvier consumers, surprise! People just don't get healthcare. Because it's too expensive. Because it's too hard to navigate. Because even finding a doctor who takes your insurance can feel like a full-time job. There is no version of myself I hate more than the one pushed to the edge of her personality on the phone with health insurance, trying to understand why I was billed for something I thought would be covered. The notion that personal responsibility could fix a system whose fundamental incentive is corporate profit, not patient care, was always a fantasy.

HSAs are just another version of the same "hey, buddy, you're on your own" and "good luck with all that" shift we saw away from pensions to the 401(k) model. Healthcare can and should be a benefit; something you receive because you have paid massive taxes to a government that should be providing it. Now it's your job to save for it, plan for it, and hope you never receive a claim denial in the mail marked with those three little words: Not Medically Necessary.

38

HOMEOWNERSHIP

Is owning a home a good investment?

In an ideal world, everyone owns a home. A cozy, safe place to sit by the fire and pet the cats, free from the whims of negligent landlords and the crushing weight of escalating rents. Unfortunately, we don't live in an ideal world. Housing prices have soared beyond what anyone could have imagined a generation ago. The dream of homeownership now feels less like a rite of adult passage and more like a luxury for the already wealthy.

In turn, this has spurred many an internet argument about whether it still makes sense to buy a home. And if you dig deep to the core of the "rent versus buy" debate, what you'll find is that much of it really comes down to how you'll afford a place to live in retirement.

Buying a home that is paid off before retirement is the traditional route, but even with a paid-off home, you'll face property taxes and the occasional roof replacement. On the flip side, if you're renting, you'll need a financial plan that accounts for climbing rents.

Here's the good news: There are multiple paths forward. If you're able to comfortably invest for retirement *and* buy a home, that's a solid option. If buying a home feels like an impossible mountain to climb—or perhaps you simply do not want to spend your weekends at Home Depot—then you'll need to redirect a larger percentage of your income into investments to cover rent in retirement. Both options are valid.

If you are like me, you may find it a tad infuriating to talk about personal compromise within a system that needs fixing, especially when we are talking about something as fundamental as having a place to live. We need massive policy shifts, starting with a push to build affordable housing at a scale we've never seen before. Doing so will require massive public investment and stronger public planning, such as creating dense, transit-connected communities built where people actually want to live.

At the same time, we have to reckon with the deeper contradiction we've built into the system: Housing is treated as an investment first and a human need second, which means that every gain in value for one owner makes it that much harder for the next person to find a home. There's a real conversation to be had about whether we're comfortable with a system where price is the organizing principle for who gets to live somewhere—locking in and deepening existing inequities.

I wish I had the answers. For now, we will focus on what's possible today. And because we are Rich Old Ladies, we will find a way to make it work—and maybe even make it beautiful.

Is a Home a Good Investment?

Although it varies by region, typically home values grow about 4% annually—less than 1% after inflation. (That said, returns were double this in the last five years.) BUT what this figure does not account for are homeownership costs—like property taxes, insurance, maintenance, repairs, the expenses of buying and selling a home, and mortgage interest.

Most people who buy a home will take a loan from a bank, which they will pay back with interest. A lot of interest. Consider a thirty-year fixed mortgage at 7%: By the time it's paid off, the interest alone will have more than doubled the home's cost. After all is said and done, it is not unusual for a house to cost three or four times more than the sticker price. And considering that a significant amount of these costs are upfront, such as closing fees (2% to 5% of the home's value), short-term homeownership (less than seven to ten years) is rarely a good deal in the traditional *return on investment (ROI)* sense.

Even long-term homeownership may produce a negative ROI once the costs of homeownership are factored in. Mortgages are celebrated as "forced investing," but they're also "forced spending." Profit isn't just your sale price minus the sticker price you paid; it's what you get once you've subtracted everything you've poured into the home. And most people don't tally up those costs honestly. When you crunch the unbiased numbers, it's hard to argue a home is a better investment than, say, a broad stock market index fund.

That said, you have to live somewhere. A home isn't just an investment; it meets the most essential needs of human beings. My friends Piggy and Kitty from the *Bitches Get Riches* blog put it best: "You cannot sleep inside a stock. You cannot pee and poop inside a bond." No matter how much money you have, some portion of it must be allocated to provide the very real and tangible place you will cook your meals and keep your troll doll collection. (Just me?) When done wisely, homeownership can be a twofer: a place to store some long-term value and a place to live.

For the purchase to be wise, it must fit within a budget that allows you to save and invest beyond the costs of owning your home. If you end up with too little liquid cash and investments to live your life, you might end up having to sell the home anyway.

But there's another reason to be cautious: a lack of investment diversification. Think back to our conversation about asset allocation. Investors spread their money not only across different asset classes but also across hundreds or thousands of individual investments within those classes. It would be an extraordinary risk to put all your money into a single stock. Putting all your money into a single piece of real estate is no different.

We cannot have an honest conversation about risk and whether a home is a good investment without acknowledging the risks of man-made climate disaster. The truth is, we don't really own our homes—the climate does—alongside the banks, insurance companies, and local and federal governments. It's a strange and heart-wrenching thing, to be writing these words as the Eaton and Palisades fires tear through Los Angeles, destroying entire neighborhoods filled with cherished homes. My deep love goes out to everyone who has lost their home to a climate disaster—and especially for those who face the secondary betrayal of being screwed over by their insurers or forced to pay a mortgage on a home that has been wiped from the earth. This has been the cruel reality for so many victims of Hawai'i's Lahaina fire. It is not hard to imagine a scenario where you spend a lifetime recovering the value of your home or a future where the cost of insuring a home doubles or triples or quadruples. So much for "stabilizing" your costs.

I'm sharing this not to discourage you from pursuing homeownership but to encourage you to approach it with eyes wide open. Risk is a fact of life, especially when you are out there doing cool shit. Trying to eliminate risk isn't possible, nor is it the goal. Instead, recognize the risks and take deliberate steps to balance and manage them wisely.

Rent-Versus-Buy Calculation

In this calculation, it is generally assumed that the two options are: (1) buy a home, or (2) rent and invest the savings in something like an S&P 500 index fund. The calculation can get somewhat complex; I suggest using *The New York Times'* rent-versus-buy calculator. I've seen many of these calculations in recent years, and I'll just tell you: Renting plus investing the difference usually comes out ahead, even when accounting for rising rents. Don't take my word for it, though.

At the same time, the results of this calculation are not handed down from the Divine Goddess of Truth and Expected Market Returns. Like any financial model, it relies on assumptions. For one, it assumes you'll actually invest the difference. Which, let's be really real, many renters don't. A mortgage, for better or worse, enforces discipline in a way that self-directed investing just . . . doesn't. The model also makes assumptions about the fate of the stock market and your dream Craftsmen bungalow. While asset prices will generally rise over time, there's no guarantee which will perform best for you and your unique timing and situation.

One final note about the ROI calculation: It doesn't account for happiness, which deserves consideration, too. For some, homeownership brings pride and stability. For others, it can be a source of significant stress or financial regret. When it comes to a decision as meaningful as buying a home, you must include your own desires and feelings in the equation. Not someone else's. Not your parents', not society's. Yours. Take them seriously, and make sure they're part of your calculus.

The Pros and Cons of Homeownership

Pros

1. Build equity while you're paying for housing anyway.
2. It partially builds "rent control" by locking in your monthly housing costs.
3. It diversifies your investments.
4. Although not ideal, you can leverage it in retirement with a *reverse mortgage* if needed.
5. Homes have been an effective way to build intergenerational wealth.
6. Emotional benefits, like stability and place attachment, can be significant.

Cons

1. It will cost more than you think. No, more than that. *More!* There you go.
2. The idea that homeownership represents a form of "rent control" is at least partially a myth, considering homeowners will *not* have control over property tax rates, insurance rates, HOA fees, and the increasing costs of repairs.
3. Renting affordably and investing the difference may be the more lucrative option.
4. A single large investment, like buying a home, can significantly increase your financial risk—especially if it requires taking on substantial debt and comes at the expense of building a diversified portfolio of assets.

5. It limits your flexibility—unlike renting, leaving a home isn't easy.

How to Prepare to Buy a House

Weeping while scrolling Zillow is an honored pastime, although probably not adequate preparation for buying a home. If it's your dream, focus your energy on financial prep:

- **Improve your credit score:** Aim for 620 or higher to secure better mortgage terms.
- **Pay down debt:** Lenders typically want your *debt-to-income (DTI) ratio* below 36%—meaning all your monthly debt payments, including your future mortgage, should be less than 36% of your gross income.
- **Increase your income:** This also has the effect of reducing your DTI—and puts you in a better position to handle the financial commitment of homeownership.
- **Save up cash:** Save 3% to 20% of the home's price for a down payment, 2% to 5% for closing costs, and a bit extra for peace of mind and unexpected costs.
- **Work out your budget:** Determine what you can realistically afford each month, and compare that against the monthly price of owning a home, including all costs. I strongly suggest talking to three to five homeowner friends about their costs of owning.
- **Consider loan options:** FHA loans for first-time homebuyers allow down payments as low as 3.5% but require additional insurance payments called *PMI (private mortgage insurance).* USDA rural development loans offer more lenient terms for rural buyers.

When you're ready, the next step is to get preapproved for a mortgage by submitting your financial documents to a lender. This process determines how much of a loan you qualify for—but be warned, this amount might be more than you can reasonably afford. The bank loves it when you take out a big ol' home loan that you will need to pay back with interest! Remember: The bank doesn't set your budget; you do.

Likewise, just because you can put down 3.5% doesn't mean you should. Smaller down payments make loans more expensive over time. Sometimes, significantly so. As part of your preparation, play around with a mortgage loan cost calculator like the one from Bankrate. Do it! See how much more interest (and insurance) you'll pay if you put 3.5% down versus 20%. While putting 20% down isn't realistic for everyone, doing so would significantly reduce your overall costs. Find a compromise that works for you.

Last, think creatively. If you're priced out of your area, consider teaming up with family or friends to buy a multiunit property. By banding together, people can better navigate affordability while also building community and resilience. Keep in mind: Unless you split the property legally, you'll usually be signing onto one joint mortgage. If so, you can sometimes explore a *condo conversion,* a legal process that allows you to split ownership into individual units if needed. Check your local laws; some places make this process easier than others. Another option: If someone you trust already owns property, many places (like California, Oregon, and Colorado) have loosened rules to allow homeowners to build secondary units in their backyard or over garages.

Whether you go down the path of homeownership or not, I hope you can be happy. If you're a renter, revel in not knowing what repointing the chimney means. Ditch out of your lease and move to Istanbul with a month's notice. If you buy a home, be proud of this financial achievement, invite me to all your house parties, and enjoy making your space lovelier and more welcoming with each passing year.

39

CHILDREN

Should I invest for my kids, and how?

You are welcome to fight me on this, but I believe that the best financial gift you can give your kids is to not become reliant on them later in life. When you don't invest for yourself, it's hardly a selfless act, because you will become someone else's responsibility. I happen to believe that investing for your kids is a pretty advanced financial move, but not because it's difficult. Anyone can open up and fund an account. I just happen to consider it advanced because it is already hard to get enough saved and invested for yourself, which I humbly offer as your first and most important order of business.

I totally get it; no one wants their child to rely on student loans to access higher education. But a strategic, judicious student loan doesn't condemn anyone to live in poverty; not investing in your own retirement will ensure that you live in poverty.

I've had lots of students, mostly moms, who are members of the sandwich generation: middle-aged people caring for both their kids and their parents. One student, Claudia, told me of the mixed emotions of "being her parents' 401(k) plan." She has profound gratitude for the sacrifices her parents made, emigrating to the US so that she could access education and opportunity. At the same time, she feels overwhelmed by their financial need. And to add to the pressure, she felt she wasn't doing enough for her kids.

She was, however, maintaining her retirement contributions to which I assured her absolutely counts as leaving a legacy. When you invest for retirement, you're not just investing in a future you; you're building a future for someone else, too. In addition to creating far less financial stress for your heirs, any money you don't use can passed to your kids, your siblings, or even a friend.

Years ago, after a particularly brutal workweek, an artist friend and I were decompressing the way we always did: eating gummy bears, venting about money, and asking life's big questions like, "Would you marry a ninety-seven-year-old billionaire oil tycoon?" When she answered "Obviously," it made me laugh—but it also stirred something in me. That was the moment I decided: I'm the Sugar Mommy now. Right then and there, I pulled up my computer and made her a *beneficiary* on one of my retirement accounts. If the gods summon me to the Eternal Sabbatical before I get the chance to retire, I am comforted by the fact that I'll be funding her art as part of my Rich Old Lady legacy. Setting your retirement account beneficiaries is a great first step to building yours, too.

Beyond beneficiary forms, a lot of parents ask me: How do I actually invest for my kids without shortchanging myself? My easy-peasy recommendation for parents who are juggling multiple goals and family commitments is always this: Instead of using a complicated account that limits how you use the money, like a 529 plan, simply invest money for yourself, in your name. If you end up ahead, you can always gift it later. This option gives you the most control to divert funds to where they need to go, on the timeline that works best for everyone. It really is easy to gift money, and the best way to do that is by investing in a no-fuss brokerage account.

For those on solid footing and who feel ready to directly invest for the children in your life—Cool Aunties, I'm also talkin' to you!—let's explore your options. But because I know moms are busy, I want to start with the summary, and then we'll expand from there.

Kids' account options, summarized for busy moms:

- **Use a Brokerage Account:** Open one in your name, even if the funds are "earmarked" for your child. This gives you the most flexibility for how the money can be used.

- **Open a 529 Plan:** This is a good option for saving for a child's college expenses—but the tax benefits really only pay off if you invest and let the funds grow over time.
- **Consider Your Timeline:** Investing may not be suitable if you need the money in a few years. A simple option is to open a high-yield savings account with your child in mind.

A 529 plan is a tax-advantaged bank account that holds investments. Yet another Caboodles! It's similar to a Roth IRA, but instead of retirement, the money must be used for education expenses to remain tax- and penalty-free. 529 plans hold stock and bond mutual funds, which is to say that investment markets power your returns. The whole point of the 529 plan is to act as a tax shelter for any profit made investing.

The discussion for kids' investment accounts might feel like a déjà vu of part II on retirement accounts. That's because the options depend on, you guessed it, taxes. As we now know, there is an inverse relationship between tax benefits and flexibility. While a 529 plan may lower your tax bill, it has complicated rules for use. If you were to invest in a brokerage account in your name—even if it's earmarked for a child—there are no tax benefits, but there are also no complicated rules. Make that decision based on whether the tax benefit is worth it to you.

Reaping the full benefit of a tax shelter means having a lot of profit to shelter. Generally, this means investing consistently and for a long time. So, before we dive into the details of these various tax-advantaged options, let's first step back and ask whether it even makes sense to use one. In my opinion, a 529 plan is not for everyone, for example parents of teenage children.

Parker, a student turned friend of mine, has two teenagers, and wanted to explore her options for saving for college. "Everyone is suggesting I open 529 plans," she said. "But I'm not sure." Since her kids were only a few years from college, we agreed that investing in the stock market didn't make sense. Why risk it? And without investment growth, a 529 offers little tax benefit. (Depending on your state, you may be able to deduct your contributions on your state taxes, but Parker lives in California, where there is no 529 state tax deduction.) Without much tax benefit, Parker would have just found herself with a very complicated bank account. Instead, she has decided to open a high-yield savings account for her kids' college expenses.

By contrast, my student Zara opened a 529 plan for her niece when she was born. Because of the long investing timeline, Zara invested the 529 plan in a combination of stock and bond index funds. The 529 plan is worth the extra effort because the expectation is that there will be lots of investment growth to shelter.

Always let your needs—your investing goals, timeline, and risk tolerance—determine your investing strategy, starting with your asset allocation. Should you invest in stocks? Bonds? Cash? Some combination? Lead with your desired investment strategy, and *then* back into the most appropriate account to hold those investments.

You're doing great, Mom. (Or Dad, Parent, Bonus Parent, Cool Auntie, Guncle, etc.!)

Account Specifics When Investing for Kids

1. Invest in a Brokerage Account in Your Name

As I mentioned before, the easiest thing you can do is invest in a brokerage account in your name, which you then gift to them when the time comes. This option gives you total control. You can give your child a gift or not. You can use the money to pay for college or something else entirely. You can do so on your timeline if and only if it's right for you. *And for them.*

There's a misconception that putting the money in a kid's name somehow amplifies the future compound growth. It doesn't! Yes, the timeline matters, and it matters that the money was invested, but it does not matter whose name is on the bank account. That said, if you sell off investments to gift money, it is true that you will (likely) have to pay a 15% tax on the profit from the sale. (The tax is only on the portion that comes from investment gains—not the full amount.)

People also often misunderstand the rules around gifting; this probably stems from confusion around the *gift tax*. It is actually very easy to give money to your kids (or to anyone). In 2025, you can gift up to $19,000 a year to someone without even letting the IRS know. Go over that, and you still don't pay gift taxes—the IRS just keeps a running total against your lifetime giving limit: $13.99 million if you're single, \$27.98 million if you're married. So, yeah, most of us probably don't need to worry about the gift tax.

Now, onto the kids' accounts. The following are all tax-advantaged options held in their name.

2. 529 Plans

A 529 qualified tuition plan is a college savings account for a chosen beneficiary, and it represents the best path if you're looking for tax savings on investment gains. The benefit is similar to a Roth IRA, where you pay federal income taxes on contributions. You do not deduct the amount you contribute on your federal taxes. (About half of states allow a partial state tax deduction.) Money that is invested grows tax-free and can be spent tax-free when used on qualified educational expenses.

529s are usually used for college, but "educational expenses" can include tuition at elementary, secondary, public, or private schools, plus fees, books, supplies, and equipment.

But what happens to your money if your kid doesn't go to college and instead decides to pursue YouTube stardom? You're not out of options! You can change the beneficiary on the account to a sibling, neighbor's kid, or even yourself. A new rule also allows the beneficiary to roll some 529 plan money into a Roth IRA. This should be somewhat comforting but as usual, there are conditions.

If you get a state tax deduction, you may need to use your state's plan. Otherwise, your 529 plan doesn't need to be your state or the state your kid goes to college. So, you could live in Washington, open a Utah 529, then go to college in Tennessee. I know. It's stupid.

Make sure your plan allows you to invest using index funds. Some state plans relegate participants to crummy, high-cost, actively managed investment options, in the same way some 401(k)s do. If index funds aren't available in your state plan, use a different state's. And if you're not beholden to your state's plan, you can easily open a 529 plan at a brokerage bank of your choice. Fidelity, Charles Schwab, and Vanguard all have low-cost plans with index funds.

3. Custodial Roth IRA

If you want to give your kid a retirement head start via investing in a Roth IRA, consider a Custodial Roth IRA. To be clear, this is not an account for college; Custodial Roth IRAs are designed for retirement and are subject to the usual rules. An adult serves as the custodian on the account and is responsible for all decision-making until the child is no longer a minor, when the Roth IRA becomes theirs.

Talking about opening a Roth IRA for your child is all the rage on the internet. But there's a pretty major catch: The child must have earned income to make contributions. That means you could put $7,000 into a Custodial Roth IRA for your toddler but only if they legitimately earned at least $7,000 that year. (Although they don't need to file a return unless they earn more than $15,000 in 2025. Just make sure you keep records, in case the IRS comes asking.)

4. Custodial Brokerage Account (UTMA/UGMA)

This is a general (non-retirement) investing account that you open on behalf of a minor. The acronyms refer to laws that cover them (UGMA = Uniform Gift to Minors Act, UTMA = Uniform Transfer to Minors Act). Depending on your state, these accounts will transfer to your kids at age eighteen or twenty-one. At that time, the money is legally theirs and they can spend it however they want. (Is it a pro or a con that the money becomes your kid's at age eighteen? I don't know the answer to that.)

With a custodial brokerage account, you get a modest tax benefit compared to investing in your own brokerage account. When filing in 2025, the first $1,350 of your child's investment income is tax-free, the next $1,350 is taxed at their (likely very low) rate, and anything above that is taxed at your rate. On the flexibility-versus-tax-benefit spectrum, UGMAs and UTMAs sit somewhere in the middle. If you go this route, you can open one at most major brokerages.

10-MINUTE MISSION

Gather the Social Security numbers and addresses of the people you want to name as beneficiaries. Then log into your retirement accounts, find the section labeled "Beneficiaries," and enter their information.

40

HIRING HELP

At what point do I hire financial help?

Unfortunately, whenever a friend tells me they've hired investing help, I brace for the worst. Why? Because most so-called wealth advisors only bother with non-wealthy clients if there's high-commission junk to sell. I've watched too many people, especially young women, have their finances wrecked by some glorified salesman LARPing as genuine investing help. So, I'll be blunt: There are excellent reasons to hire a financial professional—but investing, especially as you are first getting started, is rarely one of them.

The truth is, if you were to believe that every financial professional was going to make impartial recommendations with your best interests at heart, not only would you be wrong but you would also be leaving yourself completely vulnerable to manipulation.

A similar dynamic plays out in the pharmaceutical industry. Drug companies can offer financial incentives to doctors, which we know influences their prescribing habits. (A practice that played a central role in the opioid crisis, which has claimed over a million lives.) Further, both the pharmaceutical and financial services industries are backed by powerful lobbyists who work tirelessly to protect their interests. In financial services, that often means fighting against consumer-friendly reforms that would disrupt lucrative commission structures.

A financial professional who recommends that you buy actively managed mutual funds, an annuity, or whole life insurance is doing so because they receive a commission. It is that simple. And the commission must come from somewhere—and that somewhere is out of your pocket.

There are other good-sounding reasons your investing person might recommend products with high fees and poor performance, but few of them withstand the wash; in warm enough water, the red flags will bleed all over.

"How can this be allowed?" you'd be right to wonder. In the United States, financial regulation requires brokers, many of whom call themselves financial advisors, to meet only what is called the *suitability standard*. Think of it like this: A friend is getting married to someone you've never met, and when you ask what he's like, the only word you get back is "suitable." Not dazzling in conversation, not treating her like the goddess she is—but hey, he's got a job and a pulse. With the right spin, almost any investment product can qualify as "suitable."

Compare this to a financial professional who adheres to the *fiduciary standard*, like a *Certified Financial Planner® (CFP®)*. A fiduciary is legally and ethically obligated to make recommendations in the client's best interest. The difference in language between "suitable" and "best interest" is subtle and leaves room for interpretation, but this difference matters. If it didn't, sellers of variable annuities and other products surely wouldn't be spending millions in lobby dollars to block the SEC's implementation of the fiduciary standard across all retirement accounts.

If you have made it this far in the book, you have done exactly what you need to do to hire a professional: have baseline financial literacy and understanding of the industry so you know what questions to ask and what kind of crap to look out for. Because, these words of caution notwithstanding, there are a lot of people who can and will help you reach your financial goals.

How to Hire Someone Who Will Actually Help You

The first step in hiring the right person is clearly defining your needs. Ask yourself: What specific outcomes am I looking for by hiring help? Skipping this step can lead to wasting money on unnecessary services or even ending up in a worse situation than before.

Although there are many different titles across the industry, the two big ones to look for are *financial planners* and *financial advisors.*

Financial planners help you map out a plan for your money.

Financial advisors, also called wealth advisors, manage your investment strategy. (Confusingly, a financial planner can be a financial advisor and vice versa.)

Hire a *financial planner* because you want someone to:

- help you to map out a financial plan
- make projections for the future (are you on track to retire?)
- help you make money priority decisions and more educated choices
- help facilitate money conversations in relationships
- provide a realistic view into what is and isn't possible

If this sounds like what you want, I'd hire a *fee-only* Certified Financial Planner. Fee-only financial professionals receive their fees only from you, the client. This is good. That means no dark alleyway commissions for selling you into products that you don't need.

You can find a financial planner to work with you on a one-time or ongoing basis. Only pay on an ongoing basis if you receive ongoing service. You wouldn't pay your accountant throughout the year if they only do your taxes once, right? For a one-time financial plan, expect to spend between $2,000 and $4,000. It's expensive, but the work is time-consuming and, hopefully, thoughtful. A financial planner should spend several hours getting to know your financial situation and goals. Then they should spend another few hours going over their proposed financial plan and helping you to implement it.

Pay-by-the-hour CFPs are the industry's newest offering. It is a good thing that financial help is becoming more price accessible; plenty of folks can afford $175 for an hour but not $4,000 for a full financial plan. Nectarine (hellonectarine.com) is a great resource for finding a pay-by-the-hour CFP. That said, know that there are limitations on advice from a person who doesn't have a grasp of your total financial situation.

Hire a *financial advisor* because you want someone to:

- manage your investments

A financial advisor can be designated as a *registered investment advisor (RIA)*, as a brokerage (think stockbroker or broker), or both. An RIA is legally required to follow the fiduciary standard. Brokers (who also often call themselves financial advisors) only need to meet the suitability standard.

So yes, it's a no-brainer to hire a fiduciary RIA, but here's where it gets tricky. RIAs can also be registered as brokerages. This allows them to switch hats: Sometimes they wear their fiduciary fedora, and other times they don their suitability sombrero. So, even if you hire an RIA, you will need to ask them which standard they are adhering to. Get it in writing. Better yet, have a deep understanding of what exactly you are paying for and why.

If your advisor collects *commissions*, I'd run in the other direction. Similar to a financial planner, a *fee-only* advisor is ideal, but less common. A *fee-based* advisor, on the other hand, charges the client a fee *and* may accept commissions. (Again, notice how similar the language is here: fee-only versus fee-based.) Advisor fees are typically charged using an *assets under management (AUM)* model, where the advisor charges a percentage of the money they manage for you. A 1% AUM fee is common.

It's okay to admit that you really don't want to invest on your own. If I were hiring a fiduciary RIA, I'd look for one who builds client portfolios using low-cost index funds. (Although remember, this is a service you can access for even cheaper through a robo-advisor!) At least then you won't be paying for crappy investment products or risk very serious underperformance.

Maybe you don't need a financial planner or a financial advisor. Here are some other ideas:

Hire a *money coach* if you want someone to:

- coach you through the basics
- help you create a budget
- provide accountability

A money coach may or may not hold a credential such as an Accredited Financial Counselor® (AFC®). Money coaching certifications are issued by private organizations that create their own curricula and standards. These credentials are not subject to the same regulatory standards as financial planners and advisors. That said, the right money coach could offer meaningful support and guidance. Use your discretion and keep in mind that a credential does not necessarily mean that the coach will be the right fit for you.

Hire an *accountant* if you want someone to:

- file your taxes, perhaps because you have a business or have a complicated tax situation
- minimize your taxes

A certified public accountant (CPA) is the gold standard for tax and accounting help, though an enrolled agent (EA) is also highly qualified on tax-related matters.

Hire a *bookkeeper* if you want someone to:

- help with ongoing accounting, especially if you run a small business

This could be your accountant, but it might also not be. Sometimes bookkeeping and tax filing are packaged together, but some providers only do one or the other.

Hire an *estate planner* if you want someone to:

- help you create a plan for the distribution of assets after death
- provide guidance on minimizing taxes
- help with other end-of-life arrangements, like healthcare directives and guardianship

An estate planner either is a lawyer or works with one. For example, your financial planner may offer estate planning services, but they'd still contract a lawyer to provide legal documents.

I am going to leave you with a handy list of questions to use when hiring a financial professional. Beyond this, listen to your gut. Know when something sounds too good to be true. Beware of anyone using fear to sell you into something. Anything with a promise of a guarantee is going to cost you significantly, in both fees and upside opportunity. Good luck finding a person who feels like a member of your team and who helps you reach your dreams—they're out there, I believe it.

Questions to Ask When Hiring Financial Help

Can you tell me about what services you provide?
What are the cost of these services?
How do you get paid?
Do you earn commissions from selling me products?
What are your credentials?
Are you a fiduciary?
Do you ever make investment recommendations using the suitability standard?
(If you are using a wealth advisor:) What is your investment strategy?

41

APOCALYPSE

What if there is no future to save for?

"The apocalypse is my retirement plan!" a young woman exclaimed to her friend. The two, who appeared to be in their early twenties, sat one stool down from me at B&H Dairy, my favorite counter deli in Manhattan's Ukrainian Village. Usually, I'm just there to eat my borscht and mind my business, but it's a tight squeeze and what can I say, I love to eavesdrop. I listened as the woman explained to her friend over a tuna melt that she had recently started a new job. "I didn't sign up for my 401(k)," she said. "I'm not saving money for the future. What future?"

I didn't speak up, and I hate to think I could have helped her avert a dangerous decision. But if I'm honest, I, too, was feeling dismal about the future that day. There's a lot to be sad about, and I'm not going to tell you to be happy about things that make you sad.

Financial nihilism is growing among young people. And I get it; we haven't given them much to be hopeful about. There is an ever-growing distrust in the institutions that claim to support regular people but still allow billionaires to wreck the planet, destroy lives for profit, and buy off politicians. Societies with the widest chasms between the rich and poor have the worst mental health outcomes. Wealth inequality breeds violence and makes everyone less safe. The US wages brutal, unnecessary wars in the name of peace but really it is for profit, imperial control, and exploitation of resources that do not belong to us. How can we ever trust, let alone invest, in a society that would choose (and champion) a model where so many people suffer unnecessarily for the benefit of the few?

I don't have a simple answer to this, because I grapple with the same question every day. I teach investing because I believe in using the tools we have to help people build lives of dignity and because women need to understand their money to live securely. But let me be clear: I would gladly give up all the stock market returns, every penny, for a world where everyone has what they need.

This really isn't a contradiction; in either case, it's just wanting what is best for humanity. I believe it's possible—and necessary—to work within the system we have, caring for ourselves and those around us, while remaining fully prepared to leave it behind for an economic and political system built on care for all. Individual solutions like investing are not the final answer. Real change will come only from collective solutions that address the root causes of inequality and climate breakdown. My wealth matters to me because it represents my ability to untether from the machine. But I hold it loosely, willing to let it go if that's what it takes for the machine to crumble.

Many people have come to me without a drop of money in their retirement accounts because they believe that the financial system is destined to collapse. I don't think this is outside the realm of possibility; if it happens, I can only hope it clears the way for something better.

But I tend to believe that our political system—heavily influenced, if not outright owned, by wealth and corporate power—will do whatever is necessary to preserve the financial status quo. There is no class in the United States more zealously protected than corporations, and no right more fiercely defended than the right to profit. I feel reasonably certain that, should it ever come to a true reckoning, the government will rescue the financial system at all costs, gladly sacrificing the environment and the functioning of society itself. As the recycled cardboard sign at the climate protest says, "If the environment were a bank, we would have saved it already."

Still, even with the future as uncertain as it may be, I choose to invest. The act implies a sort of optimism, I suppose. (Or perhaps it reflects that I genuinely don't know what other choice we have.) We are worried about this possible, potential financial calamity, yet the only thing that *guarantees* calamity is doing nothing. If you choose to do nothing out of fear, you will self-fulfill your greatest fear of having nothing.

Occasionally I indulge myself and imagine a postapocalyptic *Mad Max: Fury Road* future where there are no rules (and certainly no property laws or market regulators); you play chicken in armored tanks over natural resources, and all the women somehow still look like Charlize Theron. But if we can extract ourselves from the Warner Bros. Entertainment universe and attempt to paint a realistic picture of what the future may look like, we realize that we've already seen it before. I see my friend Ginny's family, who lost a home in the Northern California wildfires in 2017 that killed forty-seven people and destroyed thousands of buildings. Life got harder, but life still remained worth living. And what Ginny, and her family, and every other person needed to keep living was money.

In every recovery effort I've witnessed, people needed more resources, not fewer. If Artificial Intelligence does indeed come for our jobs, I have a hunch we'll look back on these years and be grateful for every dollar we set aside while we could. Because the best way to prepare for an unknown future—whether shaped by AI, climate change, or authoritarianism—is to build a foundation of resilience. And that includes not only cash and investments but also practical skills and a strong community network.

And anyway, the best thing about having money invested for the future is not even that I get to use this money when I'm eighty. Investing provides a major psychological benefit to me *right now*, even though the money is earmarked for the tenuous long term. I find that there is major daily stress in living with zero fallback plan; in having no resources at all. To me, my money, community, resilience, *and* acceptance that all things are fragile are what allow me to feel protected, freeing me up to take risks and live life more fully—at least for today.

What Life Insurance Do You Need?

Everyone should consider insurance to protect their income. First, *disability insurance,* which supplements your income in the event you cannot work due to disability. Second, if you have anyone who relies on your income to survive, like children or other family members, I strongly encourage you to consider *term life insurance* that will provide income to your family in the event of your passing.

Disability Insurance

Disability is a matter of when. Good coverage ensures that if illness or injury ever keeps you from working, you'll still have a steady income. Start by checking whether your employer offers group disability coverage. Many do, though you may have to opt in. A few states, like California and New York, offer limited state disability insurance as well. And yes, there's federal Social Security disability, but qualifying is hard and the payments are far from enough. If you don't already have strong coverage through work or your state, you may want to shop for an individual policy.

Term Life Insurance

Term life insurance does exactly what you might think life insurance would do, which is to pay your beneficiaries in the event of your passing.

The idea is simple: You pay a low premium for a set number of years (the "term"), and if you pass away during that time, your family gets a tax-free lump sum. That's it. No frills, no crazy complicated conditions. And that's all most of us need; financial security for the people we love during our working years, when we're actively building wealth and raising dependents.

Now, let's talk about the alternatives, like *whole life insurance* or *universal life insurance.* These products love to market themselves as "investments," which, spoiler alert, is a huge overstatement. Sure, they allow part of your monthly premium to be "invested" alongside your insurance policy, but the fees are sky-high, the returns are piss-poor, and the lack of flexibility is astounding. While there are probably some exceptions, whole life insurance policies are generally overpriced products designed to benefit the seller more than the buyer.

A term life insurance policy, on the other hand, does not market itself as an investment and does not invest a part of the premium, and that's okay. It is incredibly affordable by comparison, and you can invest the difference. You'll likely come out way ahead—and without locking your money away in a product that penalizes you for accessing it.

As always, you are welcome to disagree with me. Perhaps you are willing to pay a premium for the comfort of a guarantee, even if it means accepting less growth. I've worked with many investors, often retirees, who found that avoiding the market's volatility was the key to their financial peace. (Even then, I'd probably consider other options, like buying a bunch of ten-year bonds directly to avoid feeling any underlying price swings.)

I will give whole life insurance credit for one thing! It sure does force you to commit. Seriously, you're locked into paying, like, $500 or $600 a month for decades, no excuses, no takebacks. If you are able to bring that level of discipline to your own investment strategy, you will build wealth faster and more flexibly than any insurance plan could ever offer.

42

COMMUNITY

What is the best alternative investment?

Sitting on the panel were two men in button-downs, another in a tech founder plain black tee and denim, and me in my shiny green hot pants. The moderator asked the question: "What *alternative investments* are interesting to you right now?" The phrase *alternative investment* refers to niche investments outside the usual suspects. The guy who answered first said cryptocurrency—as to be expected. I was next. Given his answer and the crowd's demographics, I'll admit I was feeling a bit subversive when I said, "Community. Community is a good investment, the best investment, even. We need each other and we need to start acting like it."

I realize that for many people, perhaps especially the wealthy, investing feels like a carnival game—numbers up and down on a screen, flashing lights, bobbing for apples but in pixels. But I am not investing to win stupid prizes. I am investing—my time, my energy, my money—because I want to improve the quality of my life and the lives of those around me. And we know that the quality of our lives is improved when we have meaningful connections to people and access to resources, green and third spaces, local shops, and public transportation. So then, in wellness and personal finance circles, why is no one talking about this? Why are there not robust discussions about investing in the world we want to live in? We do have to live in it, after all.

I'd risk it all to bet that at least once this month, you've dreamed of living in a commune with your platonic besties, sharing chores and making giant bubbling cauldrons of soup that you take turns stirring. If you're a parent, I bet you've wished you lived on a compound with other families with whom you can share caregiving responsibilities and food preparation. It's science: Girls need to be connected by piazzas where they can get together and have little cappuccinos.

When I say *community,* I mean any group of people who come together to support each other. It could be your extended family, your friends, your neighbors, or even a group united by a shared cause—or simply the desire to connect. A community is about looking out for one another, often sharing a space, a goal, or something meaningful in common.

And while it's fun to fantasize about our shared utopia, the work of community building is urgent—and not always glamorous. As climate change and corporate fascism intensify, we will need each other to get through. "When it all falls away, we are all we have," says Meg of Asheville, North Carolina, a city (and so-considered climate haven) upended by a hurricane in the fall of 2024. For weeks, residents had little access to clean water, electricity, cell service, and internet. Roads were blocked. "Our neighborhood immediately mobilized, made a map of all the houses in the neighborhood, checked on everyone, made sure they were okay, and redistributed resources so that everyone had access to enough food, water, and generators," recalls Meg.

Community members stepped up in ways that local and federal governments did not. As her neighbors filled the gap, it became abundantly clear to Meg how dangerous it is to believe that all you have to do is work hard and that will be enough to protect your family. "There will be a time in your life when it falls away for a short time, for a long time, forever, I don't know, and all you're going to have are the people around you."

To be clear, community-based existence isn't some new idea, nor is it necessary for us to wait until disaster strikes before we see our interconnectedness. For thousands of years, Indigenous cultures in what we now call North America and across the globe banded together to celebrate and share in the work of existence. Childcare, meals, lodging, protection, and even knowledge weren't individual burdens. They came from the people around you; your tribe, community, and shared life.

What's more, they often had no system of money or barter *not* because they were primitive, but because it simply wasn't necessary.

And while these modes of living don't get as much airtime as billionaires and their space escapades, there are places all over the world where people continue to embrace this vision of societal organization. It is a way of being that recognizes that most of our needs are the same, and instead of each person scrambling to meet them individually, they can (and should) be met collectively. It's a far more effective, efficient, and humane way of living.

Cultural, political, and economic forces conspired to dismantle the ancient model in order to sell us a different one: the individual as king and the nuclear family as the sacred cornerstone of life. Why? *Because isolation is profitable.* When we're cut off from community, every basic need becomes a transaction, and a corporation is always there to cash in. Capitalism is nothing if not paywalls around everything we used to provide for ourselves for free. And when you're on your own, you're not just paying for your own housing, your own washer and dryer, your own childcare, your own meals, and your own entertainment—you're also paying for the connection and convenience that used to come naturally. Like, *of course* you had a full rotisserie chicken delivered to your doorstep last night. It is not reasonable to work full-time *and* make every meal for yourself!

Nothing keeps us more exhausted—and spending more money—than our commitment to "rugged individualism." (It is worth noting here that for folks whose family and political systems have failed them, the intense desire to "do it on one's own" can be a trauma response. This is further evidence of the need for better social structures beyond the very fragile nuclear family unit.)

Now, you might be thinking, "Wow, this lady needs to get real. I live in a cramped apartment with two roommates who eat my granola with their bare fingers, and I'm over it." Or "Yeah, welcome to the rest of the world, where everyone already lives with their extended family crammed into one house." Or "Actually, I love my nuclear family unit, thank you very much." And to that, I say: I hear you. You deserve privacy and to live safely. Nor am I blaming any individual for our collective isolation. That blame is reserved for policy failures, capitalist exploitation, poor urban planning, and our relentless undervaluing of the care work done mostly by women.

Instead, I'm only asking you to consider that the version of success we're being sold might not align with what's truly best for us. People spend their whole lives with their entire identities wrapped around their careers and the material items they were able to buy because of them. The lure is strong, but we must be vigilant not to isolate ourselves from the very success we wish for. While wealth can buy privacy, autonomy, and convenience, wealth can also buy loneliness. We are taught to seek meaning and abundance through endless capital accumulation, rather than through love, deep relationships, creative work, and community.

Back in 1938, a study began tracking a group of about 270 Harvard sophomores (all men because, well, 1938) to see what might be learned about adult happiness from following them across their adult lives. The study went on for eighty years, following the men into their nineties, and it revealed what I think we already know: Close relationships, more than money or fame, are the key to a happy life. These relationships "protect people from life's discontents, help delay mental and physical decline, and are better predictors of long and happy lives than social class, IQ, or even genes," the study concludes. Dr. Robert Waldinger, the study's director, adds, "Taking care of your body is important, but tending to your relationships is a form of self-care too."

As a palliative care nurse, the author Bronnie Ware observed similar lessons. In her book, the dying people she worked with most regretted losing touch with their friends and working too hard, especially in pursuit of a lifestyle that really did not, in fact, make them happier. It's better, she concludes, to keep your life materially simpler and to have more time for friends and to pursue your interests and passions.

Finding a new path forward means challenging the systems we've built and unlearning the individualism and materialism we've been taught. It won't be easy, and it won't happen overnight. But when we are loud, persistent, and actively engaged—when we invest in our communities—we can create meaningful change, not just in the world around us, but in our own lives. When we get serious about investing in each other, we can build a world that isn't just about generating capital for a few wealthy individuals. We can create a world where everyone benefits. And the best part? We can start today.

My apologies to all spreadsheet enthusiasts because, no, there will be no predictable ROI calculation on community. There's not even a promise that you'll get back what you put in! Even then, the investment will be worth it—because you gain something by giving, too.

How to Invest in Community

- Make time for your friends. All friendships require prioritization and care. Make the next move (and perhaps the one after that). Don't let people use you, but try not to keep score, either.
- Feed people. People just want to be fed, listen to a good playlist, and be heard.
- Extend care to your neighbors. Introduce yourself with a flower and your contact information.
- Shop locally. All the time. This is a straightforward investment in the type of community you want to live in, and you will build relationships with the people in your weekly orbit.
- Own less and share more.
- Participate in *mutual aid*—the sharing of resources in the spirit of solidarity, not charity. Look for a local organization near you. Or start a local *mutual aid pod.*
- Join your union, a volunteer organization, or a social movement, and attend in-person meetings.
- Join a hobby group, writing or coworking group, community garden, or sports league.
- If you are struggling with grief or addiction, find a local or online support group.
- Find ways to be in consistent contact with people who are different from you. In both community and investing, diversification is the key to richness.
- Advocate for policies and vote for local politicians who want to build and protect community spaces, public transit, public bathrooms, and walkable, bikeable cities.

- Advocate for zoning reforms that allow building multiunit and affordable housing.
- Advocate for policies prioritizing the care of children and families, including paid parental leave, universal childcare, universal healthcare, and equitable funding models for schools.
- Challenge what we've been taught to accept as "normal" in organizing our lives. I've watched my LGBTQ+ friends forge chosen families when they weren't accepted by theirs. They've shown me how to build inclusive networks of support beyond the nuclear family and political structures.
- Advocate for legal and financial support for communities beyond marriage, especially those that center around caretaking. Because when you think about it, it is wild that tax breaks are mostly reserved for relationships where there is presumed genital contact.
- Question the rules of ownership. Learn about democratic socialism. Today's system of private ownership concentrates wealth and power in the hands of a few, giving them outsized control over the labor and lives of the working class. Collective models of ownership may offer a path toward real economic democracy and create the conditions communities need to thrive. Read Marx ☺.

PART VI HOMEWORK: Party Time

Throw a party. That's right, your last and final piece of homework is to throw a party. Because *it's an investment.*

Oh, you think I'm kidding? I'm not. I am so serious. You have to plan a party and you have to do it *now*. There is no need for specialty table linens or personalized flabongos or whatever it is you think makes a party. Start small and have a few friends over for tea or wine. Nothing fancy. Pick a date, send a text, and put it in the calendar.

Repeat monthly.

I mean, c'mon! What are you going to be, a Rich Old Lady who *doesn't* host parties? I don't think so.

THE END (DELIGHT)

Money carries with it a pain that is both universal and individual. It is the ache of uncertainty and the worry that there won't be enough. And if you're like most people, there's a little voice in your head whispering, *What if I never figure this all out? What if I never get it right?*

Here's the thing: You might not figure it all out. You might never feel like you've "won" at money. And that's okay. Yes, I want you to do your best to use money as a tool to build a wild, beautiful life—but we cannot let the pursuit of money stop you from enjoying the wild, beautiful life that you have right now. To do so would undermine the very thing you are trying to achieve.

Financial independence subreddits provide a seemingly never-ending stream of stories from people who are retired at age fifty and have no idea how to have fun. A man with unlimited free time who can't think of a single hobby, volunteer organization, or activity to do besides vaping, watching TV, and consuming online content. Another who is on pace for early retirement and was invited on a trip with friends but cannot bring himself to spend the cash on it. These are extreme examples, of course, and it's easy to believe that there's not a lesson here for you. But there is.

If you put off living your life, waiting until you feel "good" about your money or reach financial independence, you risk not only your joy now but also the future joy you are purportedly working toward. Spending the next twenty years in severe restriction mode might get you to a number on the screen, but it will also shape you into someone who struggles to relax, act with generosity, or savor experiences. Your habits and values will harden, and slipping into a life of travel, creativity, leisure, or service won't come naturally. The person you are now, who dreams of enjoying the fruits of your labor, will have fundamentally changed. You will be a different person.

We have talked about risk a lot in this book, and I'm a big fan of risk. It can be a well from which our very aliveness springs. But there are some risks you just cannot take. One is doing nothing to prepare for the future, but just as dangerous is postponing pleasure for a future that may never materialize.

It's so easy to let money—its presence, its absence, its mysteries, its absurdity—get in the way of living well. Even in abundance, money can warp us, teaching us to prioritize our own money over people, pushing us into relentless self-optimization with no true ceiling, and flooding us with cheap dopamine that leaves us hollow. The endless pursuit of money can create a haze that obscures that our existence here is a sheer fucking miracle; a metaphysical wonder. And assuming you are currently safe, you do not need to reach any financial goal to see it and to see it right now.

I believe in everything I've outlined in this book, but even then, I cannot tell you whether these strategies will hold, or whether markets will be up or down, or how the financial future will unfold.

What I can tell you is that elephants exist, and so do babies. I can tell you that this morning, I had a bagel so delicious I pounded the table and said "YUM" so loud it scared the family next to me. I can remind you how good it feels to get warm after you've been cold from swimming in the sea. About the smell of pine or how the rush of laughter between friends can make you forget everything else you were worried about. I can tell you that this experience is one hell of a glorious ride regardless of how frustrating and heartbreaking this world can be, and that it would be a damn shame if you didn't appreciate it while it lasts.

Would it be great to have all your money stuff sorted? Sure. But you don't have to wait until that happens to find joy or to be a good parent or neighbor. You don't have to wait until your retirement account is maxed out, your debt is gone, or your emergency fund is fully stocked. You can start noticing the magic of life right now, as it is. And in doing so, you'll realize that the most precious wealth you'll ever have is already yours: time, love, connection, and the delight of taking a bite into a hot, toasted bagel.

Bridget Casey, a personal finance creator, posed the following question to her audience: Would you rather have five million dollars or would you rather wake up tomorrow? You'd choose to wake up tomorrow, she reminded us. And you will wake up tomorrow. You're alive on this ridiculous, messy planet with another day to notice how good the coffee smells and how alive you feel when you dance to your favorite song. Because that's really the essence of being a Rich Old Lady.

Part of this journey is learning to love and trust yourself. To me, the fact that you read this technical book on investing is a sign that you already do. If you find yourself angry or frustrated with money, I encourage you to remember it's because your pain is rooted in love. Somewhere deep down, you love yourself and want the best for yourself, as you should. Some days, you may want to sit with the pain. Other days, you may want to use that roiling, burning self-love as motivation to action—to stand up for yourself, to do something scary, to ask for more money because, seriously, who made up these rules, anyway?!

I am providing you with personal finance advice in the context of complex economic and political systems because I want you to see that many of the outcomes we deem "failures" are not actually ours to own. My hope is that with this knowledge you can shift your frustration outward, toward the broader frameworks that were never designed to ensure the success of regular people. As you find yourself opening, may there be space for empathy for yourself and for others navigating the same challenges. I hope that by having seen a flawed system, you learn not to define or measure yourself by any setbacks you've faced within the system.

Yes, take the next step on your financial journey. Continue on with your education, knowing that I am just one teacher and this is just one perspective. But don't wait until you know everything, because that will never happen. Invest, yes—but don't forget to live. Investing in yourself is about much more than index funds and compound returns. Be deeply invested in *you* and making the most of your one shot on this insane cosmic marble. Live a life of true romance. Don't let the pressure of money rob you of the exquisite joy of being here, now. Wake up tomorrow, take a deep breath, notice something beautiful, do something wild. That's the gift.

RICH OLD LADY RESOURCES

Want to continue your learning? Here are a few of my favorite ways:

Personal Finance Foundations

- *Finance for the People,* a book by Paco de Leon
- *Bitches Get Riches,* a blog by Lauren Torres and Jess Fickett
- Everything by *The Financial Diet* and Chelsea Fagan—start with their YouTube channel
- The Personal Finance Club website and on Instagram
- *Get Good with Money,* a book by Tiffany Aliche

Investing

- *The Little Book of Common Sense Investing,* a book by John C. Bogle
- *The Four Pillars of Investing,* a book by William J. Bernstein

If you would like to learn from me in a course format, which includes office hours for all your questions, consider my Invested Development online course!

Financial Independence

- *Cashing Out,* a book by Julien and Kiersten Saunders
- *Work Optional,* a book by Tanja Hester

Financial Independence (while considering women's unique financial challenges)

- *Rich Girl Nation,* a book by Katie Gatti Tassin

Using Your Money for Good

- *Wallet Activism,* a book by Tanja Hester
- *Consumed,* a book by Aja Barber
- *The Story of Stuff,* a book by Annie Leonard
- *Money for Change,* a book by Kara Perez
- *Feminist City,* a book by Leslie Kern

Economics

- *Talking to My Daughter About the Economy,* a book by Yanis Varoufakis
- *The Shock Doctrine,* a book by Naomi Klein
- *In This Economy?,* a book by Kyla Scanlon—also Kyla's newsletter
- *Vulture Capitalism,* a book by Grace Blakeley
- *Poverty, By America,* a book by Matthew Desmond

ACKNOWLEDGMENTS

Thank you to:

Mom and Dad, for my early inheritances: from Dad, the hair and the math; from Mom, the creativity and the devotion; and from both of you, the humor and the generosity. Thank you for the steadfast (if sometimes confused) support of all the strange decisions that have shaped my life and career.

My sister, Madelaine, I sometimes can't believe that you're mine. No other sister would do. To the next many decades of troll doll–collecting, costumes, and having each other's backs.

My brother, Clay, my hero. To the next many decades of hangin' in the Man Cave, calling you anything but your actual name, and being in love with your beautiful heart.

My editors, Julianna Haubner and Carolyn Kelly. Julianna, I can't thank you enough for believing in me and in this book. You took a chance on "investing explained by your slightly unhinged friend," and because of you, I know many women will feel seen, maybe for the first time. Carolyn, thank you for jumping in and guiding this book across the finish line with clarity, energy, and a sharp sense of what the reader needed from me. I admire you both so much, and more than that, I just really like you.

My agent, Jamie Carr. I'll never forget emailing you from Mumbai on my birthday, slightly hallucinatory (I ate the lettuce), but certain I couldn't miss the chance to work with you. I wasn't wrong. Your savvy and talent brought both this book and my dream to life. Thank you for seeing me. Additional thanks to Brettne Bloom and all the icons at The Book Group.

The team at Avid Reader Press: Meredith Vilarello, Stephanie Evans, Annalea Manalili, Katya Wiegmann, Kayla Dee, Ilana Gold, Eva Kerins, Alison Forner, Clay Smith, Sydney Newman, Ruth Lee-Mui, Allison Green, and Hana Handzija, for your hard work behind the scenes. It is beyond magical to have so many cool, brilliant people invested in this project.

The data providers: Accessing primary source data for this book was an incredible challenge. (Not the financial gatekeeping I discuss in these very pages!) I am endlessly grateful to Alexander Poukchanski, Margaret Mahlke, Matthew Harrison, and Diane Roman at the Center for Research in Security Prices (CRSP), and to Paul Marsh, Elroy Dimson, and Mike Staunton—quite simply the most generous academics I've ever encountered. For anyone interested in a rousing history of markets, their book *Triumph of the Optimists* is a masterpiece.

Carrie Frye, a certified genius and the best ally. Getting to work with you was the creative collaboration of my dreams.

Lisa Brown, to whom I owe all of this. Thank you for teaching me everything that matters.

Emma Pattee. Writing and publishing alongside you has been one of my life's great joys. Thank you for your endless hours, care, and brilliance. I'm in awe of you.

Emma, Jess Astrella, and Jamie Hall: my big-brained, bighearted, funnygirl friends. Not just for your wise, generous edits, but for keeping me from going completely bonkers. As multiple genocides unfolded on our phones and speaking out became a risk, I could not have made it through these last two years without you three. Your support—for me, for the book, for Palestine, and for people you'll never meet—carried me on all fronts. I will never forget it.

Tara Ketner, for your work on the cover and for the seven-minute, 6:00 a.m. voice notes, always perfectly timed. **Chloe Devine,** for your work on the cover and for your endless artistic guidance.

Sophia June, to whom I owe a debt of gratitude. Thank you for your research, fact-checking, sourcing, and for always being down to clown.

Bronwyn Isaac, Melissa Hunter, Tanja Hester, Mark Meroney, and Chris Konzen, who each read different versions of this book and provided invaluable help, punched-up jokes, and saw what I missed.

My many, many, many girlfriends. You are the crown jewels of my life. Special thanks to **Steph Petry,** for your attempts at wrangling my attention span with color-coded spreadsheets; **Dana Baldwin,** for your sisterly love; **Alexis Hensel,** for our weekly laugh sessions; and **Paula Tobo** and **Liza Miller,** for your endless appetites for diner coffee and book talk.

My FI comrades, who patiently taught me the ways of this strange financial world and always looked out for me. I'll love you all forever. *xo, Trash Sticks*

NOTES

INTRODUCTION

xi *As recently as the late 1980s: New Economic Realities: The Role of Women Entrepreneurs; Hearings before the House of Representatives Committee on Small Business,* 100th Congress, Second Session (April 26–27, May 10, 11, 17, and 19, 1988), https://files.eric.ed.gov/fulltext/ED304524.pdf.

xi *refused property ownership:* "The Horrifying History of Sexist Housing Policies You Might Not Know About," *National Women's Law Center* (blog), August 22, 2023, https://nwlc.org/the-horrifying-history-of-sexist-housing-policies-you-might-not-know-about/.

credit cards: John W. Cairns, "Credit Equality Comes to Women: An Analysis of the Equal Credit Opportunity Act," *San Diego Law Review* 13, no. 4 (1976): 960–77.

banking privileges: "Voices on Independence: Four Oral Histories About Building Women's Economic Power," *Smithsonian American Women's History Museum* (blog), October 25, 2024, https://womenshistory.si.edu/blog/voices-independence-four-oral-histories-about-building-womens-economic-power.

xi *"head and master" laws:* "Timeline of Legal History of Women in the United States," National Women's History Alliance, https://nationalwomenshistoryalliance.org/resources/womens-rights-movement/detailed-timeline.

xii *majority of the household labor:* Richard Fry et al., *In a Growing Share of U.S. Marriages, Husbands and Wives Earn About the Same* (Pew Research Center, April 13, 2023), https://www.pewresearch.org/social-trends/2023/04/13/in-a-growing-share-of-u-s-marriages-husbands-and-wives-earn-about-the-same/.

xii *A savagely titled study:* "Daughters Provide as Much Elderly Parent Care as They Can, Sons Do as Little as Possible," American Sociological Association,

August 19, 2014, https://www.asanet.org/daughters-provide-much-elderly-parent-care-they-can-sons-do-little-possible.

xii *lose an estimated $324,000: The Female Face of Family Caregiving* (National Partnership for Women & Families, November 2018), https://nationalpartnership.org/wp-content/uploads/2023/02/female-face-family-caregiving.pdf.

xii *half a million dollars in lifetime earnings:* Alex Gailey, "The Motherhood Penalty: Mothers Earn 35 Percent Less Than Fathers in 2024," edited by Tori Rubloff, Bankrate, May 9, 2025, originally published June 26, 2024 as "Study: Women Can Miss Out on Over $500,000 in Career Earnings—Just by Being Mothers," https://www.bankrate.com/banking/savings/motherhood-penalty-study/.

xii *He gets a salary bump:* Gailey, "Motherhood Penalty."

xii *systemic devaluation:* Asaf Levanon et al., "Occupational Feminization and Pay: Assessing Causal Dynamics Using 1950–2000 U.S. Census Data," *Social Forces* 88, no. 2 (December 2009), 865–891, https://doi.org/10.1353/sof.0.0264.

xii *People born into wealth:* Fabian T. Pfeffer and Alexandra Killewald, "Generations of Advantage: Multigenerational Correlations in Family Wealth." *Social Forces* 96, no. 4 (June 2018): 1411–1442. https://doi.org/10.1093/sf/sox086.

xiii *Wage gaps are far worse:* "Racial Wealth Snapshot: Women and the Racial Wealth Divide," Inequality.org, https://inequality.org/racial-wealth-divide-snapshot-women/.

trans: Trans, Queer & Underpaid: Emerging LGBTQI+ Pay Gap Data (National Women's Law Center, June 2023), https://nwlc.org/wp-content/uploads/2023/06/NWLC_LGBTQI-Equal-Pay-Day-FS_FINAL.pdf.

disabled women: Marissa Ditkowsky et al., *Disabled Women and the Wage Gap* (National Partnership for Women & Families, October 2024), https://nationalpartnership.org/report/disabled-women-wage-gap/.

xiii *women overall own just thirty-two cents:* Nicole Torres, "Closing the Gender Wealth Gap," *Harvard Business Review*, October 3, 2019, https://hbr.org/2019/10/closing-the-gender-wealth-gap.

xiii *Black and Latina women own less than one penny:* Torres, "Gender Wealth Gap."

xiii *majority of the low-wage workforce: Women in the Low-Wage Workforce by State* (National Women's Law Center, June 2018), https://nwlc.org/wp-content/uploads/2018/06/women-in-low-wage-workforce-by-state-2018-2.pdf.

xiii *the easiest people to exploit:* Nicole Aschoff, "Why Capitalism and Feminism Can't Coexist," *Jacobin*, September 24, 2019, https://jacobin.com/2019/09/capitalism-socialist-feminism-inequality-sexism.

xiii *comes at an enormous cost:* Claire Savage, "Q&A: Jessica Calarco on 'How Women Became America's Social Safety Net,'" AP News, updated July 3, 2024.

xiii *investment risk-taking is largely:* John E. Grable and Abed Rabbani, "The Moderating Effect of Financial Knowledge on Financial Risk Tolerance," *Journal of Risk and Financial Management* 16, no. 2 (February 2023), 137, https://www.mdpi.com/1911-8074/16/2/137.

xiv *better at it than men*: *2021 Woman and Investing Study* (Fidelity Investments, 2021), https://www.fidelity.com/bin-public/060_www_fidelity_com/documents/about-fidelity/FidelityInvestmentsWomen&InvestingStudy2021.pdf.

xiv *don't take as many stupid ones:* Yu Kuramoto et al., "Behavioral Biases in Panic Selling: Exploring the Role of Framing during the COVID-19 Market Crisis," *Risks* 12, no. 10 (2024): 162, https://doi.org/10.3390/risks12100162.

xiv *Even though men splurge more, spend more:* Evan Sheehan et al., "For Consumers, Splurges Aren't Just Lipstick," *Deloitte Insights*, April 27, 2023, https://www2.deloitte.com/us/en/insights/industry/retail-distribution/consumer-behavior-trends-state-of-the-consumer-tracker/splurge-spending-inflation-lipstick-index.html.

xiv *more credit card debt than women:* Marianne Bertrand et al., "Gender Identity and Relative Income within Households," Working Paper No. 19023, National Bureau of Economic Research, May 2013, https://www.nber.org/papers/w19023.

xiv *The share of Republican men:* Michael Tesler, John Side, and Colette Mar cellin, "Republican Men and Women Are Changing Their Minds About How Women Should Behave," *New York Times*, February 27, 2025, https://www.nytimes.com/2025/02/27/opinion/trump-republicans-masculinity-gender-traditional.html

xiv *69% of millennial heterosexual marriages: Own Your Worth 2021: Building Bridges, Breaking Barriers* (UBS, 2022), https://advisors.ubs.com/ftb/mediahandler/media/591175/Own%20Your%20Worth%202021%20w%202022%20approval.pdf.

xv *this practice is about:* "What Our Work Can Do for You," About Paco, The Hell Yeah Group, https://thehellyeahgroup.com/about.

xvii *with the death of the company pension:* Elizabeth A. Myers and John J. Topoleski, *A Visual Depiction of the Shift from Defined Benefit (DB) to Defined Contribution (DC) Pension Plans in the Private Sector* (Congressional Research Service, December 27, 2021), accessed May 1, 2025, https://www.congress.gov/crs-product/IF12007.

xvii *assaults on Social Security:* Molly Weston Williamson, "Cuts to the Social Security Administration Threaten Millions of Americans' Retirement and Disability Benefits," The Center for American Progress," March 12, 2025, https://www.americanprogress.org/article/cuts-to-the-social-security-administration-threaten-millions-of-americans-retirement-and-disability-benefits/.

PART I

Chapter 2: WHAT FIRST

6 *should be your first priority:* "Pay Off Debt or Save for the Future?" Ramsey Solutions, April 17, 2025, https://www.ramseysolutions.com/debt/pay-off-debt-before-retirement.

6 *filed for bankruptcy:* "A Note from Dave," Ramsey Solutions, https://www.ramseysolutions.com/dave-ramsey#.

Chapter 3: EMERGENCY FUND

9 *a term coined by Paulette Perhach:* Paulette Perhach, "A Story of a Fuck Off Fund," *Billfold*, January 20, 2016, https://www.thebillfold.com/2016/01/a-story-of-a-fuck-off-fund/.

11 *Chase pays an insulting .01% APY:* "Consumer Deposit Rates," Chase.com, April 25, 2025, https://www.chase.com/content/dam/chase-ux/ratesheets/pdfs/rdfl1.pdf.

11 *a HYSA is currently paying 4%:* Margarette Burnette, "Best High-Yield Savings Accounts of May 2025: Up to 4.66%," NerdWallet, May 1, 2025, https://www.nerdwallet.com/best/banking/high-yield-online-savings-accounts.

12 *JPMorgan Chase bankrolls:* Banking on Climate Chaos (BOCC) coalition, "Banking on Climate Chaos: Fossil Fuel Finance Report," 2025, https://www.bankingonclimatechaos.org/wp-content/uploads/2025/06/BOCC_2025_FINAL-4.pdf.

Chapter 4: DEBT VERSUS INVEST

14 *Forty-five percent of American adults: Changes in U.S. Family Finances from 2019 to 2022: Evidence from the Survey of Consumer Finances* (Board of Governors of the Federal Reserve System, October 2023), accessed May 1, 2025, https://www.federalreserve.gov/publications/files/scf23.pdf.

14 *average balance of nearly $6,100: Changes in U.S. Family Finances.*

15 *Americans paid over $130 billion: The Consumer Credit Card Market* (Consumer Finance Protection Bureau, October 2023), https://files.consumerfinance.gov/f/documents/cfpb_consumer-credit-card-market-report_2023.pdf.

15 *the average interest rate:* "Consumer Credit - G.19," Board of Governors of the Federal Reserve System, April 7, 2025, https://www.federalreserve.gov/releases/g19/current/.

15 *you can be charged a* penalty: Alexandria White, "What Is a Penalty APR—And How to Avoid It," CNBC, April 25, 2025, https://www.cnbc.com/select/what-is-penalty-apr/.

Chapter 6: SPENDING

30 *describes beauty as a system that stratifies:* Tressie McMillan Cottom, *Thick: And Other Essays* (New York: The New Press, 2019), 37–72.

31 *undeniable benefits to "beautiful privilege":* Kelsey P. Yonce, "Attractiveness Privilege: The Unearned Advantages of Physical Attractiveness" (master's thesis, Smith College, 2014), https://scholarworks.smith.edu/cgi/viewcontent.cgi?article=1822&context=theses.

31 *As humans, we commonly exhibit a cognitive bias:* Christoph Klebl, "Physical Attractiveness Influences Perceptions of Morality," *Psychology Today,* March 31, 2022, https://www.psychologytoday.com/us/blog/prejudice-and-morality/202203/physical-attractiveness-influences-perceptions-morality.

32 *"Hot Girl Hamster Wheel,":* Katie Gatti Tassin, host, *The Money with Katie Show,* podcast, season 2, episode 117, "Beauty Is $$$: How to Hop Off the 'Hot Girl Hamster Wheel,'" Morning Brew Podcasts, August 9, 2023, https://podcasts.apple.com/us/podcast/beauty-is-%24%24%24-how-to-hop-off-the-hot-girl-hamster-wheel/id1589146097?i=1000623890048.

32 *Gatti Tassin writes:* Katie Gatti Tassin, "We're Having Fun, Right?" *Money with Katie* (blog), https://moneywithkatie.com/blog/were-having-fun-right.

33 *That is why "'I just like what I like':* McMillan Cottom, *Thick,* 58.

Chapter 7: INCOME

38 *A study on gendered language: Summary Report: Gendered Representations of Money in Visual Media, a Study* (Starling Bank, May 2021), https://www.starlingbank.com/docs/reports-research/StarlingGenderRepresentationReport.pdf.

40 *this advice may be effective only:* Katherine Bindley and Lynn Cook, "Job Seekers Hit Wall of Salary Deflation," *Wall Street Journal,* March 16, 2025, https://www.wsj.com/lifestyle/careers/salary-deflation-workers-new-jobs-0b2e1a1f.

40 *with many companies slashing salaries:* Ray A. Smith et al., "Bosses Are Finding Ways to Pay Workers Less," *Wall Street Journal,* August 29, 2024, https://www.wsj.com/lifestyle/careers/salary-workers-pay-cuts-2024-54101d66.

41 *women* do *negotiate:* Benjamin Artz et al., "Research: Women Ask for Raises as Often as Men, but Are Less Likely to Get Them," *Harvard*

Business Review, June 25, 2018, https://hbr.org/2018/06/research-women-ask-for-raises-as-often-as-men-but-are-less-likely-to-get-them.

41 *And yet another observed:* Hannah Riley Bowles et al., "Social Incentives for Gender Differences in the Propensity to Initiate Negotiations: Sometimes It Does Hurt to Ask," *Organizational Behavior and Human Decision Processes* 103, no. 1 (2007): 84–103, https://dash.harvard.edu/entities/publication/23da8023-2ef1-4ebc-b0a8-921d0a994073.

41 *shown to actively undermine:* Laura J. Kray et al., "Now, Women Do Ask: A Call to Update Beliefs about the Gender Pay Gap," *Academy of Management* 10, no. 1 (March 2024): 11–37, https://journals.aom.org/doi/full/10.5465/amd.2022.0021.

43 *women in unions in the US:* Chuxuan Sun et al., *Stronger Together: Union Membership Boosts Women's Earnings and Economic Security* (Institute for Women's Policy Research, September 2021), https://uaw.org/wp-content/uploads/2024/02/Stronger-Together-Union-Membership-Boosts-Womens-Earnings-and-Economic-Security_FINAL-1.pdf.

43 *The gender wage gap between:* Elise Gould and Celine McNicholas, "Unions Help Narrow the Gender Wage Gap," *Working Economics Blog*, Economic Policy Institute, April 3, 2017, https://www.epi.org/blog/unions-help-narrow-the-gender-wage-gap/.

43 *The racial pay gap narrows: Unions Provide Major Economic Benefits for Workers and Families* (Joint Economic Committee, June 10, 2022), https://www.jec.senate.gov/public/index.cfm/democrats/issue-briefs?ID=A608604E-AAF6-4867-A080-648B29198E24

43 *Union members are also three and a half:* "Union Workers More Likely Than Nonunion Workers to Have Retirement Benefits in 2019," U.S. Bureau of Labor Statistics, U.S. Department of Labor, *The Economics Daily*, October 25, 2019, https://www.bls.gov/opub/ted/2019/union-workers-more-likely-than-nonunion-workers-to-have-retirement-benefits-in-2019.htm.

44 *found to actively resist:* Billy Perrigo, "Inside Facebook's African Sweatshop," *Time*, updated February 17, 2022, https://time.com/6147458/facebook-africa-content-moderation-employee-treatment/.

PART II

Chapter 8: RETIREMENT ACCOUNTS

53 *some accountant man discovered:* Ted Benna, "The Day I Designed the First 401(k) Savings Plan," A Brief History of 401k, Benna401k, http://benna401k.com/401k-history.html.

54 *corporations moved away from pensions:* Elizabeth A. Myers and John J. Topoleski, *A Visual Depiction of the Shift from Defined Benefit (DB) to*

Defined Contribution (DC) Pension Plans in the Private Sector (Congressional Research Service December 27, 2021), accessed May 1, 2025, https://www.congress.gov/crs-product/IF12007.

Chapter 9: ROTH VERSUS TRADITIONAL

Note about IRS rules and regulations: All retirement account rules and other tax-related information in this book are sourced from the IRS website (IRS.gov). Please use this book as a starting point, and refer to IRS.gov for the most current figures and updates.

65 *her highest marginal rates:* Andrey Yushkov and Katherine Loughead, "State Individual Income Tax Rates and Brackets, 2025," Tax Foundation, February 18, 2025, https://taxfoundation.org/data/all/state/state-income-tax-rates.

PART III

Chapter 11: STOCKS & BONDS

Note on sources for tables, charts, and graphs: To keep the main bibliography focused on textual references, the data sources used to construct charts, graphs, and tables are listed separately, immediately following the endnotes.

81 *Beanie Bubble of '99:* Anne Vandermey, "Lessons From the Great Beanie Babies Crash," *Fortune*, March 11, 2015, https://fortune.com/2015/03/11/beanie-babies-failure-lessons/.

83 *now worth $2.5 million:* "Apple IPO Anniversary: A $1000 Investment 44 Years Ago Would Have Made You Richer by 249,900% by Now," *Economic Times*, December 12, 2024, https://economictimes.indiatimes.com/news/international/global-trends/apple-ipo-anniversary-apple-stock-price-surge-a-1000-investment-44-years-ago-would-have-made-you-richer-by-249900-by-now/articleshow/116285177.cms?from=mdr.

Chapter 13: RISK

91 *spike in demand for sweatpants:* "From Suits to Sweatpants During and After the Pandemic," CBI Ministry of Foreign Affairs, December 2, 2021, https://www.cbi.eu/news/suits-sweatpants-during-and-after-pandemic.

91 *Enron, Lehman Brothers, and Sears:* Allana Akhtar, "Thomas Cook's Failure Has Left Half a Million People Stranded Abroad. Here Are 9 of the Worst Company Collapses in History," *Business Insider*, September 23, 2019, https://www.businessinsider.com/thomas-cook-enron-lehman-the-worst-company-collapses-bankruptcies-2019-9.

93 *historical inflation rate is about 3%:* Center for Research in Security Prices, LLC (CRSP), *CRSP Consumer Price Index (INDNO 1000709)* [data file] (CRSP, 1925–present). Author's calculation.

Chapter 15: INDEX

101 *They were journalists:* Angel Vu and Ellen Terrell, "This Month in Business History: Dow Jones Industrial Average First Published," Library of Congress, Research Guides, April 2017, updated April 2025, https://guides.loc.gov/this-month-in-business-history/may/djia-first-published.

101 *ultimately became* The Wall Street Journal: "July 8, 1889: The First WSJ," *Wall Street Journal,* July 8, 2014, https://www.wsj.com/articles/BL-267B-183.

101 *created the first stock market index:* Vu and Terrell, "Dow Jones Industrial Average First Published."

102 *added a second index:* Vu and Terrell, "Dow Jones Industrial Average First Published."

102 *Of the twelve industrial stocks:* Steve Schaefer, "The First 12 Dow Components: Where Are They Now?" *Forbes,* July 15, 2011, https://www.forbes.com/sites/steveschaefer/2011/07/15/the-first-12-dow-components-where-are-they-now/.

103 *Microsoft makes up 6.8%:* Sasirekha Subramanian, "The Top 10 S&P 500 Stocks by Weight—A Boon or Bane?" *Forbes,* May 22, 2024, https://www.forbes.com/sites/investor-hub/article/top-sp-500-stocks-by-weight.

103 *while Chipotle accounts for just .15%:* "S&P 500 Index Components," Slickcharts, April 28, 2025, https://www.slickcharts.com/sp500.

Chapter 16: INDEX FUNDS

105 *sought investing advice:* Fred Imbert, "Warren Buffett's Advice to LeBron James," CNBC, March 2, 2015, https://www.cnbc.com/2015/03/02/warren-buffetts-advice-to-lebron-james.html.

107 *Index funds are also the choice:* Charles Schwab, *Invested: Changing Forever the Way Americans Invest* (New York: Crown Currency, 2019), 190.

107 *A dogpile of the country's:* William Watson, "Economists Unanimous—Index Funds Are 'Investing 101,'" Fraser Institute, February 1, 2019, https://www.fraserinstitute.org/commentary/economists-unanimous-index-funds-are-investing-101.

107 *Almost everyone should be investing:* Anil Kashyap, "Diversification," panel, Kent A. Clark Center for Global Markets, University of Chicago Booth School of Business, November 20, 2013, https://www.kentclarkcenter.org/surveys/diversification/.

109 *ETFs are more tax-efficient:* Christine Benz, "The Best Investments for Taxable Accounts," Morningstar, January 23, 2024, https://www.morningstar.com/personal-finance/best-investments-taxable-accounts.

Chapter 17: DIVERSIFICATION & THE THREE-FUND PORTFOLIO

110 *championed using a single US stock market index fund:* Emmie Martin, "Warren Buffett Just Won a $1 Million Bet—And Highlighted One of the Best Ways to Grow Wealth," CNBC, January 3, 2018, https://www.cnbc.com/2018/01/03/why-warren-buffett-says-index-funds-are-the-best-investment.html.

111 *Markets shift over time:* Melissa Saphier et al., *Geographic Diversification Can Be a Lifesaver, Yet Most Portfolios Are Highly Geographically Concentrated* (Bridgewater, February 2019), https://mebfaber.com/wp-content/uploads/2020/01/Geographic-Diversification-Can-Be-a-Lifesaver-1.pdf.

111 *strategy popularized by the Bogleheads:* Taylor Larimore, *The Bogleheads' Guide to the Three-Fund Portfolio: How a Simple Portfolio of Three Total Market Index Funds Outperforms Most Investors with Less Risk* (Hoboken, NJ: Wiley, 2018).

113 *emerging market countries have:* Aubrey Capital Management, "A Trip Down Memory Lane in the Emerging Markets," *Aubrey Capital Management Research*, March 19, 2021, https://www.aubreycm.co.uk/research/a-trip-down-memory-lane-in-the-emerging-markets/.

114 *China dominates market-weighted:* Srinivasan Sivabalan, "China Dominating Emerging Markets Again as MSCI Weight Soars," *Bloomberg*, October 1, 2024, https://www.bloomberg.com/news/articles/2024-10-02/china-back-to-dominating-emerging-markets-as-msci-weight-soars.

114 *its government intervenes:* Sophie Kiderlin, "China's Crackdown on Education Providers Sends Stocks Tumbling. JPMorgan Says the New Rules Could Make the Sector 'Un-Investable,'" *Business Insider*, July 26, 2021, https://markets.businessinsider.com/news/stocks/china-education-stocks-tutoring-regulations-tech-shares-jpmorgan-2021-7.

114 *US treasuries may be a better hedge:* William J. Bernstein, *The Four Pillars of Investing: Lessons for Building a Winning Portfolio*, 2nd ed. (McGraw-Hill, 2023).

Chapter 18: TARGET-DATE FUNDS

118 *becoming more common:* "Quick Facts on Target Date Funds," Investment Company Institute, October 2024, https://www.ici.org/system/files/2024-10/quick-facts-tdfs.pdf.

119 *compares buying an index TDF:* Jeremy Schneider, "Four Identical Portfolios—Why to Keep It Simple," Personal Finance Club, February 8, 2023, https://www.personalfinanceclub.com/four-identical-portfolios-why-to-keep-it-simple/.

119 *holds something like*: Vanguard Target Retirement 2035 Fund," Vanguard, March 31, 2025, https://investor.vanguard.com/investment-products/mutual-funds/profile/vtthx#portfolio-composition.

119 *Compare that to a 2070:* "VTTSX: Vanguard Target Retirement 2060 Fund," Vanguard, March 31, 2025, https://investor.vanguard.com/investment-products/mutual-funds/profile/vttsx#portfolio-composition.

120 glide path: "Target-Date Fund Glide Path," Vanguard, https://institutional.vanguard.com/investment/strategies/tdf-glide-path.html.

121 *Vanguard Target-Date Index Fund 2030:* "VTHRX: Vanguard Target Retirement 2030 Fund," Vanguard, March 31, 2025, https://investor.vanguard.com/investment-products/mutual-funds/profile/vthrx#portfolio-composition.

122 *Vanguard Target-Date Index Fund 2070:* "VSVNX: Vanguard Target Retirement 2070 Fund," Vanguard, March 31, 2025, https://investor.vanguard.com/investment-products/mutual-funds/profile/vsvnx#portfolio-composition.

123 *Fidelity Freedom® Index 2060 Fund:* "Fidelity Freedom® Index 2060 Fund Investor Class," Fidelity, https://fundresearch.fidelity.com/mutual-funds/summary/315793695.

123 *Fidelity Freedom® 2060 Fund:* "Fidelity Freedom®Fund," Fidelity, https://fundresearch.fidelity.com/mutual-funds/summary/315793729.

Chapter 19: EXPECTATIONS

126 *when the US stock market returned a negative 18%:* Aswath Damodaran, "Historical Returns on Stocks, Bonds, and Bills with Premiums," NYU Stern School of Business, January 1, 2025, https://pages.stern.nyu.edu/~adamodar/New_Home_Page/datafile/histretSP.html.

128 *The stock market is negative:* Bob Pisani, "Long-Term Investors Shouldn't Worry Too Much about Stocks Being 10% Off Their Highs," CNBC, January 25, 2022, https://www.cnbc.com/2022/01/25/long-term-investors-shouldnt-worry-too-much-about-stocks-being-10percent-off-their-highs.html

129 *shares surged 52.5%:* Whitney Kisling, "Eisenhower Rally Repeating as S&P 500 Tracks Gains of '54," *Bloomberg*, September 30, 2013, https://www.bloomberg.com/news/articles/2013-09-29/eisenhower-rally-repeating-as-s-p-500-moves-in-lockstep-with-54.

131 *US stock market lost about 9%:* "S&P 500 Total Return Index (SPXT Index)," Bloomberg Finance, data retrieved via Bloomberg Terminal, accessed March 2024.

131 *roughly -1% per year:* "S&P 500 Total Return Index."

131 *the market roared back with an incredible 256% gain:* "S&P 500 Total Return Index."

132 *other times they won't:* Christine Benz, "What's the Best-Performing Asset Type During a Recession?" Morningstar, May 9, 2023, https://www.morningstar.com/portfolios/whats-best-equity-ballast-during-recessions.

132 *about 27% of calendar-year:* "Time, Not Timing, Is What Matters," Capital Group, https://www.capitalgroup.com/individual/planning/investing-fundamentals/time-not-timing-is-what-matters.html.

Chapter 20: MARKET CRASHES

134 *57% of its value:* Robert Rich, "The Great Recession: December 2007–June 2009," Federal Reserve History, November 22, 2013, https://www.federalreservehistory.org/essays/great-recession-of-200709.

135 *would have boomed back:* "S&P 500 Total Return Index (SPXT Index)," Bloomberg Finance, data retrieved via Bloomberg Terminal, accessed March 2024.

136 *climbed 86% in 1999:* Jim Probasco, "Exploring Nasdaq: The Digital Stock Market Powerhouse," *Business Insider*, July 18, 2024, https://www.businessinsider.com/personal-finance/investing/what-is-nasdaq.

136 *explains such investment manias:* Robert Shiller, *Irrational Exuberance* (Princeton, NJ: Princeton University Press, 2016).

137 *market began to boil over:* "The Late 1990s Dot-Com Bubble Implodes in 2000," Goldman Sachs, https://www.goldmansachs.com/our-firm/history/moments/2000-dot-com-bubble.

137 *lost 77% from its peak:* "Late 1990s Dot-Com Bubble Implodes."

137 *half of all tech companies:* Leslie Berlin, "Lessons of Survival, From the Dot-Com Attic," *New York Times*, November 21, 2008, https://www.nytimes.com/2008/11/23/business/23proto.html.

138 *Boo.com:* Richard Wray, "Boo.com Spent Fast and Died Young but Its Legacy Shaped Internet Retailing," *The Guardian*, May 16, 2005, https://www.theguardian.com/technology/2005/may/16/media.business.

138 *Flooz.com:* Robert McMillan, "Turns Out the Dot-Com Bust's Worst Flops Were Actually Fantastic Ideas," *Wired*, December 8, 2014, https://www.wired.com/2014/12/da-bom/.

140 *As Morgan Housel writes*: Morgan Housel, *The Psychology of Money: Timeless Lessons on Wealth, Greed, and Happiness* (Harriman House, 2020).

Chapter 21: UNDERPERFORMANCE (STOCK PICKING)

144 *4% accounted for all:* Hendrik Bessembinder, "Do Stocks Outperform Treasury Bills?" *Journal of Financial Economics* (May 28, 2018), http://dx.doi.org/10.2139/ssrn.2900447.

145 *more than half delivered negative lifetime returns:* Bessembinder, "Do Stocks Outperform Treasury Bills?"

145 *most common outcome:* Bessembinder, "Do Stocks Outperform Treasury Bills?"

146 *97% of actively managed:* Anu R. Ganti, CFA, et al., *SPIVA® U.S. Scorecard* (S&P Dow Jones Indices, 2024), https://www.spglobal.com/spdji/en/documents/spiva/spiva-us-year-end-2024.pdf.

146 *some economists and market observers:* Kenechukwu Anadu et al., *The Shift from Active to Passive Investing: Potential Risks to Financial Stability?* Finance and Economics Discussion Series 2018-060r1 (Board of Governors of the Federal Reserve System, May 15, 2020), https://www.federalreserve.gov/econres/feds/files/2018060r1pap.pdf.

147 *But what's good for individual investors:* Andrew Lipstein, "What Goes Up: Does the Rise of Index Funds Spell Catastrophe?" *Harper's,* June 2024, https://harpers.org/archive/2024/06/what-goes-up-andrew-lipstein-401k-doomsday-index-fund-catastrophe.

147 *when a company is added:* Yen-cheng Chang et al., "Regression Discontinuity and the Price Effects of Stock Market Indexing," Working Paper No. 19290, National Bureau of Economic Research, August 2013, https://www.nber.org/papers/w19290.

147 *active investors still own about half:* Jeff Cox, "Passive Investing Automatically Tracking Indexes Now Controls Nearly Half the US Stock Market," CNBC, March 19, 2019, https://www.cnbc.com/2019/03/19/passive-investing-now-controls-nearly-half-the-us-stock-market.html.

Chapter 22: FEES

151 *brokerage account at Morgan Stanley:* "Morgan Stanley Wealth Management Schedule of Miscellaneous Account and Service Fees," Morgan Stanley, December 2024, https://www.morganstanley.com/wealth-relationshipwithms/pdfs/account_and_service_fees.pdf.

152 *Fidelity now has zero-fee index funds:* "Fidelity ZERO® Total Market Index Fund," Fidelity, https://fundresearch.fidelity.com/mutual-funds/fees-and-prices/31635T708.

152 *expense ratios like .01% or .04%:* James Duvall and Casey Rybak, "Trends in the Expenses and Fees of Funds, 2022," *ICI Research Perspective* 29, no. 3 (March 2023): 1–28, https://www.ici.org/system/files/2023-03/per29-03.pdf.

160 *hedge funds lose to a basket of stocks:* Richard M. Ennis, "Hedge Funds: A Poor Choice for Most Long Term Investors?" *Enterprising Investor* (CFA Institute), June 26, 2024, https://blogs.cfainstitute.org/investor/2024/06/26/hedge-funds-a-poor-choice-for-most-long-term-investors.

PART IV
Chapter 24: BANKS

164 *insures $500,000 per brokerage account per bank:* "What SIPC Protects," Securities Investor Protection Corporation, https://www.sipc.org/for-investors/what-sipc-protects.

165 *designed to encourage harmful behaviors:* Sheelah Kolhatkar, "Robinhood's Big Gamble," *New Yorker*, May 10, 2021, https://www.newyorker.com/magazine/2021/05/17/robinhoods-big-gamble.

166 *a process called* gamification*:* Eric Platt and Madison Darbyshire, "Robinhood Faces Legal Action over 'Gamification' of Investing," *Financial Times*, December 16, 2020, https://www.ft.com/content/0e451231-fa4c-4686-bf2f-a5e107f337b9.

166 *selling your trade orders:* Simone Foxman and Suzanne Woolley, "Robinhood Said to Get 40% of Revenue from Firms Like Citadel," *Bloomberg Law*, October 15, 2018, https://news.bloomberglaw.com/securities-law/robinhood-said-to-get-40-of-revenue-from-firms-like-citadel.

166 *One report in early 2020 revealed:* Nathaniel Popper, "Robinhood Has Lured Young Traders, Sometimes with Devastating Results," *New York Times*, July 8, 2020, https://www.nytimes.com/2020/07/08/technology/robinhood-risky-trading.html.

Chapter 25: RESEARCH

169 *FZROX:* "Fidelity ZERO Total Market Index (FZROX)," Yahoo Finance, https://finance.yahoo.com/quote/FZROX/.

172 *Financial firms targeted school districts and nonprofits:* Elena Barone Chism and Mitra Surrell, "Teachers and Nurses Deserve Access to the Same Investment Options as 401(k) Savers," Investment Company Institute, February 10, 2025, https://www.ici.org/viewpoints/25-view-retirement-fairness.

Chapter 28: UPKEEP

190 *On an episode of his show called: Last Week Tonight with John Oliver*, season 3, episode 15, "Money," written by Tim Carvell et al., aired June 12, 2016, on HBO.

Chapter 29: ROBO-ADVISORS

193 *typical robo management fee:* Lan Anh Tran and Emelia Fredlick, "Are Robo-Advisors Still Worth It?" Morningstar, May 2, 2025, https://www.morningstar.com/personal-finance/are-robo-advisors-still-worth-it.

194 *is both real and probably overstated:* Michael Kitces, "Evaluating the Tax Deferral and Tax Bracket Arbitrage Benefits of Tax Loss Harvesting," Kitces .com, December 3, 2014, https://www.kitces.com/blog/evaluating-the-tax-deferral-and-tax-bracket-arbitrage-benefits-of-tax-loss-harvesting/.

PART V

Chapter 30: ETHICAL INVESTING

204 *Under a more just system: The Case for Employee Ownership* (Project Equity, 2019), https://project-equity.org/wp-content/uploads/2023/07/Copy-of-The-Case-For-Employee-Ownership-Executive-Summary-2019-Project-Equity-1.pdf.

205 *companies now actively profiting from:* Francesca Albanese, *From an Economy of Occupation to an Economy of Genocide: The Impact of Israel's Military Operation in Gaza on the Palestinian People,* Report presented to the United Nations Human Rights Council, Fifty-ninth session, Agenda Item 2, A/HRC/59/23. March 3, 2025, https://www.un.org/unispal/document/a-hrc-59-23-from-economy-of-occupation-to-economy-of-genocide-report-special-rapporteur-francesca-albanese-palestine-2025/.

207 *accused of being a* greenwashed *solution:* Heather Fambrough, "Reports Says Too Many ESG Funds Are Greenwashing and Misleading," *Forbes,* February 28, 2025, https://www.forbes.com/sites/heatherfarmbrough/2025/02/28/reports-says-too-many-esg-funds-are-greenwashing-and-misleading/.

207 *ESG investing is hardly enough:* Kenneth P. Pucker and Andrew King, "ESG Investing Isn't Designed to Save the Planet," *Harvard Business Review,* August 1, 2022, https://hbr.org/2022/08/esg-investing-isnt-designed-to-save-the-planet.

208 *explains that divestment aims not to:* Bill McKibben, "Turning Colleges' Partners Into Pariahs," *New York Times,* February 11, 2014, https://www.nytimes.com/roomfordebate/2013/01/27/is-divestment-an-effective-means-of-protest/turning-colleges-partners-into-pariahs.

Chapter 31: MARKET CATEGORIES

210 *11.2% of the US stock market:* "S&P 500® Quick Facts," S&P Global, April 30, 2025, https://www.spglobal.com/spdji/en/indices/equity/sp-500/#data.

211 *small- and mid-cap companies also have more room:* Fei Mei Chan and Craig Lazzara, CFA, *Mid Cap: A Sweet Spot for Performance* (S&P Dow Jones Indices, September 2015), https://www.spglobal.com/spdji/en

/documents/education/practice-essentials-mid-cap-a-sweet-spot-for-performance.pdf.

211 *dominate our market weighted indices:* Weston Lewis, "U.S. Equity Index Families: Understanding the Differences," *Callan,* February 6, 2025, https://www.callan.com/blog-archive/us-equity-index-families/.

214 *Warren Buffett is famously a value investor:* Lucy Handley, "A Complete Guide to Value Investing—How Warren Buffett Made His Money," CNBC, February 10, 2025, https://www.cnbc.com/2025/02/11/what-is-value-investing-how-warren-buffett-made-his-money.html.

214 *are growth stocks in the tech industry:* "S&P 500® Quick Facts," S&P Global.

214 *doubted that everyday investors:* Fidelity Investments, "Types of ETFs by Style and Capitalization," Fidelity Learning Center, Fidelity Investments, www.fidelity.com/learning-center/investment-products/etf/types-etfs-style-capitalization.

215 *eleven stock market* sectors*: GICS® Global Industry Classification Standard* (S&P Global Marketing Intelligence, MSCI, 2018), https://www.spglobal.com/marketintelligence/en/documents/112727-gics-mapbook_2018_v3_letter_digitalspreads.pdf.

Chapter 32: REAL ESTATE (REITS)

219 *REITs are required to return at least 90% : Investor Bulletin: Real Estate Investment Trusts (REITs),* Securities and Exchange Commission Office of Investor Education and Advocacy, December 2011, https://www.sec.gov/files/reits.pdf.

219 *Equity REITs are the most popular:* "The Role of REITs in Diversifying Your Investment Portfolio," *Steers Center for Global Real Estate* (blog), February 4, 2025, https://globalrealestate.georgetown.edu/insight/the-role-of-reits-in-diversifying-your-investment-portfolio/.

219 *Proponents for REITs point to the added diversification:* "Role of REITs."

219 *outperformed bonds:* "Annual Index Values and Returns," Nareit, https://www.reit.com/data-research/reit-indexes/annual-index-values-returns.

220 *both stocks and REITs got pummeled:* "Annual Index Values and Returns."

221 *Typically, around 3% to 4%: MSCI US IMI Real Estate 25/50 Index (USD)* (Morgan Stanley Capital International, March 31, 2025), https://www.msci.com/documents/10199/255599/msci-usa-imi-real-estate-2550-index-usd-gross.pdf.

221 *Apartment buildings represent another 9% to 10%: Real Estate 25/50 Index.*

221 *notoriously racist history of redlining:* City of Portland, Bureau of Planning and Sustainability, "Historical Context of Racist Planning: A History of How Planning Segregated Portland," https://www.portland.gov/bps/planning/adap/history-racist-planning-portland.

Chapter 33: CRYPTOCURRENCY

222 *more pronounced than even the worst volatility in the stock market:* Andrey Sergeenkov, "How Volatile Is Bitcoin Compared to Other Assets," *Forbes*, August 16, 2024, https://www.forbes.com/sites/digital-assets/2024/08/16/how-volatile-is-bitcoin-compared-to-other-assets/.

222 *primary purpose seems to be:* Tressie McMillan Cottom, "Wealth Inequality Drives the Appeal of Crypto," *New York Times*, January 31, 2022, https://www.nytimes.com/2022/01/31/opinion/crypto-nfts-inequality.html.

223 *print ever more money for wars:* Saifedean Ammous, *The Bitcoin Standard: The Decentralized Alternative to Central Banking* (Wiley, 2018).

224 *the president's blindly corrupt:* Ezra Klein and Kevin Roose. "How the Trump 'Meme Coin' Became a National Security Question." *The Ezra Klein Show, The New York Times*, May 21, 2024, https://www.nytimes.com/2024/05/21/opinion/ezra-klein-podcast-trump-meme-coin.html.

224 greater fool theory*:* Stacey Vanek Smith and Darian Woods, "The Origin of Value: The Greater Fools Theory," NPR, August 4, 2021, https://www.npr.org/2021/08/04/1024881179/the-origin-of-value-the-greater-fools-theory.

224 *extract profit for elite asset holders at the top:* Tressie McMillan Cottom, "Crypto and the Power of Folk Economics," *New York Times*, February 7, 2022, https://www.nytimes.com/2022/02/07/opinion/crypto-nfts-folk-economics.html.

PART VI

Chapter 34: RETIREMENT CALCULATIONS

232 *like the one on investor.gov:* Compound Interest Calculator, Investor.gov, https://www.investor.gov/financial-tools-calculators/calculators/compound-interest-calculator.

234 *nearly $2,000 per month: 2025 Social Security Changes*, fact sheet (Social Security Administration), https://www.ssa.gov/news/press/factsheets/colafacts2025.pdf.

234 *from the Trinity study:* Philip L. Cooley et al., "Retirement Savings: Choosing a Withdrawal Rate That Is Sustainable," *AAII Journal* 20, no. 2 (1998): 16–21, https://www.aaii.com/journal/199802/feature.pdf.

235 *Not everyone believes that 4% is a* safe withdrawal rate*:* Karyl B. Leggio et al., "The Death of the 4% Rule: New Market Conditions and Retiree Needs Require Rethinking Retirement Spending," *The Journal of Retirement* 11, no. 4 (2024): 40–60, 10.3905/jor.2024.1.154.

235 *some market optimists think:* Paul Squirrell, "Why the 4% Rule Shouldn't Be 'The Tail That Wags the Dog,'" Fidelity International, October 18,

2024, https://adviserservices.fidelity.co.uk/news-insights/financial-advisor-insights/insights-and-opinions/why-the-four-rule-shouldnt-be-the-tail-that-wags-the-dog/#.

235 *asks too much of the average investor:* Rob Williams and Chris Kawashima, "The 4% Rule: How Much Can You Spend in Retirement?" Charles Schwab, April 18, 2015, https://www.schwab.com/learn/story/beyond-4-rule-how-much-can-you-spend-retirement.

Chapter 35: SOCIAL SECURITY

237 *only used to pay:* "What are the Trust Funds?" Social Security Administration, https://www.ssa.gov/news/press/factsheets/WhatAreTheTrust.htm.

237 funding shortfall: "The 2024 Annual Report of the Board of Trustees of the Federal Old-Age and Survivors Insurance and Federal Disability Insurance Trust Funds," Social Security Administration, https://www.ssa.gov/OACT/TR/2024/.

237 *designed as what we call a "pay as you go" pension system:* "Are the Social Security Trust Funds Real?" Tax Policy Center, Urban Institute and Brookings Institution, January 2024, https://taxpolicycenter.org/briefing-book/are-social-security-trust-funds-real.

237 *slowdown in population growth:* Gayle L. Reznik et al., "Coping with the Demographic Challenge: Fewer Children and Living Longer," *Social Security Bulletin* 66, no. 4 (April 2007), https://www.ssa.gov/policy/docs/ssb/v66n4/v66n4p37.html.

238 *shortage of wages to fund the program:* "The 2024 Annual Report of the Board of Trustees," Social Security Administration.

238 *birthrate declining in recent years:* "U.S. Fertility Rate Drops to Another Historic Low," US Centers for Disease Control and Prevention/National Health Statistics, April 25, 2024, https://www.cdc.gov/nchs/pressroom/nchs_press_releases/2024/20240525.htm.

238 *From now until the year 2033:* Janet Yellen et al., *A Summary of the 2024 Annual Reports* (Social Security Administration), https://www.ssa.gov/oact/trsum/#:~:text=Based%20on%20our%20best%20estimates,of%20that%20report's%20projection%20period.

238 *incoming taxes will fund a majority but not all: Will Social Security Be There for Me?* (Social Security Administration, October 2023) https://www.ssa.gov/pubs/marketing/fact-sheets/will-social-security-be-there-for-me.pdf.

238 *a gradual decline in benefits from 79% to 69%:* Yellen, *A Summary of the 2024 Annual Reports.*

238 *allowing for more legal immigration:* Tara Watson, "How Immigration Reforms Could Bolster Social Security and Medicare Solvency and Address

Direct Care Workforce Issues," Brookings Institute, April 16, 2024, https://www.brookings.edu/articles/how-immigration-reforms-could-bolster-social-security-and-medicare-solvency-and-address-direct-care-workforce-issues/.

238 *removing the Social Security tax cap:* "Increase the Maximum Taxable Earnings for the Social Security Payroll Tax," *Options for Reducing the Deficit: 2021 to 2030* (Congressional Budget Office, December 9, 2020), https://www.cbo.gov/budget-options/56862.

238 *especially to benefit the rich:* "After Decades of Costly, Regressive, and Ineffective Tax Cuts, a New Course Is Needed," *The Rich Get Richer, Deficits Get Bigger: How Tax Cuts for the Wealthy and Corporations Drive the National Debt; Hearing Before the US Senate Committee on the Budget* (May 17, 2023) (testimony of Samantha Jacoby, Senior Tax Legal Analyst, Center on Budget and Policy Priorities), https://www.cbpp.org/research/federal-tax/after-decades-of-costly-regressive-and-ineffective-tax-cuts-a-new-course-is.

238 *only possible to become ultrawealthy:* Fred Magdoff and John Bellamy Foster, "Grand Theft Capital: The Increasing Exploitation and Robbery of the U.S. Working Class," *Monthly Review*, May 1, 2023, https://monthlyreview.org/2023/05/01/grand-theft-capital-the-increasing-exploitation-and-robbery-of-the-u-s-working-class/.

238 *particularly elder women:* Amber Christ and Tracey Gronniger, *Older Women and Poverty* (Justice in Aging, December 2018), https://justiceinaging.org/wp-content/uploads/2020/08/Older-Women-and-Poverty.pdf.

239 *Social Security will be eliminated:* Justin Glawe, "Social Security Insiders Warn Trump and Musk Could Break the Program," *Rolling Stone*, March 10, 2025, https://www.rollingstone.com/politics/politics-features/trump-musk-doge-social-security-omalley-1235292652/.

Chapter 36: WHAT NEXT

242 *contribute approximately 20%:* "SEP Retirement Plans For Small Businesses," Employee Benefits Security Administration, U.S. Department of Labor, https://www.dol.gov/agencies/ebsa/about-ebsa/our-activities/resource-center/publications/sep-retirement-plans-for-small-businesses.

244 *"back door":* Elizabeth A. Myers, *Rollovers and Conversions to Roth IRAs and Designated Roth Accounts: Proposed Changes in Budget Reconciliation* (Congressional Research Service, Congress.gov, May 6, 2025), https://www.congress.gov/crs-product/IF11963.

244 *mega backdoor maneuver:* "What Is a 'Mega Backdoor Roth'?" Fidelity, February 8, 2025, https://www.fidelity.com/learning-center/personal-finance/mega-backdoor-roth.

245 pro rata rule: "Rollovers of After-Tax Contributions in Retirement Plans," February 26, 2025, https://www.irs.gov/retirement-plans/rollovers-of-after-tax-contributions-in-retirement-plans.

246 FIRE (Financial Independence, Retire Early) *movement:* Shubhangi Goel, "The Lonely March to Early Retirement," *Business Insider*, February 24, 2025, https://www.businessinsider.com/financial-independence-retire-early-saving-loneliness-retreat-bali-making-friends-2025-2.

246 *investing up to 70% of their income:* Anisa Purbasari, "These People Are Making the 'Financial Independence, Retire Early' Movement More Inclusive by Challenging Norms Around Saving, Debt, and Living Frugally," *Business Insider*, December 7, 2020, https://www.businessinsider.com/individuals-making-fire-movement-inclusive-diverse-saving-money-retirement-2020-11.

Chapter 37: HEALTH SAVINGS ACCOUNTS

249 *you are likely picking the plan:* "A Brief Overview of the Major Flaws with Health Savings Accounts," Center on Budget and Policy Priorities, April 5, 2006, https://www.cbpp.org/sites/default/files/atoms/files/hsa-overview.pdf.

249 *they frequently put off the care:* Jennifer Tolbert et al., "Key Facts about the Uninsured Population," Kaiser Family Foundation, https://www.kff.org/uninsured/issue-brief/key-facts-about-the-uninsured-population/.

250 *product of conservative efforts:* Julie Appleby, "HSAs: 'Tax-Break Trifecta' or Insurance Gimmick Benefiting the Wealthy?" Kaiser Family Foundation Health News, https://kffhealthnews.org/news/hsas-tax-break-trifecta-or-insurance-gimmick-benefiting-the-wealthy/.

250 *Healthcare costs exploded:* Matthew McGough et al., "How Has U.S. Spending on Healthcare Changed Over Time?" Petersen Kaiser Family Foundation Health System Tracker, December 20, 2024, https://www.healthsystemtracker.org/chart-collection/u-s-spending-healthcare-changed-time/.

250 *system designed to be opaque and confusing:* John Cassidy, "How Did We End Up with Such an Opaque and Costly Health-Care System?" *New Yorker*, December 16, 2024, https://www.newyorker.com/news/the-financial-page/how-did-we-end-up-with-such-an-opaque-and-costly-health-care-system.

250 *People just don't get healthcare:* Sara R. Collins and Avni Gupta, "The State of Health Insurance Coverage in the U.S.," The Commonwealth Fund, November 21, 2024, https://www.commonwealthfund.org/publications/surveys/2024/nov/state-health-insurance-coverage-us-2024-biennial-survey.

Chapter 38: HOMEOWNERSHIP

251 *Housing prices have soared:* Anna Kodé, "The American Dream Without a House? Believe It," *New York Times*, September 7, 2024, https://www.nytimes.com/2024/09/07/realestate/american-dream-homeowner-young-people.html.

252 *locking in and deepening existing inequities:* Gökhan Ünalan et al., "The Impact of Increases in Housing Prices on Income Inequality: A Perspective on Sustainable Urban Development," *Sustainability* 17, no. 9: 4024, https://doi.org/10.3390/su17094024.

252 *typically home values grow about 4% annually:* Robert McAllister, "Average Home Value Increase Per Year in the US, 5 Years, 10 Years," North American Community Hub Statistics, April 10, 2025, https://nchstats.com/average-home-value-increase-us/.

252 *will take a loan from a bank:* "Highlights From the Profile of Home Buyers and Sellers 2024," National Association of Realtors, https://www.nar.realtor/research-and-statistics/research-reports/highlights-from-the-profile-of-home-buyers-and-sellers.

252 *interest alone will have more than doubled:* Max Fay, "30-Year Fixed Rate Mortgage," Debt.org, https://www.debt.org/real-estate/mortgages/30-year-fixed.

252 *2% to 5% of the home's value:* Meaghan Hunt, "Closing Costs: What Are They and How Much Are They?" Bankrate, May 23, 2025, https://www.bankrate.com/mortgages/what-are-closing-costs/.

252 *may produce a negative ROI:* Kelley C. Long, "Being Realistic About Homeownership as an Investment," *Journal of Accountancy, Personal Financial Planning Digest*, April 28, 2025, https://www.journalofaccountancy.com/newsletters/pfp-digest/being-realistic-about-homeownership-as-an-investment/.

253 Bitches Get Riches *blog put it best:* Lauren Torres, "Bullshit Reasons Not to Buy a House: Refuted," *Bitches Get Riches* (blog), December 5, 2016, https://www.bitchesgetriches.com/bullshit-reasons-not-buy-house-refuted/.

254 *the reality for so many victims:* Cassie Ordonio, "Lāhainā Fire Victims Struggle to Make Mortgage Payments on Destroyed Houses," Hawaiʻi Public Radio, October 23, 2023, https://www.hawaiipublicradio.org/local-news/2023-10-23/lahaina-fire-victims-struggle-to-make-mortgage-payments-on-destroyed-houses.

254 *rent-versus-buy calculator:* David Leonhardt, "A New Rent-Versus-Buy Calculator," *New York Times*, June 17, 2024, https://www.nytimes.com/2024/05/13/briefing/a-new-rent-versus-buy-calculator.html.

256 *below 36%:* Libby Wells, "What Is a Debt-to-Income Ratio for a Mortgage?" Bankrate, February 20, 2025, https://www.bankrate.com/mortgages/why-debt-to-income-matters-in-mortgages.

256 *Save 3% to 20% of the home's price for:* "Determine Your Down Payment," Consumer Financial Protection Bureau, December 12, 2024, https://www.consumerfinance.gov/owning-a-home/prepare/determine-your-down-payment.

256 *allow down payments as low as 3.5%:* "FHA Loans," Consumer Financial Protection Bureau, October 16, 2024, https://www.consumerfinance.gov/owning-a-home/fha-loans/.

256 *offer more lenient terms for rural buyers:* "Single Family Housing Direct Home Loans," U.S. Department of Agriculture Rural Development, https://www.rd.usda.gov/programs-services/single-family-housing-programs/single-family-housing-direct-home-loans.

257 *mortgage loan cost calculator:* Mortgage Calculator, Bankrate, https://www.bankrate.com/mortgages/mortgage-calculator/.

257 *explore a* condo conversion: "Understanding the Condo Conversion Process," *Old Republic Title* (blog), https://www.oldrepublictitle.com/blog/condo-conversion-process/.

257 *have loosened rules:* Alex Horowitz et al., "Most Western States Have Eased Zoning Rules to Promote Housing," *Governing*, February 10, 2025, https://www.governing.com/urban/most-western-states-have-eased-zoning-rules-to-promote-housing.

Chapter 39: CHILDREN

258 *sandwich generation:* Kim Parker and Eileen Patten, *The Sandwich Generation: Rising Financial Burdens for Middle-Aged Americans* (Pew Research Center, January 30, 2013), https://www.pewresearch.org/social-trends/2013/01/30/the-sandwich-generation/.

260 *must be used for education expenses:* "529 Plans: Questions and Answers," Internal Revenue Service, November 15, 2024, https://www.irs.gov/newsroom/529-plans-questions-and-answers.

260 *no 529 state tax deduction:* "What Kind of Benefits Do I Get?" CalABLE, https://calable.ca.gov/faqs/what-kind-of-benefits-do-i-get.

260 *you may be able to deduct:* Matthew Toner, "How Much Is Your State's 529 Tax Deduction Really Worth?," Saving for College, February 17, 2025, https://www.savingforcollege.com/article/how-much-is-your-state-s-529-plan-tax-deduction-really-worth.

262 *About half of states allow a partial state tax deduction:* Toner, "Your State's 529 Tax Deduction."

262 *doesn't need to be your state:* Toner, "Your State's 529 Tax Deduction."

263 *the child must have:* Taylor Freitas, "Custodial Roth IRA: How and Why to Start a Roth IRA for Kids," Bankrate, May 14, 2025, https://www.bankrate.com/retirement/custodial-roth-ira-starting-ira-for-your-child/.

263 *the first $1,350:* "What to Know About the Kiddie Tax," Fidelity, April 15, 2025, https://www.fidelity.com/learning-center/personal-finance/kiddie-tax.

Chapter 40: HIRING HELP

264 *high-commission junk to sell:* Simon Gervais and John E. Thanassoulis, *Ethics and Trust in the Market for Financial Advisors,* SSRN, January 8, 2025, http://dx.doi.org/10.2139/ssrn.4812676.

264 *which we know influences their prescribing habits:* Hannah Fresques, "Doctors Prescribe More of a Drug If They Receive Money from a Pharma Company Tied to It," *ProPublica,* December 20, 2019, https://www.propublica.org/article/doctors-prescribe-more-of-a-drug-if-they-receive-money-from-a-pharma-company-tied-to-it.

264 *central role in the opioid crisis:* Charles Ornstein and Ryann Grochowski Jones, "Opioid Makers, Blamed for Overdose Epidemic, Cut Back on Marketing Payments to Doctors," *ProPublica,* June 28, 2018, https://www.propublica.org/article/opioid-makers-blamed-for-overdose-epidemic-cut-back-on-marketing-payments-to-doctors.

264 *both the pharmaceutical:* Olivier J. Wouters, "Lobbying Expenditures and Campaign Contributions by the Pharmaceutical and Health Product Industry in the United States 1999–2018," *JAMA Internal Medicine* 180, no. 5 (2020): 688–697, https://doi.org/10.1001/jamainternmed.2020.0146.

264 *financial services industries:* Douglas Gillison, "US Bank Lobbyists Ranks Swell to Post-Crisis High Amid Regulatory Pushback," Reuters, February 8, 2024, https://www.reuters.com/business/finance/us-bank-lobbyists-ranks-swell-post-crisis-high-amid-regulatory-pushback-2024-02-08/.

264 *fighting against consumer-friendly reforms:* Tony Romm, "Insurance Lobbyists Block Federal Crackdown on Costly Retirement Advice," *Washington Post,* August 11, 2024, https://www.washingtonpost.com/business/2024/08/11/insurance-lobbyists-block-fiduciary-rule/.

264 *is doing so because they receive a commission:* Julie Pinkerton, "What to Know About Financial Advisor Fees & Costs," *U.S. News and World Report,* March 27, 2025, https://money.usnews.com/financial-advisors/articles/what-to-know-about-financial-advisor-fees-and-costs.

265 suitability standard: "2111. Suitability," FINRA, https://www.finra.org/rules-guidance/rulebooks/finra-rules/2111.

265 fiduciary standard: *Code of Ethics and Standards of Conduct* (CFP Board, 2018), https://www.cfp.net/ethics/code-of-ethics-and-standards-of-conduct.

265 *spending millions in lobby dollars:* Tara Siegel Bernard, "Obama-Era Investor Protection Rule Is Dead," *New York Times,* June 22, 2018, https://www.nytimes.com/2018/06/22/your-money/fiduciary-rule-dies.html.

266 *a* fee-only *Certified Financial Planner:* "What is Fee-Only Financial Planning?," National Association of Personal Financial Advisors, https://www.napfa.org/financial-planning/what-is-fee-only-advising.

267 *A financial advisor can be designated:* Adam Hayes, "Registered Investment Advisor (RIA): Definition, Duties, and Responsibilities," Investopedia, July 7, 2024, https://www.investopedia.com/terms/r/ria.asp.

Chapter 41: APOCALYPSE

270 *Financial nihilism is growing:* Paulina Cachero and Claire Ballentine, "Nearly Half of All Young Adults Live With Mom and Dad—And They Like It," *Bloomberg,* September 20, 2023, https://www.bloomberg.com/news/articles/2023-09-20/nearly-half-of-young-adults-are-living-back-home-with-parents.

270 *have the worst mental health outcomes:* Richard Wilkinson and Kate Pickett, "Income Inequality and the Damage Done," *Reflections,* issue "No More Excuses: Confronting Poverty" (Fall 2010), https://reflections.yale.edu/article/no-more-excuses-confronting-poverty/income-inequality-and-damage-done.

270 *Wealth inequality breeds violence:* Theresa L. Armstead et al., "Structural and Social Determinants of Inequities in Violence Risk: A Review of Indicators," *Journal of Community Psychology* 49, no. 4 (2021): 878–906, https://doi.org/10.1002/jcop.22232.

271 *more zealously protected than corporations:* Nina Totenberg, "When Did Companies Become People? Excavating the Legal Evolution," NPR, July 28, 2014, https://www.npr.org/2014/07/28/335288388/when-did-companies-become-people-excavating-the-legal-evolution.

271 *no right more fiercely defended than the right to profit:* Daniel O'Rourke, "Corporations Want Profits Without Consequences. Courts Are Giving It to Them," Emergency Workplace Organizing Committee, September 9, 2024, https://workerorganizing.org/corporations-want-profits-without-consequences-courts-are-giving-it-to-them-8807/.

272 *Northern California wildfires:* Peter Fimrite and Jenna Lyons, "Tubbs Fire in Sonoma County is Most Destructive in State History," *SF Gate,* October 20, 2017, https://www.sfgate.com/bayarea/article/Little-tears-of-joy-falling-from-the-skies-12293647.php.

273 *limited state disability insurance:* "Comparison of Federal vs. State vs. Private Disability Benefits," Patient Advocate Foundation, https://www.patientadvocate.org/explore-our-resources/preserving-income-federal-benefits/comparison-of-federal-vs-state-vs-private-disability-benefits.

273 *qualifying is hard: Annual Statistical Report on the Social Security Disability Insurance Program, 2023* (Social Security Administration) https://www.ssa.gov/policy/docs/statcomps/di_asr/2023/sect04.html.

Chapter 42: COMMUNITY

276 *For thousands of years, Indigenous cultures:* Delwin Fiddler, Jr, "Native American Family: It Takes a Village," *Native Hope* (blog), March 11, 2021, https://blog.nativehope.org/native-american-family-it-takes-a-village.

277 *the individual as king:* Ashley Humphrey and Ana-Maria Bliuc, "Western Individualism and the Psychological Wellbeing of Young People: A Systematic Review of Their Associations," *Youth* 2, no. 1 (2022): 1–11, https://doi.org/10.3390/youth2010001.

277 *the sacred cornerstone of life:* Ryan McMaken, "The Rise of the Western Nuclear Family and the 'European Miracle,'" Mises Institute, September 13, 2024, https://mises.org/mises-wire/rise-western-nuclear-family-and-european-miracle.

277 *can be a trauma response:* Zuri White-Gibson, "Can Hyper-Independence Be a Trauma Response?," medically reviewed by Marney A. White, *PsychCentral,* February 18, 2022, https://psychcentral.com/health/hyper-independence-trauma.

278 *Back in 1938, a study:* Liz Mineo, "Good Genes Are Nice, But Joy Is Better," *Harvard Gazette,* April 11, 2017, https://news.harvard.edu/gazette/story/2017/04/over-nearly-80-years-harvard-study-has-been-showing-how-to-live-a-healthy-and-happy-life/.

278 *observed similar lessons:* Bronnie Ware, *Top Five Regrets of the Dying: A Life Transformed by the Dearly Departing* (Hay House, 2019).

Charts, Graphs, and Tables

Note on the presentation of historical data: There are many institutions and researchers that attempt to measure financial markets, and no single measure is universally agreed upon. Different sources may present slightly different figures depending on methodology and scope. In this book, I've used my discretion in selecting sources and, where helpful, I've rounded values—not just for ease and readability, but in some cases to reflect the natural variation across different measures.

Further, comparisons across different measures and timeframes, as I've provided in this book, are not always perfectly "fair." Still, I've aimed to present the data as responsibly as possible.

82 Historical Annualized Returns:

Aswath Damodaran, "Historical Returns on Stocks, Bonds, and Bills with Premiums," NYU Stern School of Business, last modified January 1, 2025, https://pages.stern.nyu.edu/~adamodar/New_Home_Page/datafile/histretSP.html.

Center for Research in Security Prices, LLC (CRSP), *CRSP NYSE/NYSE American/NASDAQ/Arca Value-Weighted Market Index* [data file] (CRSP, 1925–present). Author's calculation.

"Consumer Deposit Rates," Chase, accessed September 6, 2025, https://www.chase.com/personal/savings/savings-account/interest-rates.

CRSP 10-Year Bond Returns (INDNO 1000702) [data file] (CRSP, 1925–present). Author's calculation.

CRSP 30-Day Bill Returns (INDNO 1000708) [data file] (CRSP, 1925–present). Author's calculation.

Elroy Dimson, Paul Marsh, and Mike Staunton, *US Equity Returns, 1900–2024: Calculation from the DMS Database,* unpublished calculation, London Business School. Email to the author, August 25, 2025.

Dimson, Marsh, and Staunton, *World ex-US Equity Returns, 1900–2024: Calculation from the DMS Database,* unpublished calculation. Email to the author, August 25, 2025.

Dimson, Marsh, and Staunton, *US Bond Returns, 1900–2024: Calculation from the DMS Database,* unpublished calculation, London Business School. Email to the author, August 25, 2025.

Dimson, Marsh, and Staunton, *US Treasury Bills Returns, 1900–2024: Calculation from the DMS Database,* unpublished calculation, London Business School. Email to the author, August 25, 2025.

Note on calculation for "Cash earning interest:" It is common to use something like thirty-day treasury bills as a proxy for cash returns. Short-term bills offer a safe, liquid, and cash-like place to store money, and are frequently treated as the benchmark for short-term interest rates.

Note on annualized returns calculation: Calculate the compound annual growth rate (CAGR) using this formula:

CAGR = (Ending value / Beginning value)^(1 / *n*) - 1

Here, *n* is the number of years. For example, growing $100 to $150 in the first year (+50%) and then dropping to $75 in the second (-50%) yields a CAGR of: (75 / 100)^(1 / 2) – 1 = -13.4%.

90 Value of $100 Invested in 1928: Damodaran, "Historical Returns."

94 Real Returns (After Inflation):

CRSP Consumer Price Index (INDNO 1000709) [data file] (CRSP, 1925–present). Author's calculation.

Dimson, Marsh, and Staunton, *US Inflation, 1900–2024: Calculation from the DMS Database,* unpublished calculation, London Business School. Email to the author, August 25, 2025.

Note on calculating the effect of inflation on returns: Subtracting the inflation rate from the nominal rate gives a close-enough estimate for most purposes. However, the proper way to calculate real returns is using this equation:

(1 + nominal rate) / (1 + inflation rate) - 1

For a nominal return of 10% and an inflation rate of 3%, the real return is 1.1/ 1.03 - 1 = 6.8%.

114 Developed International and Emerging Markets:

Dimson, Marsh, and Staunton, *Developed ex-US Equity Returns, 1900–2024: Calculation from the DMS Database,* unpublished calculation, London Business School. Email to the author, August 25, 2025.

Dimson, Marsh, and Staunton, *Emerging Markets Equity Returns, 1900–2024: Calculation from the DMS Database,* unpublished calculation, London Business School. Email to the author, August 25, 2025.

127 Stock and Bond Returns by Year, 1990–2024: Damodaran, "Historical Returns."

129 Annual Returns of the S&P 500 Index: Damodaran, "Historical Returns."

130 Annualized Returns over Rolling Periods + Volatility: *CRSP NYSE/NYSE American/NASDAQ/Arca Value Weighted Market Index (INDNO 1000200)* [data file] (CRSP, 1925–present). Author's calculation.

138 "Good" and "Bad" Markets: *CRSP NYSE/NYSE American/NASDAQ/Arca Value Weighted Market Index (INDNO 1000200)* [data file] (CRSP, 1980–present).

211 Large-Cap and Small-Cap Returns:

Damodaran, "Historical Returns."

William J. Bernstein, *The Four Pillars of Investing: Lessons for Building a Winning Portfolio*. 2nd ed. (McGraw-Hill, 2023).

214 Growth and Value Returns:

Bernstein, *The Four Pillars of Investing.*

Dimson, Marsh, and Staunton, *US Value vs. Growth Stock Returns, 1927–2024: Summary of Returns Based on Fama-French Data,* unpublished calculation, London Business School. Email to the author, August 28, 2025.

Fidelity Investments, "Types of ETFs by Style and Capitalization," *Fidelity Learning Center,* Fidelity Investments, www.fidelity.com/learning-center/investment-products/etf/types-etfs-style-capitalization.

Kenneth R. French, *Data Library,* Amos Tuck School of Business, Dartmouth College, accessed September 6, 2025, https://mba.tuck.dartmouth.edu/pages/faculty/ken.french/data_library.html. Author's calculations.

219 REIT Returns:

CRSP Ziman REIT Value Weighted Index (INDNO 1000800) [data file] (CRSP, 1980–present). Author's calculation.

FTSE Nareit All Equity REITs Index [data file], 1972–2024, Nareit, accessed May 5, 2025, https://www.reit.com/data-research/reit-market-data. Author's calculation.

ABOUT THE AUTHOR

Amanda Holden is the founder of Invested Development, an investing education business. Before becoming a leading voice on women and money, she earned degrees in economics and communications from UCLA and worked in investment management. Known online as @dumpster.doggy, she shares financial literacy alongside her activism work and signature secondhand "trashion" outfits.

Avid Reader Press, an imprint of Simon & Schuster, is built on the idea that the most rewarding publishing has three common denominators: great books, published with intense focus, in true partnership. Thank you to the Avid Reader Press colleagues who collaborated on *How to Be a Rich Old Lady*, as well as to the hundreds of professionals in the Simon & Schuster advertising, audio, communications, design, ebook, finance, human resources, legal, marketing, operations, production, sales, supply chain, subsidiary rights, and warehouse departments whose invaluable support and expertise benefit every one of our titles.

Editorial
Carolyn Kelly, *Editor*

Jacket Design
Alison Forner, *Senior Art Director*
Clay Smith, *Senior Designer*
Sydney Newman, *Art Associate*

Marketing
Meredith Vilarello, *VP and Associate Publisher*
Kayla Dee, *Associate Marketing Manager*
Katya Wiegmann, *Marketing and Publishing Assistant*

Production
Allison Green, *Managing Editor*
Hana Handzija, *Managing Editorial Assistant*
Jessica Chin, *Senior Manager of Copyediting*
Annalea Manalili, *Senior Production Editor*
Alicia Brancato, *Production Manager*
Ruth Lee-Mui, *Interior Text Designer*
Cait Lamborne, *Ebook Developer*

Publicity
Ilana Gold, *Publicity Director*
Eva Kerins, *Publicity Assistant*
Lily Soroka, *Publicity Assistant*

Subsidiary Rights
Paul O'Halloran, *VP and Director of Subsidiary Rights*
Fiona Sharp, *Subsidiary Rights Coordinator*